VERANDA

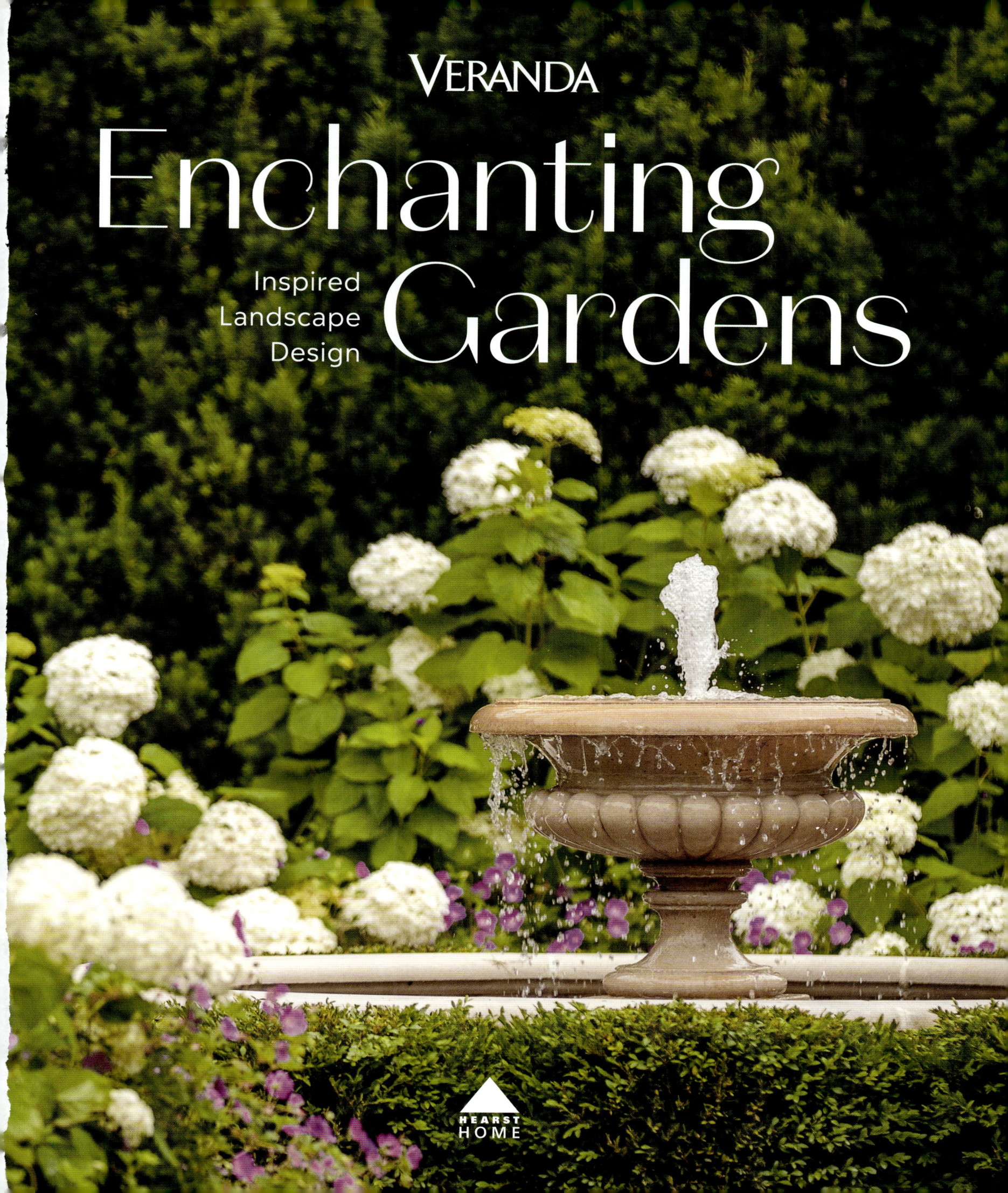

Enchanting Gardens

Inspired Landscape Design

HEARST HOME

VERANDA
Enchanting Gardens

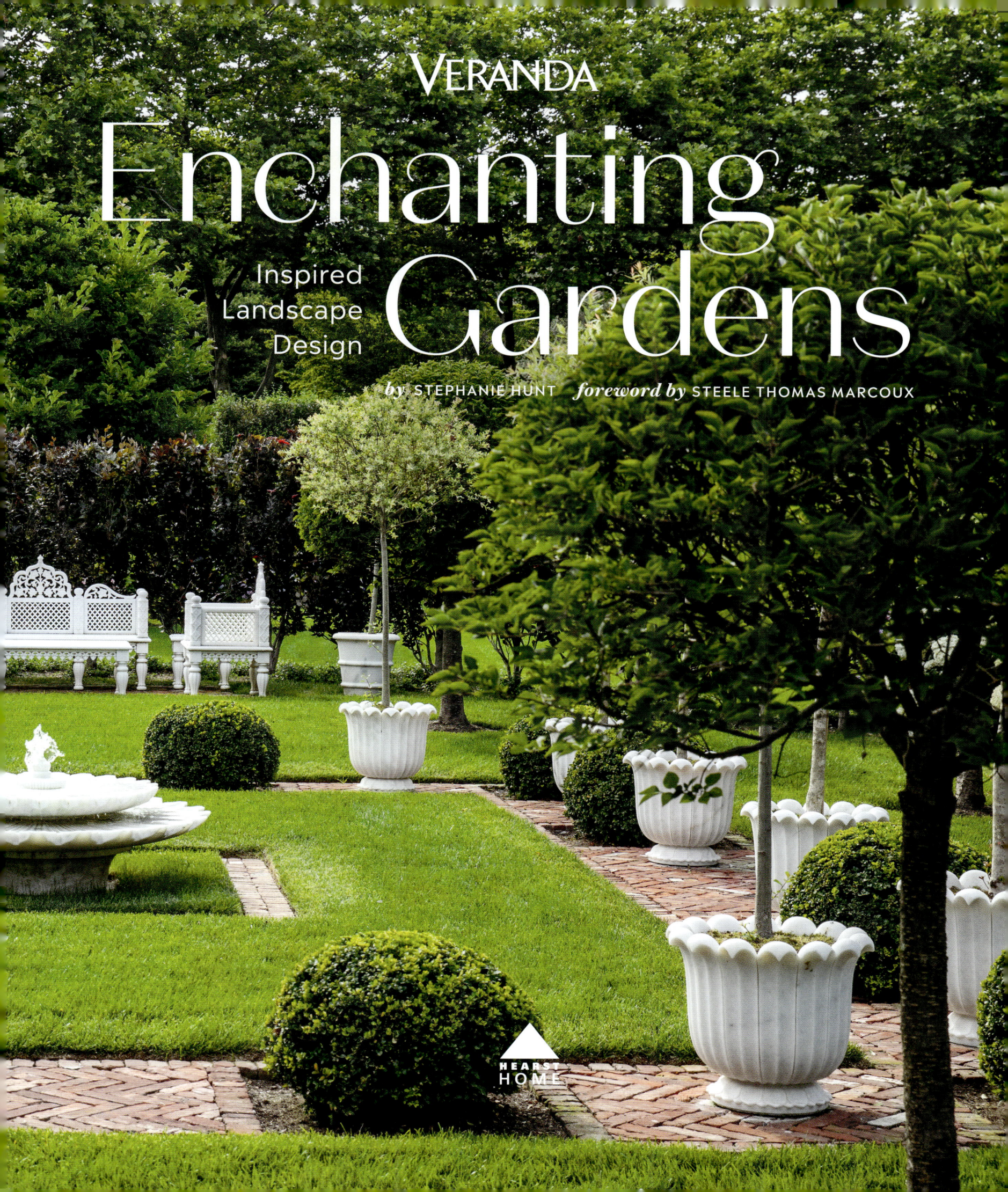

Inspired Landscape Design

by STEPHANIE HUNT   *foreword by* STEELE THOMAS MARCOUX

HEARST HOME

contents

FOREWORD 7 INTRODUCTION 8
INDEX 220 PHOTOGRAPHY CREDITS 223

CHAPTER 1
Rooted in the Past
page 10

CHAPTER 2
Cottage Romance
page 68

CHAPTER 3
Country Escapes
page 128

CHAPTER 4
Waterside Idylls
page 172

CHAPTER 5
Walled Sanctuaries
page 196

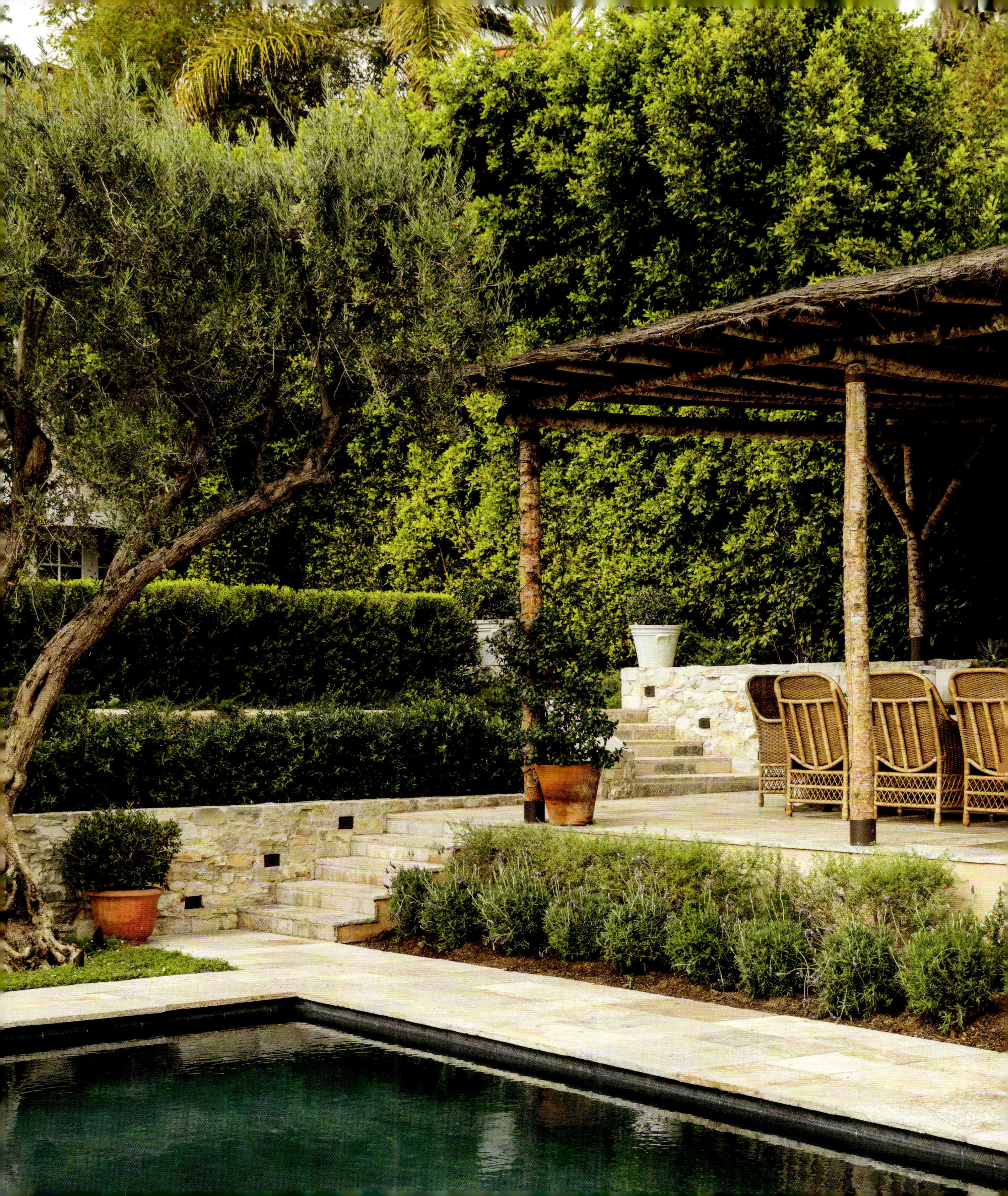

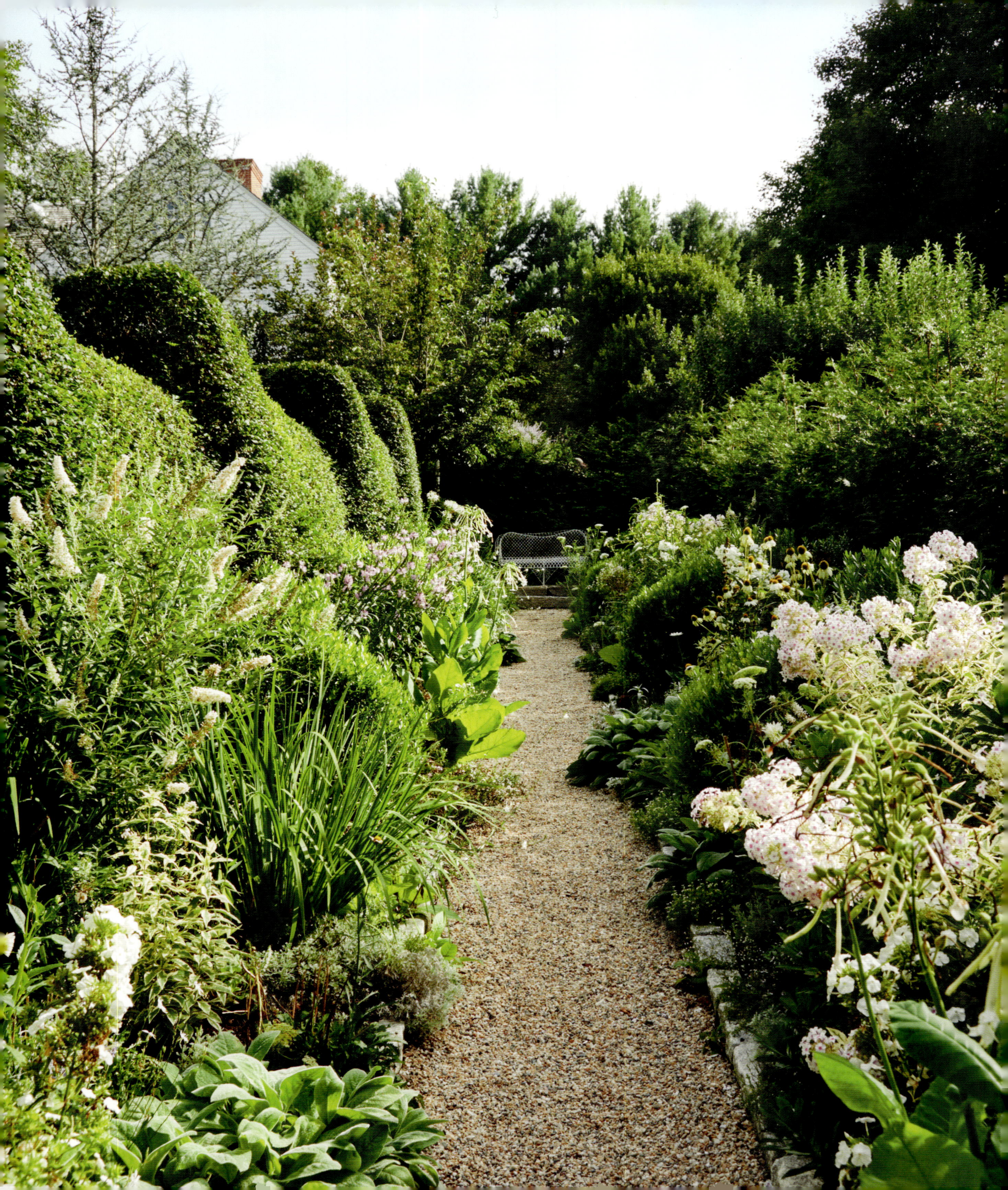

FOREWORD

" *To plant a garden is to believe in tomorrow.*" —ACTRESS AUDREY HEPBURN

Having spent the past two years planning—and now planting—a garden with my husband and our dear friend and landscape designer Zachary Westall, the words of Hepburn ring especially true. Gardens require just the right mix of dreaming and doing: dreams of tomorrow, of future family celebrations like birthdays, graduations, engagements, inspire us to "do" more gardening today. But as any seasoned gardener will tell you, it's the doing of gardens where the real magic happens. Planting a garden has taught me so much about patience, resilience, enjoying the moment (a critical lesson for a dreamer like me), even selflessness. In a more meaningful way than ever before, gardens have become, for me, living symbols of hope.

VERANDA celebrates the best in garden and outdoor living design with our World's Most Beautiful Gardens awards. We bestow the honor annually to spaces created by professionals and enthusiasts alike, with the help of our expert judges, interior designer Bunny Williams and Peter Lyden, director of the Institute of Classical Architecture & Art. Many of those winning gardens, from a riot of perennial color by English garden designer Jo Thompson to a lush poolside retreat designed by L.A.'s Inner Gardens, are included here, as well as Williams's own garden, a Connecticut countryside idyll she has been cultivating for more than 30 years.

Of course, outdoor living has always been a part of VERANDA—as our name suggests. Our founder and editor emeritus, Lisa Newsom, nurtured a passion for flowers, gardens, and conservation among our readers from the early days of the magazine, showcasing floral arrangements and breathtaking outdoor living spaces. We are delighted to continue to share with you the most beautiful gardens in the world, offering verdant places of respite and escape. These serene spaces remind us of the peace that can be found in nature, bringing joy and inspiration—and hope—to all who visit.

STEELE THOMAS MARCOUX

PAGE 5 An alderwood pergola offers shade to a West Hollywood poolside living room designed by landscape architect Anna Hoffman, whose client wanted to "re-create the feel of their favorite Tuscan hotel, the Castiglion del Bosco."

LEFT A "white garden" flourishes with fair-blooming perennials like yarrow, Casablanca lilies, milkweed, roses, and Lindheimer's beeblossom on Bill Reynolds's and Robb Nestor's Southeastern Connecticut property.

INTRODUCTION

GARDENS GROUND US. In the garden, we return to root and bud; we frolic with leaf and flower; we connect back to the essential Eden, the primordial paradise found across cultures. The garden is a place of beginnings and blossoming, but also of decay and death. A sanctuary made holy by seasons and cycles of life, by the sacred elements of dirt and light, water and seed. We plant, prune, weed, water, compost, hope, wait. We harvest, or when humbled, we admit failure—then dig in again. "Clearly, nature calls to something very deep in us... Hortophilia, the desire to interact with, manage, and tend nature, is also deeply instilled in us," says the late neurologist and best-selling author Oliver Sacks. But we don't really need a scientist to tell us that, do we?

While numerous studies now prove that getting dirt under our fingernails boosts everything from our immune system to our cognitive function, we've all known intuitively that it just feels good to be outside, nurturing life (or trying to). Virginia Woolf, whose friend and lover was Vita Sackville-West, the famous gardener of Sissinghurst Castle Garden, wrote that even on gray English days, "one feels lit up" gazing at the garden's "vast white lilies and such a blaze of dahlias." That endorphin rush from gardening outweighs bug bites or an achy back from bending over perennial beds. So we plant. We tend. We thumb through seed catalogues and dream. And we look to the masters in the field (literally).

That's what these pages offer—a chance to explore some of the finest, lushest, most inventive and classic gardens around the world. You'll be transported to England (of course), but also to California and Connecticut, to Mexico and Texas, to Ireland, Canada, and beyond. You'll be introduced to leading landscape architects and designers who share their inspiration and, sometimes, their secrets. The iconic Bunny Williams is fond of quoting horticultural writer and landscape architect Elizabeth Lawrence from *Through the Garden Gate*: "There's a garden in every childhood," Lawrence writes, "an enchanted place where colors are brighter, the air softer, and the morning more fragrant than ever again." Welcome, fellow garden lovers, to some truly enchanted places.

STEPHANIE HUNT

RIGHT Grey Gardens' ivory-covered gate door is painted aquatic blue to echo the Hamptons historic home's shutters.

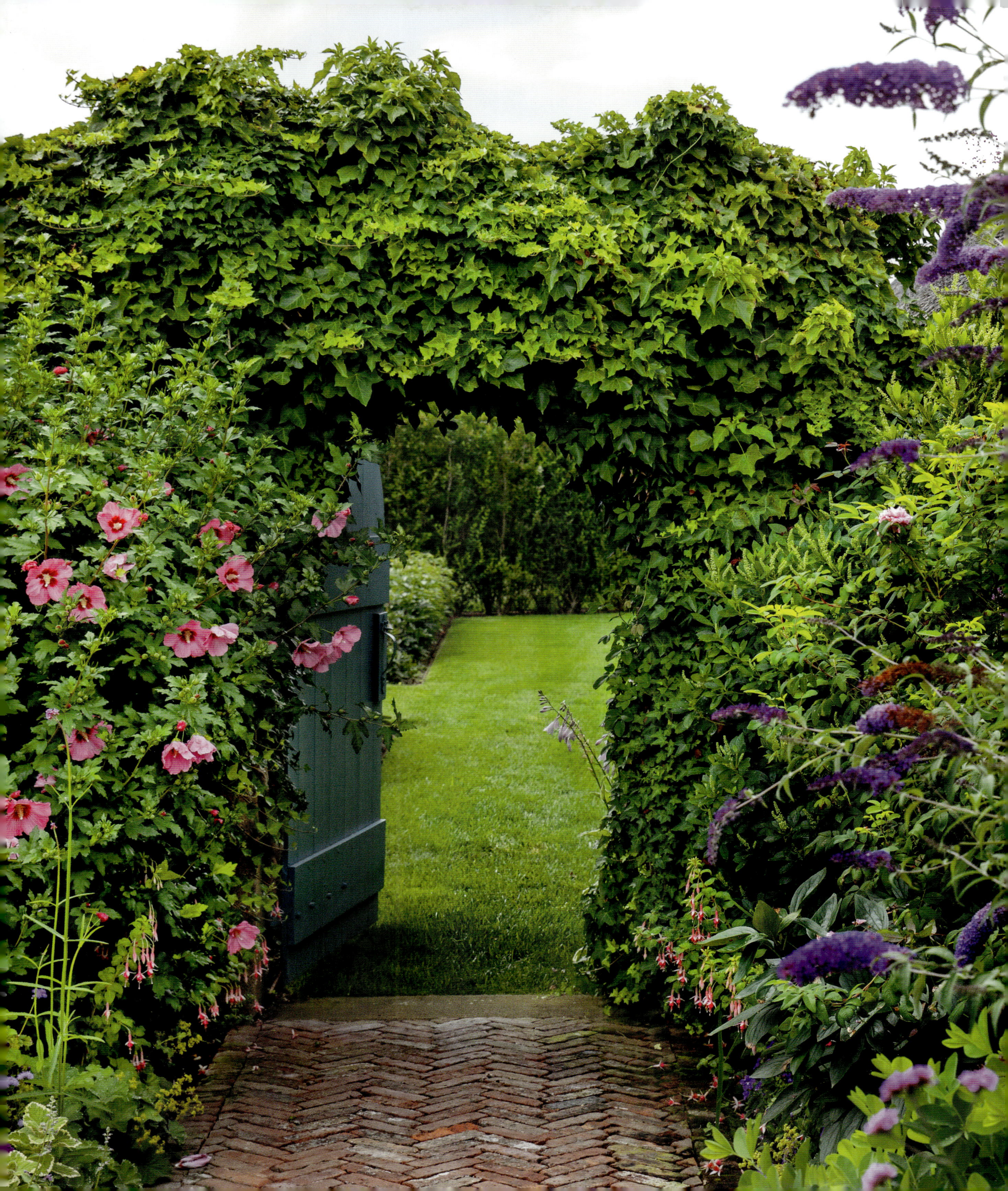

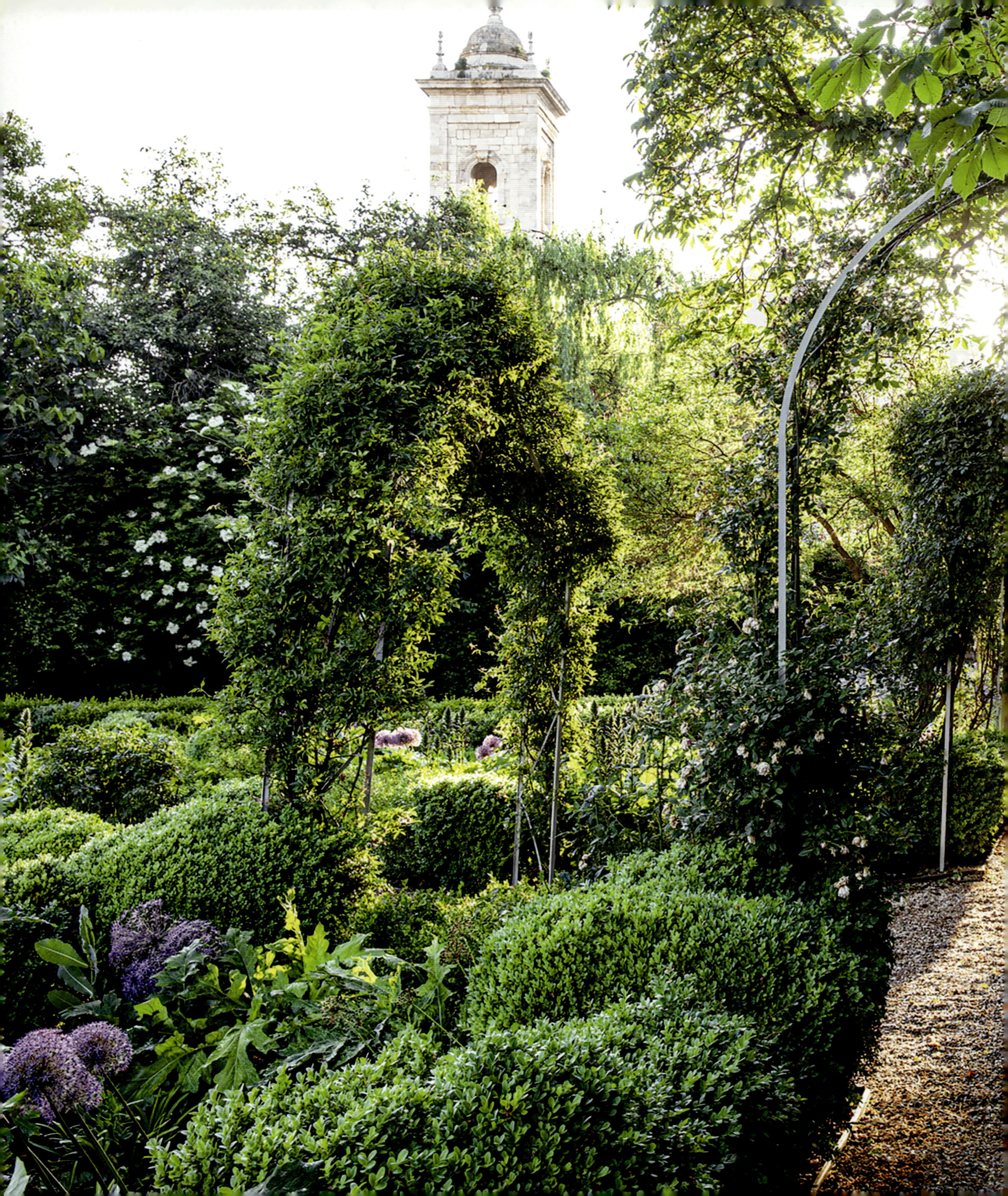

CHAPTER 1

ROOTED IN THE PAST

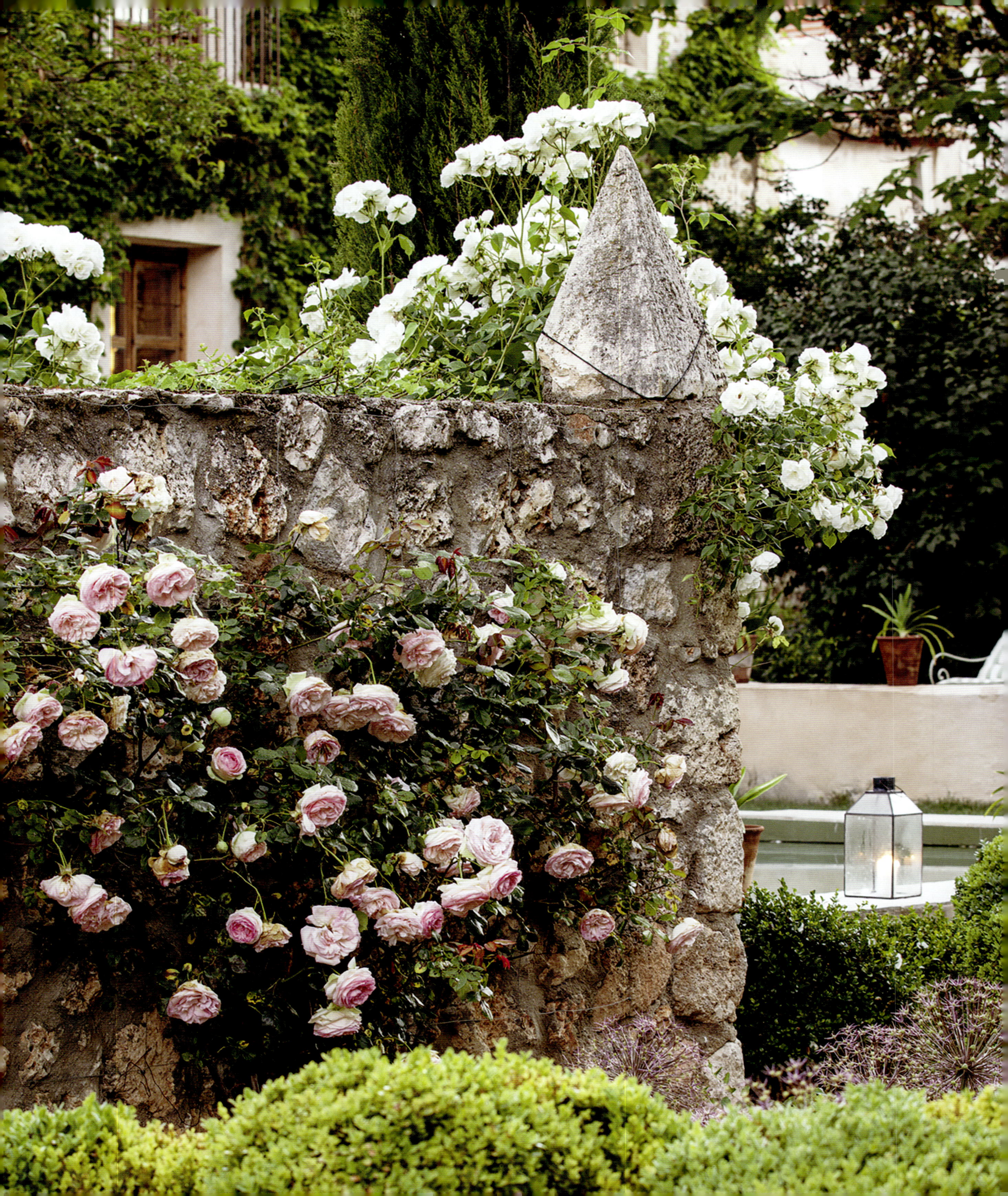

ROOTED IN THE PAST

t

O GARDEN IS TO TIME TRAVEL. The act itself is meditative: immersion in the present, with an eye toward what's to come. We bury bulbs and sow tiny seeds as acts of hope and optimism, digging down to reach toward the future.

Gardening also plants us firmly in the past. Indeed, what is soil itself but the rich, fertile dwindling down of geological eons. Soil is our oldest story—growth out of decay, the return of seasons, new buds from fallow fields, the relentless march of time. So there's particular poignancy when a garden blooms with a sense of history. When the cuttings from your late grandmother's rose bush spring to fragrant life, or the gnarled old olive tree planted maybe three centuries ago still miraculously fruits. Oh how beautifully a garden can ground us, in innumerable ways, in all that came before. Certainly the ones we visit within this chapter do.

You'll traverse shady allées and pebble paths that others have traveled before us—from a 16th-century manor outside Paris that once belonged to Hubert de Givenchy to the storied grounds of a Scottish castle to the garden of one of America's famed garden writers that had, ironically, never been documented—with eyes open and ears tuned to birdsong, listening to the timeless stories that these landscapes tell. Reviving, or in some cases reenvisioning, a historic garden often entails research and forensic digging. Gabriela Yariv and Álvaro Sampedro both celebrated the "a ha" moments of discovering the pentimento of a long-forgotten garden axis and the faded outlines of overgrown beds. Others plant anew, bringing fresh vision, or in the case of Cris Briger, a fresh batch of trees, to invigorate their surroundings. Whatever the approach, be it pruning old growth or fertilizing for the future, the garden is where our sense of time both collapses and expands. These outdoor havens are rooted in the past yet blossom in our present.

LEFT Madame Alfred Carrière and Eden roses climb one of many repointed stone walls that landscape designer Álvaro Sampedro restored on the grounds of a 17th-century palace outside Madrid, home of interior designer Luis Puerta.

PAGES 10-11 Through archival research, Sampedro discovered hints of an orchard and creeks, all of which had turned into a "jungle" that obscured an "incredible paradise," he says. He created gravel paths lined with arches and Lady Banks roses leading to garden rooms that blend with the expansive vistas.

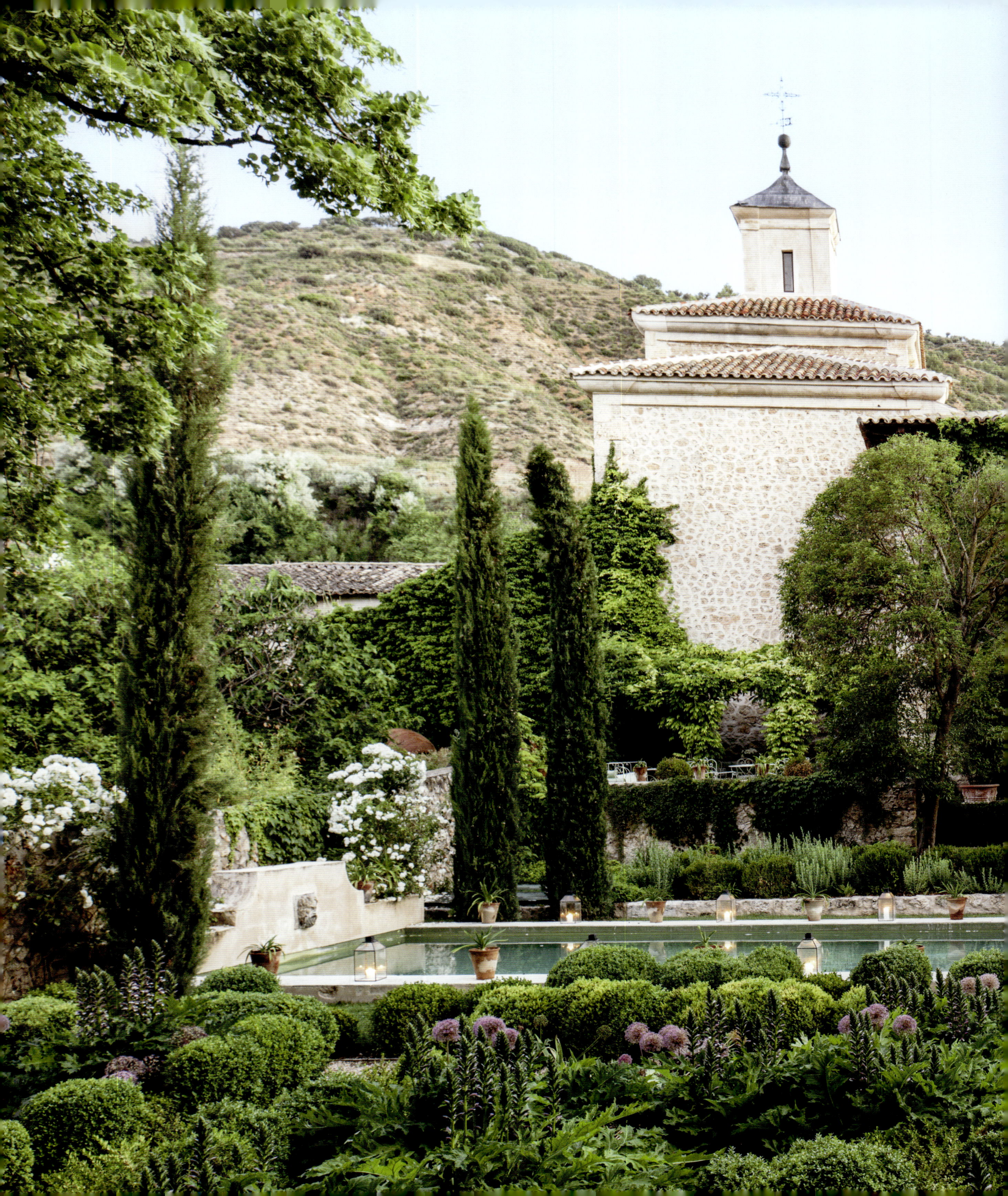

Spanish Revival

With equal parts research, imagination, and kismet, Álvero Sampedro transforms 17th-century ruins into blooming splendor.

LEFT "My client is a creator of magnificent spaces, a lover of beauty and tranquility, so I approached this garden similarly, as if it was an interior space, with places to nap, have tea with friends, to eat and play," Sampedro says. Here, a cloak of wisteria creates a cozy dining room. The gravel was meticulously mixed until it made "just the right sound underfoot," he adds.

RIGHT The sculptural fountain crowning the rectangular pool doubles as a soothing auditory feature, underscoring Sampedro's belief that a garden should delight every sense. Mounded boxwoods add structure to the space, while linden trees and Italian cypress "give vertical lift, unifying ground and sky," says the landscape designer, who salvaged and moved many old trees in addition to planting new ones.

PAGES 14-15 The grounds of this ancient Spanish estate outside of Madrid were in need of rescue so Sampedro began excavating to uncover remnants of earlier designs. He planted Italian cypress and linden trees to give height and gravitas in the courtyard, where Boston ivy climbs the palace façade.

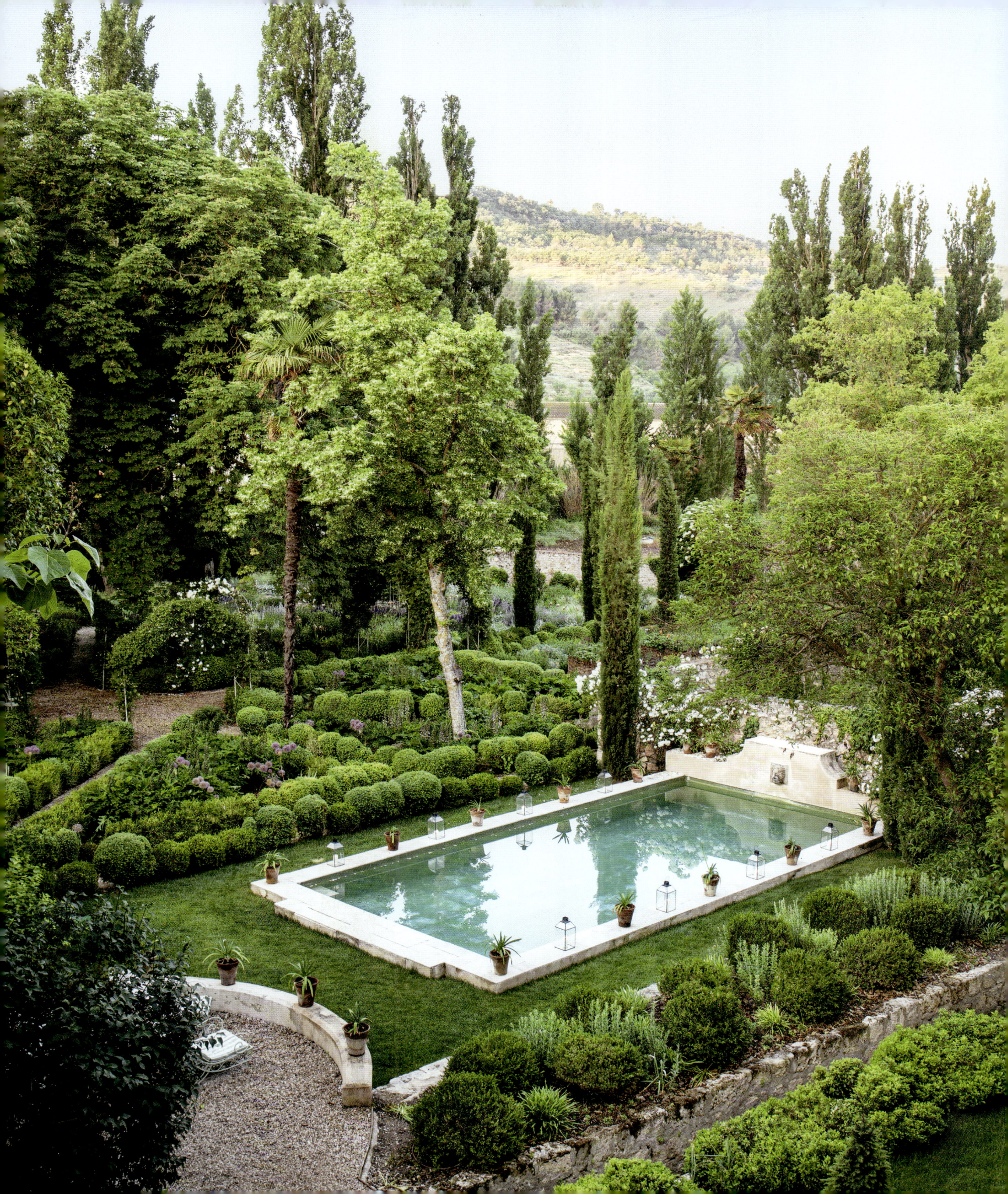

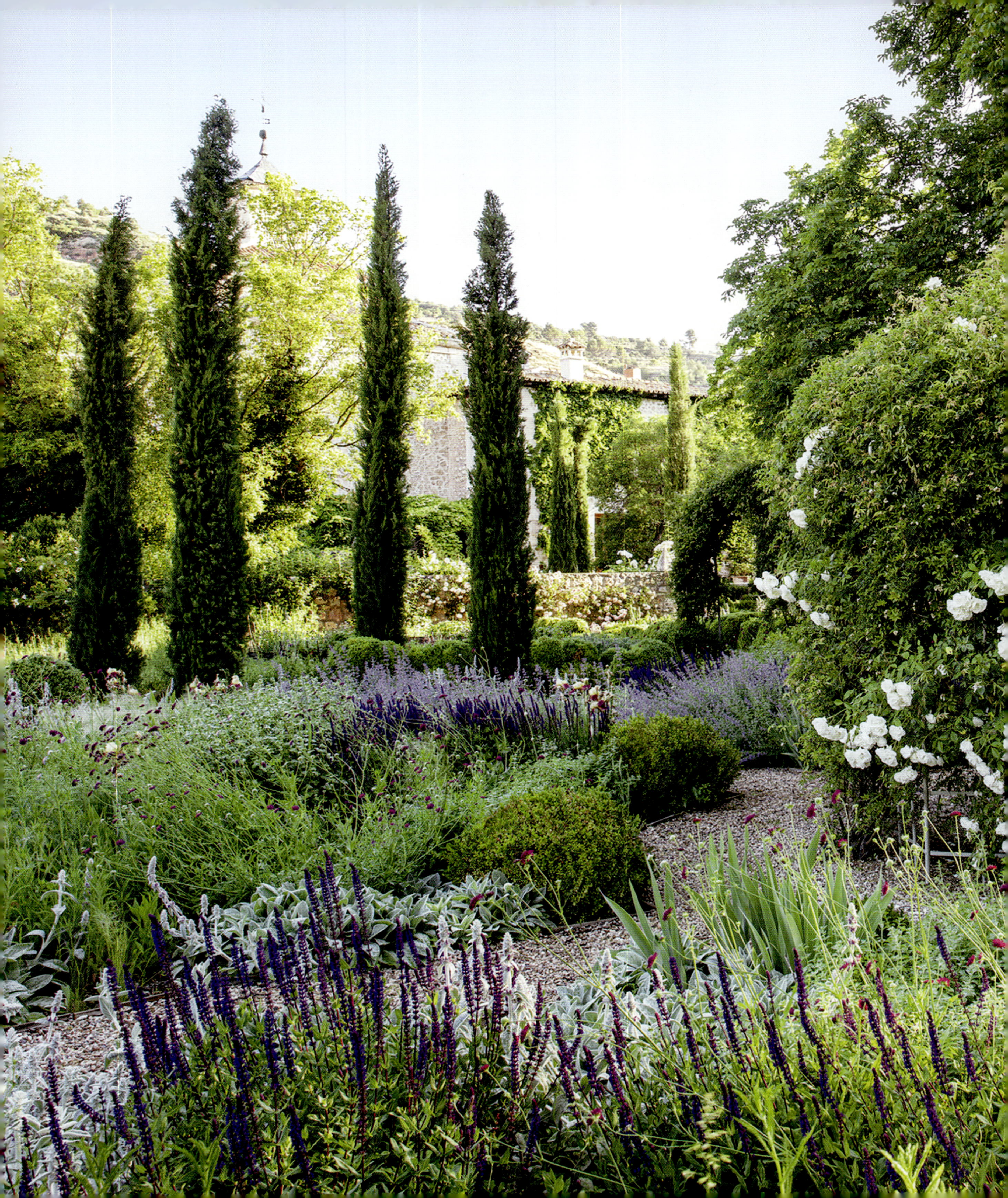

LEFT Soft, wispy layers of grasses, nepeta, salvia, yarrow, and irises delight in a lush perennial garden punctuated by Italian cypress. "I like these serene blues and purples and creating a sense of quiet order, especially near the house," says Sampedro. He spent six years on this restoration project. "I love how a garden is never finished and always changing—something curious and amazing all year long."

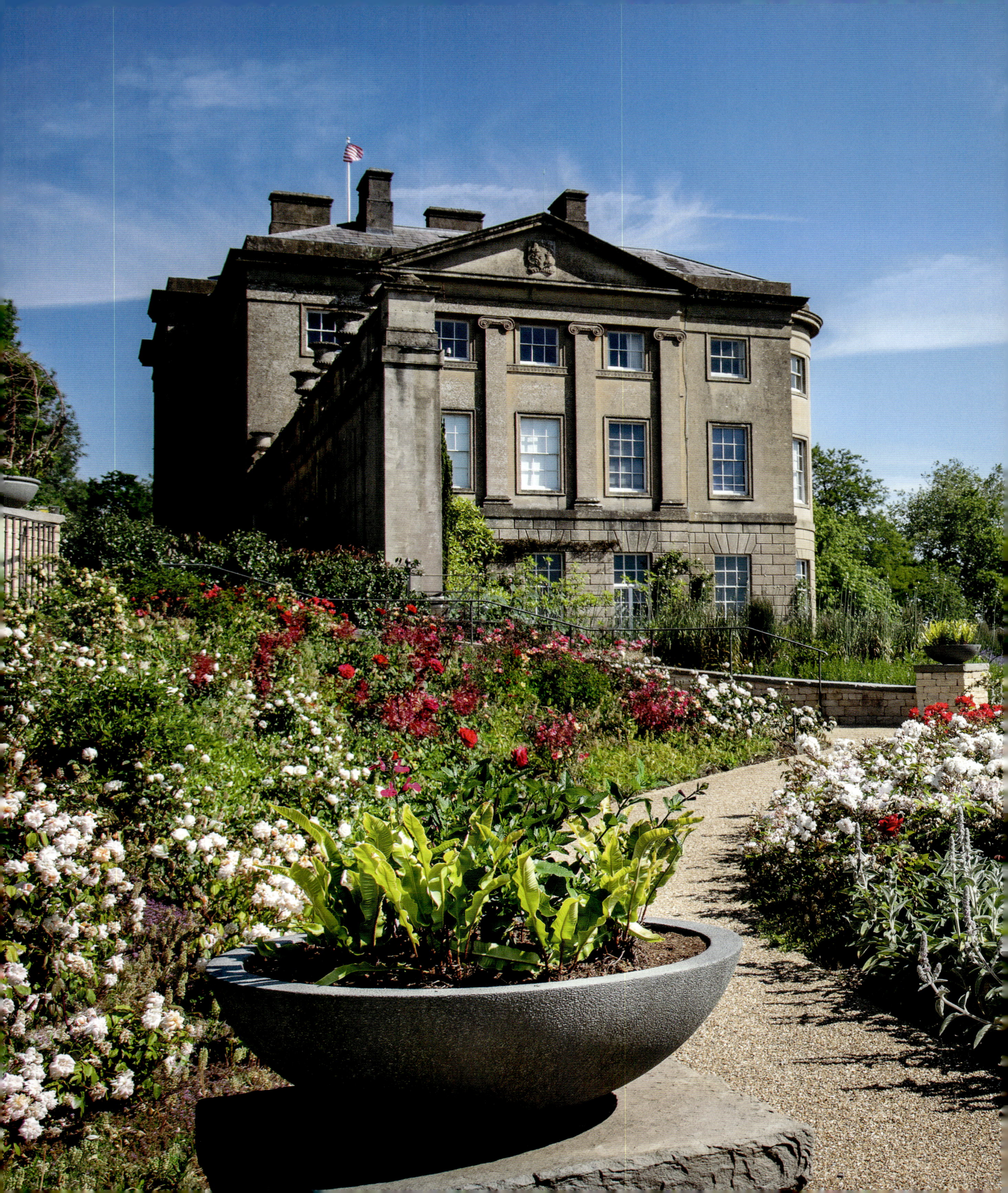

Ode to the Motherland

At Bath's Claverton Manor, American sensibilities bring fresh audacity to a British landmark overlooking River Avon.

ABOVE Washington, D.C.–based landscape design firm Oehme, van Sweden reenvisioned 125 rolling acres surrounding the American Museums & Gardens, including the Mount Vernon Garden, an ode to George Washington's 18th-century home, complete with eagle statuary.

BELOW Bulbs create nonstop seasonal wow. In early spring, 40,000 daffodils reign, and then lavender and white alliums steal the show by late spring. "The garden is so bold and graphic that it works well with the contours of the landscape," says Andy Cannell, the Royal Horticultural Society–trained head gardener.

22 ENCHANTING GARDENS

ABOVE The lumpy terrain between the ticketing pavilion and the 1820s Italianate manor house welcomes visitors with sweeping lawns and Limpley Stoke Valley vistas. In celebration of the American meadow, the team interspersed prairie-style perennials with grasses like catnip and marsh spurge. The result is a profusion of color, texture, and movement throughout the seasons.

PAGES 20-21 Claverton's gardens, including the Barbara Bovender American Rose Garden, offer unparalleled Cotswolds valley views and colorful borders with varying blooms every season. Remnants of the circa 1820 manorial pleasure gardens, including the balustrade and curtain walling, are still evident.

ABOVE The museum was founded by an Anglo-American couple in 1961 to showcase American decorative arts and "dispel stereotypes of American culture," according to its website. The gardens, including an amphitheater terraced into the hillside, do just that by displaying the diversity and breadth of American horticulture. "We hear a lot of 'wows,'" says Cannell. "I think this experience really challenges the way British people look at gardens."

ABOVE Sculptor Angela Conners's bust of President Abraham Lincoln enjoys an ongoing conversation with Lucy Ball alliums. Elsewhere, more than 30 cultivars of ornamental American grasses unite the expansive borders, and numerous species of American trees dot the landscape as well as the property's arboretum.

BELOW Principal designer Eric Groft referenced Thomas Jefferson's Monticello, another monumental American hilltop garden, when creating this "winding way." Blue-purple salvia and other ornamentals grace the 430-yard meandering path overlooking the Cotswolds National Landscape.

ROOTED IN THE PAST 25

California Comeback

Landscape designer Gabriela Yariv revives a rose-infused garden of a legendary writer, returning the private sanctuary to its 1930s heyday.

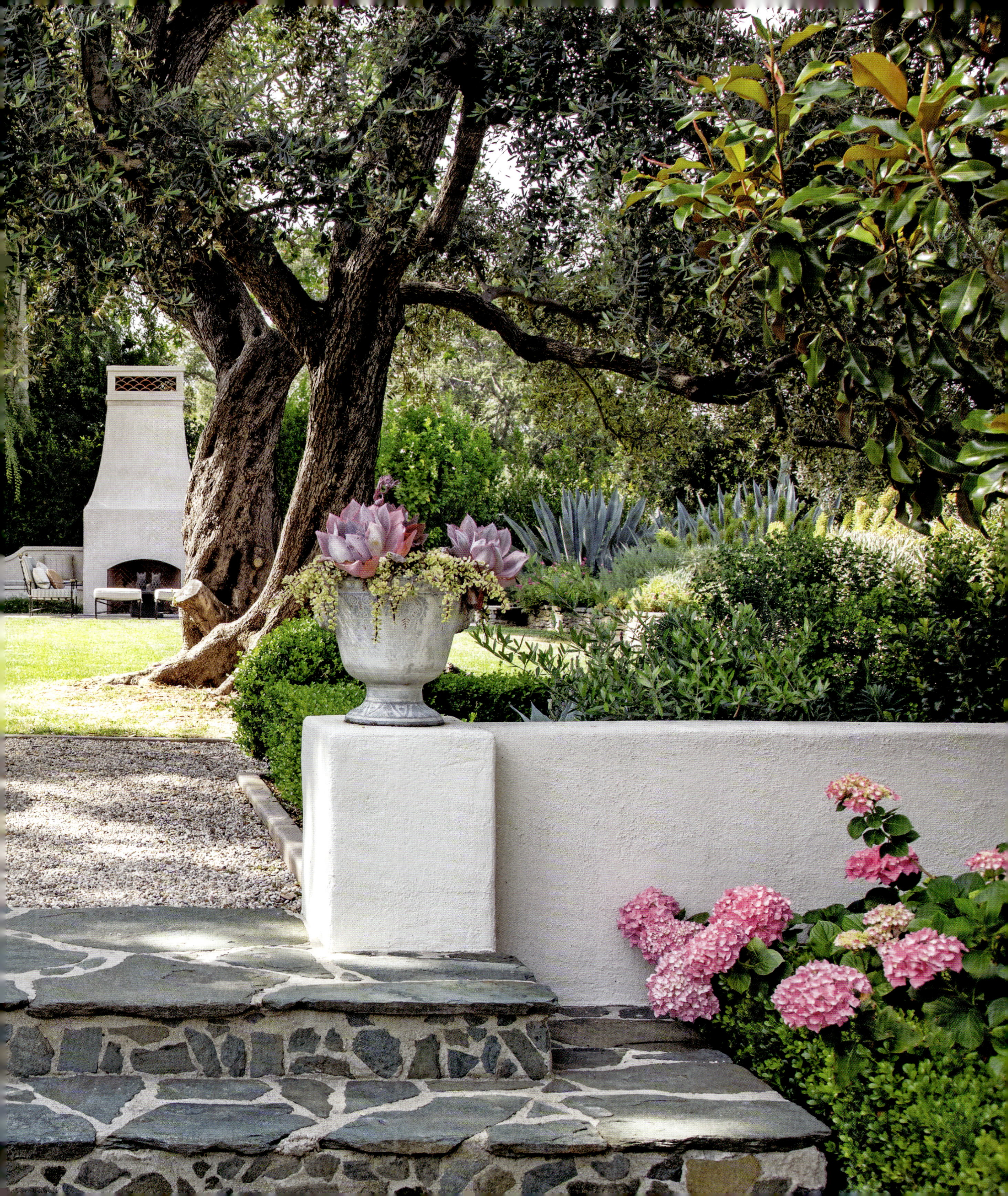

PAGES 26-27 When revitalizing the garden that once belonged to Winifred Starr Dobyns, author of the seminal 1931 book *California Gardens*, Yariv sleuthed: despite chronicling so many other gardens, Dobyns failed to document her own. Magnificent old trees and agave were benchmarks, but Yariv filled in gaps with new additions, like an outdoor pizza oven.

ABOVE Yariv removed and restored every paver around an octagonal fountain, puzzled it all back together, and then added loose plantings at the base. Manicured low boxwoods outline beds of perennials and olive trees nestled around the guesthouse, where Yariv trained bougainvillea to climb the stucco.

RIGHT In the back garden of the Period Revival house, designed by noted California architect Joseph Kucera, era-accurate boxwood hedges outline close beds and potted agave add Mediterranean flavor. Yariv removed overgrown shrubbery to re-create the axial and symmetrical vistas. Outdoor seating invites year-round relaxing in the ideal climate.

ROOTED IN THE PAST 29

RIGHT Fragrant rosemary, Greek sage, variegated pittosporum, and Little Ollie adorn a pathway leading to a side gate. Based on her research, Yariv chose plants that would have been used in Dobyns's day but are also fitting for Southern California's dry climate. "Dobyns copied the greats," says Yariv, who in turn did her best to imitate Dobyns.

PAGES 32-33 With the assistance of architectural historian Dr. Barbara Lamprecht, Yariv determined it was highly probable that Dobyns had a circular fountain. She reinstated the water feature and surrounded it with roses following the old rose-bed outlines Yariv uncovered. "To get my hands on Dobyns's own garden and to sleuth using her book—this is what I trained for my whole life," she says.

ROOTED IN THE PAST 31

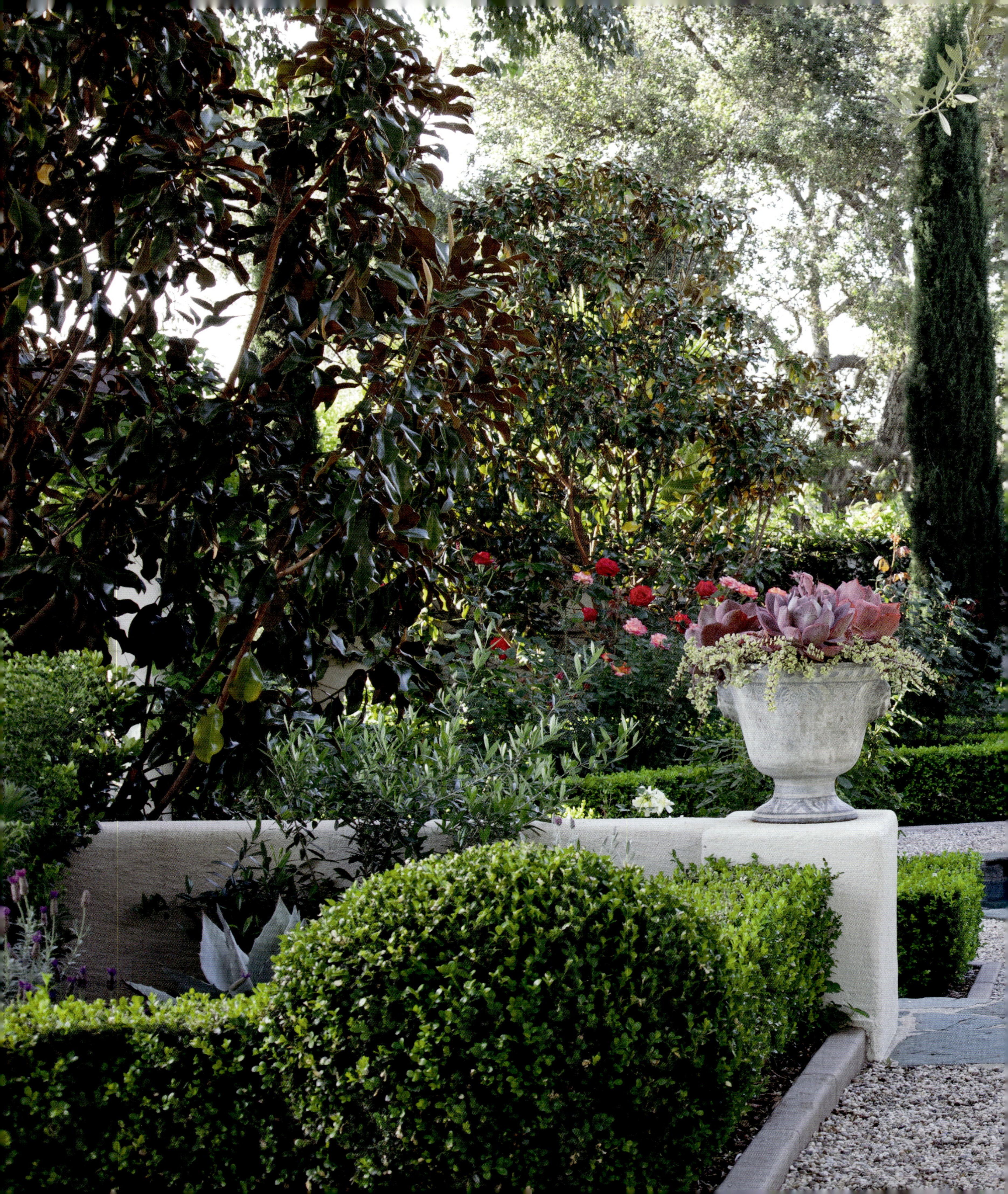

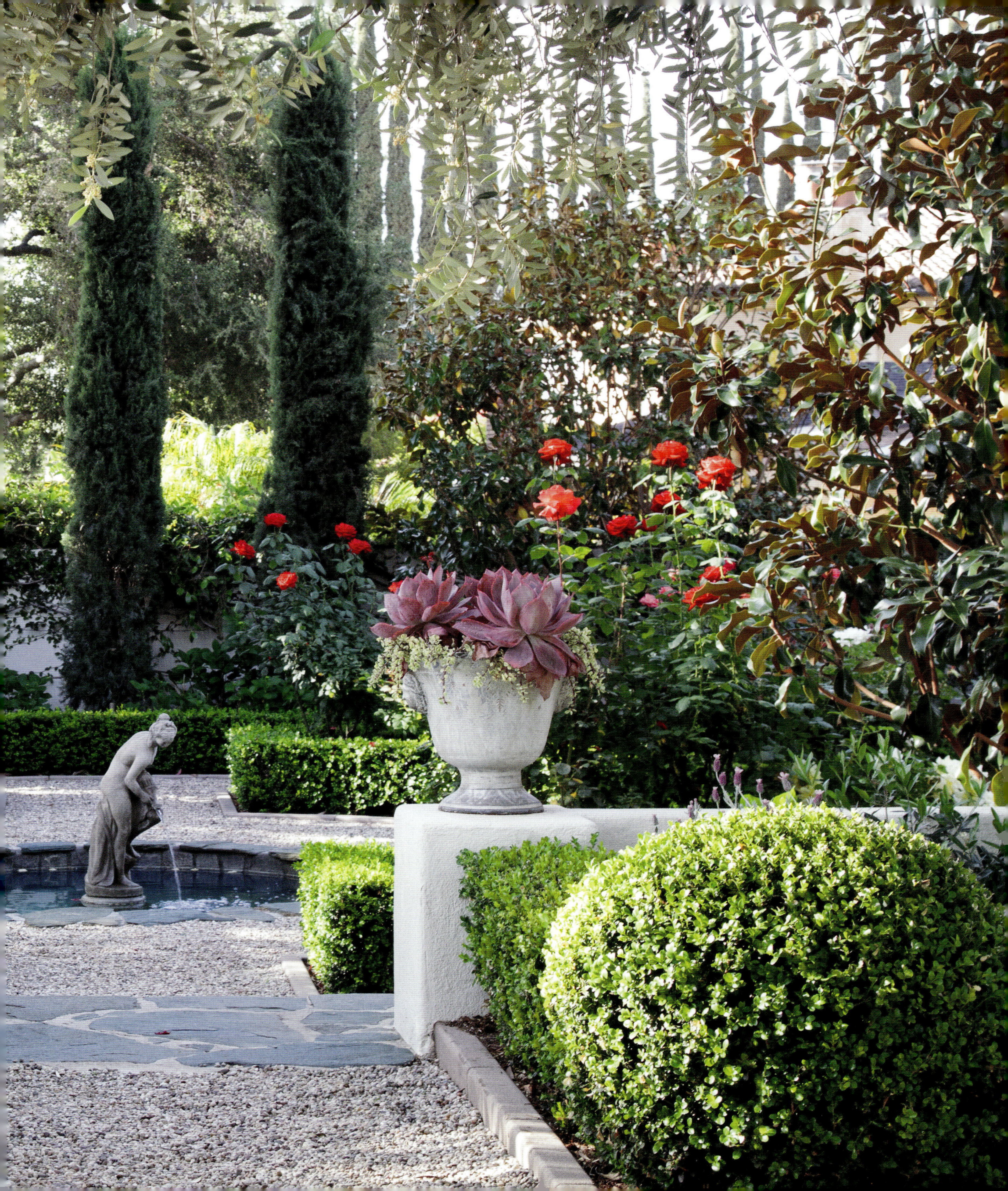

Noble Undertaking

Angus and Zara Gordon Lennox dig in at Gordon Castle, giving the vast eight-acre Scottish garden, one of the United Kingdom's largest, its royal horticultural status.

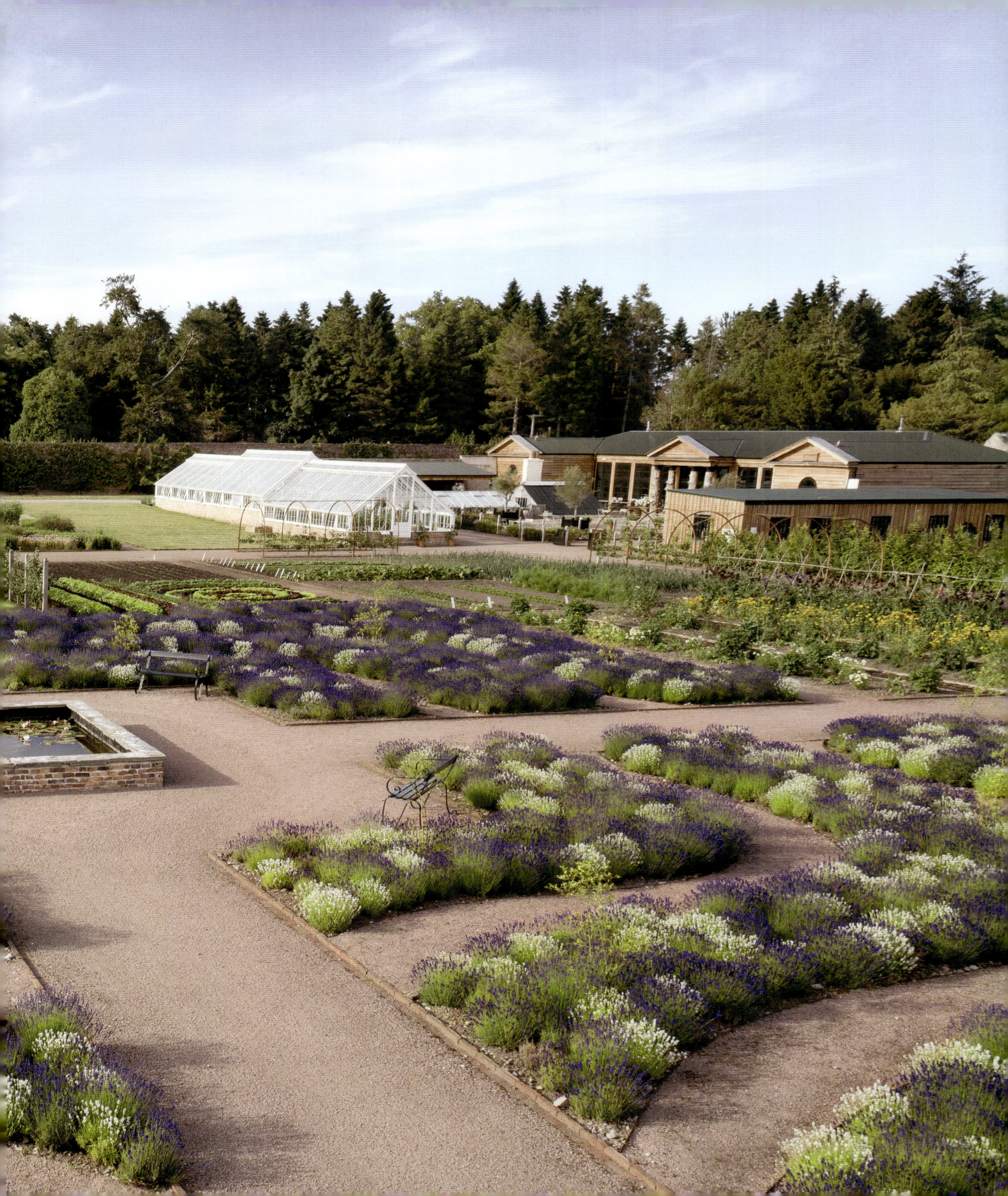

36 ENCHANTING GARDENS

ABOVE Thirty-five varieties of tulips add pops of magenta and golden orange to the vast garden. Zara and her husband, Angus Gordon Lennox, a descendant of the fourth Duke of Gordon who built the Scottish estate, are the hands-on workhorses who keep it up, pruning and weeding daily.

LEFT Noted U.K. landscape designer Arne Maynard revived the brick-walled garden, which at around eight acres is one of the largest in the country today. "I subdivided it into more intimate areas, stitching together different textures, atmospheres and heights," says Maynard. A circular grass maze anchors the far end, while heritage fruit trees, herbs, and other crops are interspersed.

ABOVE Two-hundred-some heritage fruit trees, including this Laxton Superb apple tree, trained against the existing 15-foot brick walls, were part of the garden inheritance. One of nine Edwardian glass houses also survives.

PAGE 34-35 Drifts of English lavender gently ripple out from the brick dipping pond at the heart of the Gordon Castle garden. Maynard conceived of the formal grid of wide paths, anchored at one end by the head gardener's house.

ROOTED IN THE PAST 37

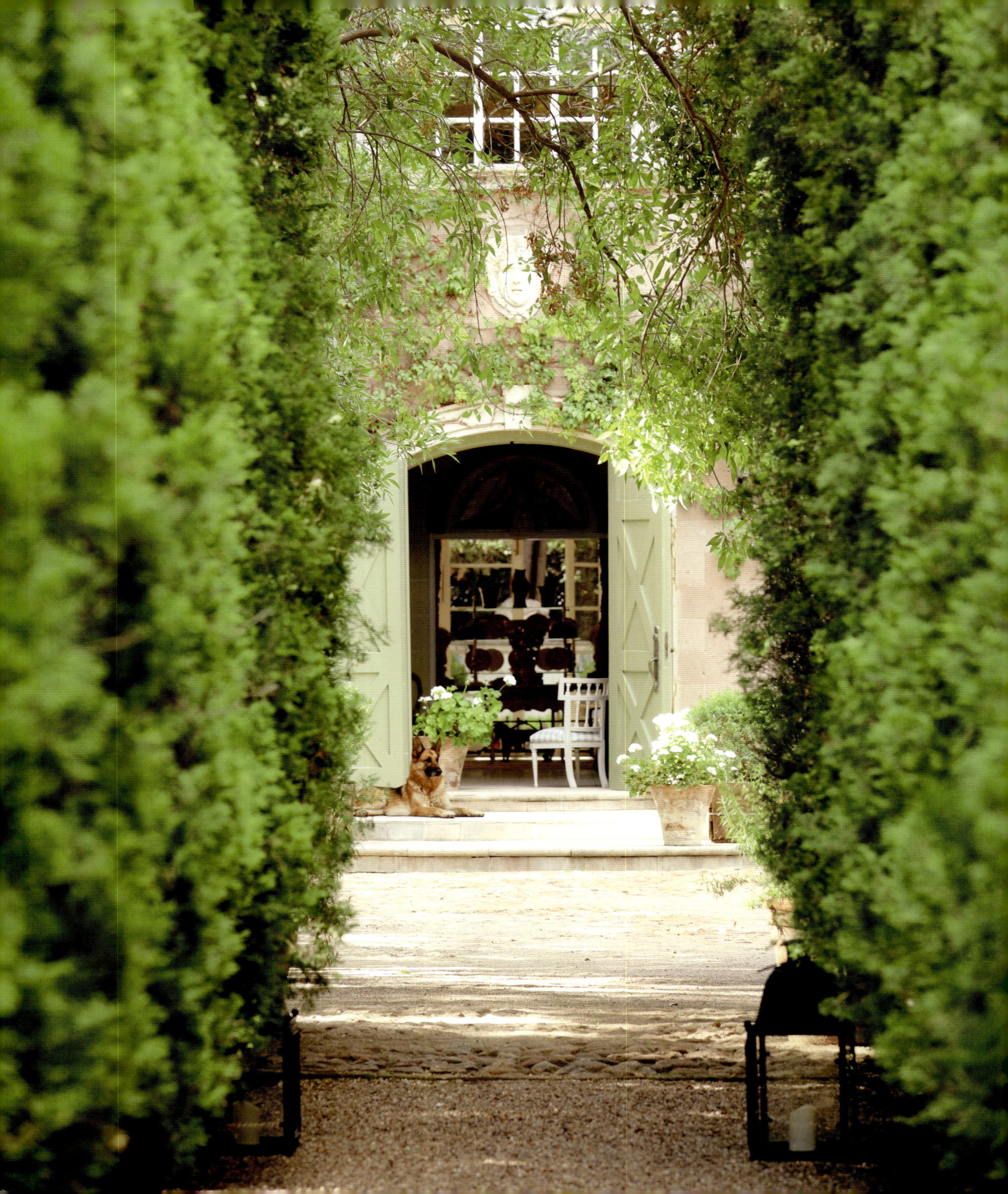

Grown with Gusto

On the grounds of a restored San Miguel de Allende hacienda, Cris Briger and sons cultivate a verdant oasis, one tree (or 72!) at a time.

LEFT On a historic property on the outskirts of San Miguel de Allende, Mexico, Briger, the interior designer and owner of Casa Gusto, the Palm Beach antiques and decorating emporium, says she and her sons have created "our own little oasis." A boxwood allée leads to the entry, where one of family's German shepherds makes itself at home.

RIGHT "The idea is that wherever you are on the property, you look ahead and there's a destination," says Briger. She's a consummate hostess and entertainer who hangs a candlelit chandelier from juniper trees for a pop-up alfresco dinner spot. "It's a movable feast," her son Charles Peed adds.

ROOTED IN THE PAST 39

RIGHT Ash trees, boxwood, and lavender grace the entrance to the guest cottage and surrounding brick-and-gravel courtyard. Briger and her late husband, Paul, originally envisioned this as a formal French garden, but the space has since evolved into "more sweet randomness," says son Augie Briger.

ABOVE Trees, including these cottonwoods, give grace and gravitas to the property. "It's an arboretum now, or will be," Briger says. She rolled up her sleeves, and so did her sons, to plant 72 new trees on one visit. "Everything here was built or made by hand, no heavy machinery," she says.

40 ENCHANTING GARDENS

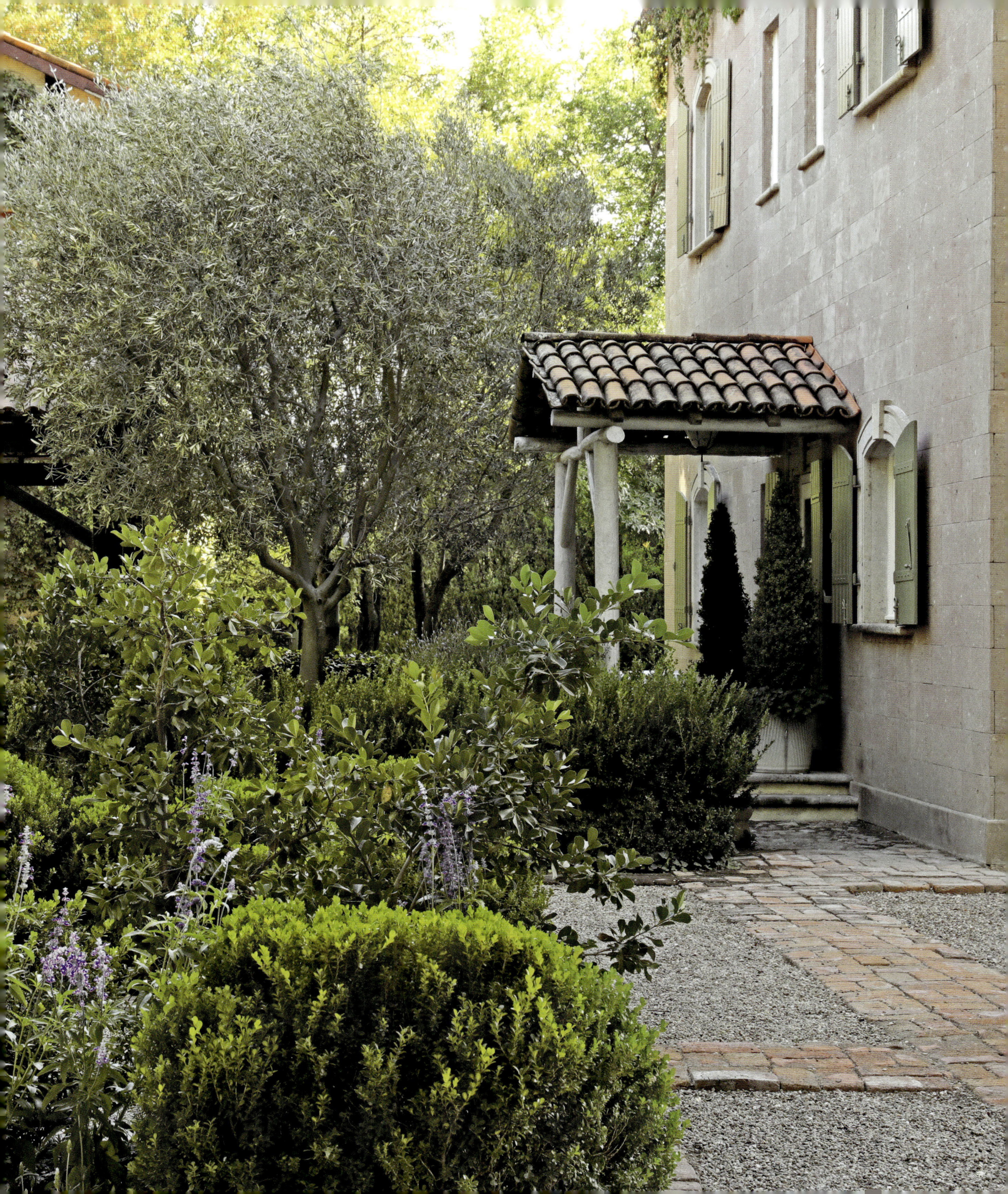

LEFT Apple trees, maples, oak, ash, and other fruit trees, which arch over enticing shady paths, comprise the expanding arboretum. Briger savors both the sweat equity and the serenity of tending and enjoying this garden—loving "the ceaseless amazement of it all," she says.

RIGHT The garden's tendrils extend indoors, where a Casa Gusto papier-mâché fig vine crowns the dining room and rattan chairs plant a "gardeny" feel, says Peed. Acanthus leaves grown in the garden will become future papier-mâché models, he adds. "This is literally where we grow Casa Gusto."

ENCHANTING GARDENS

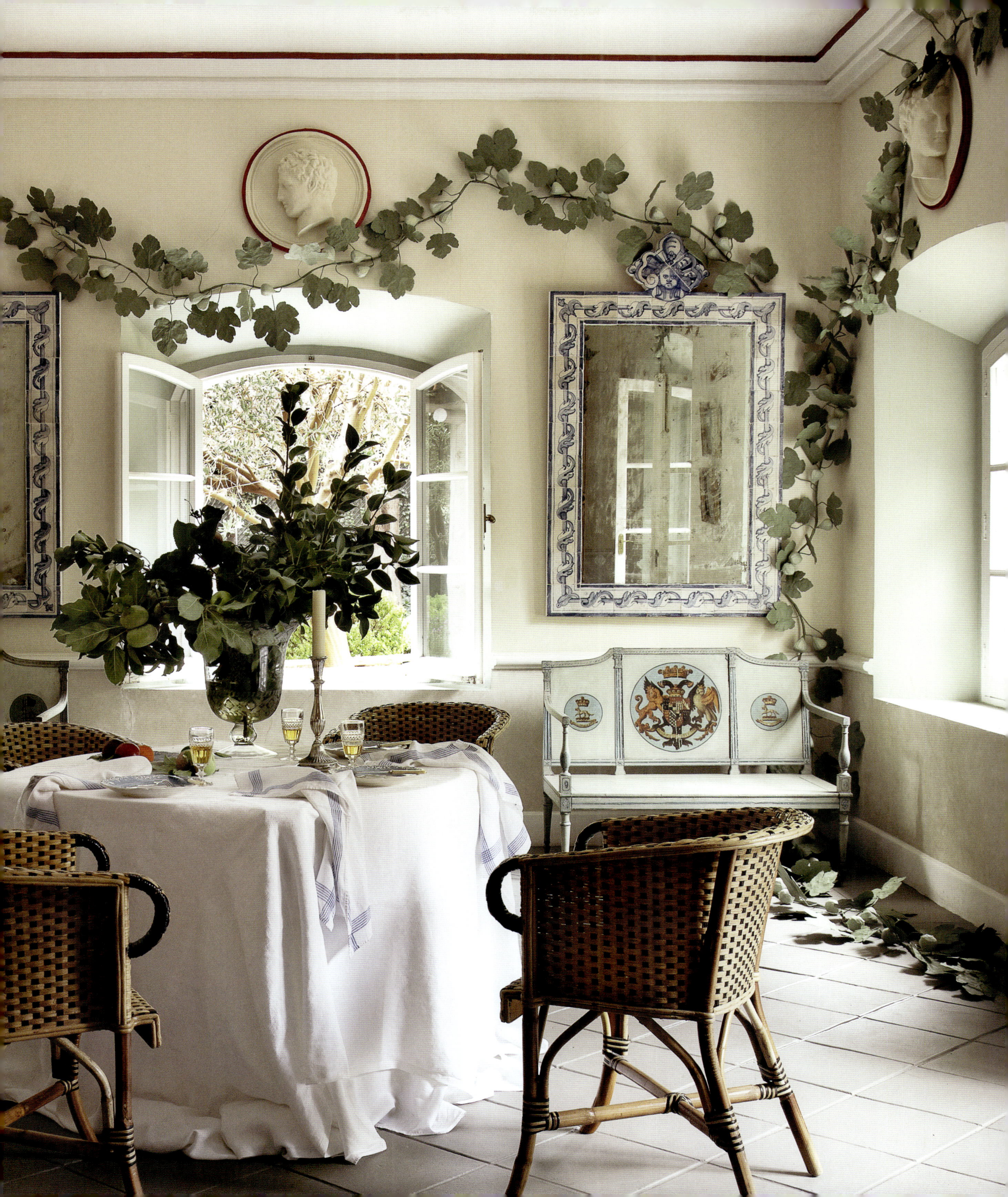

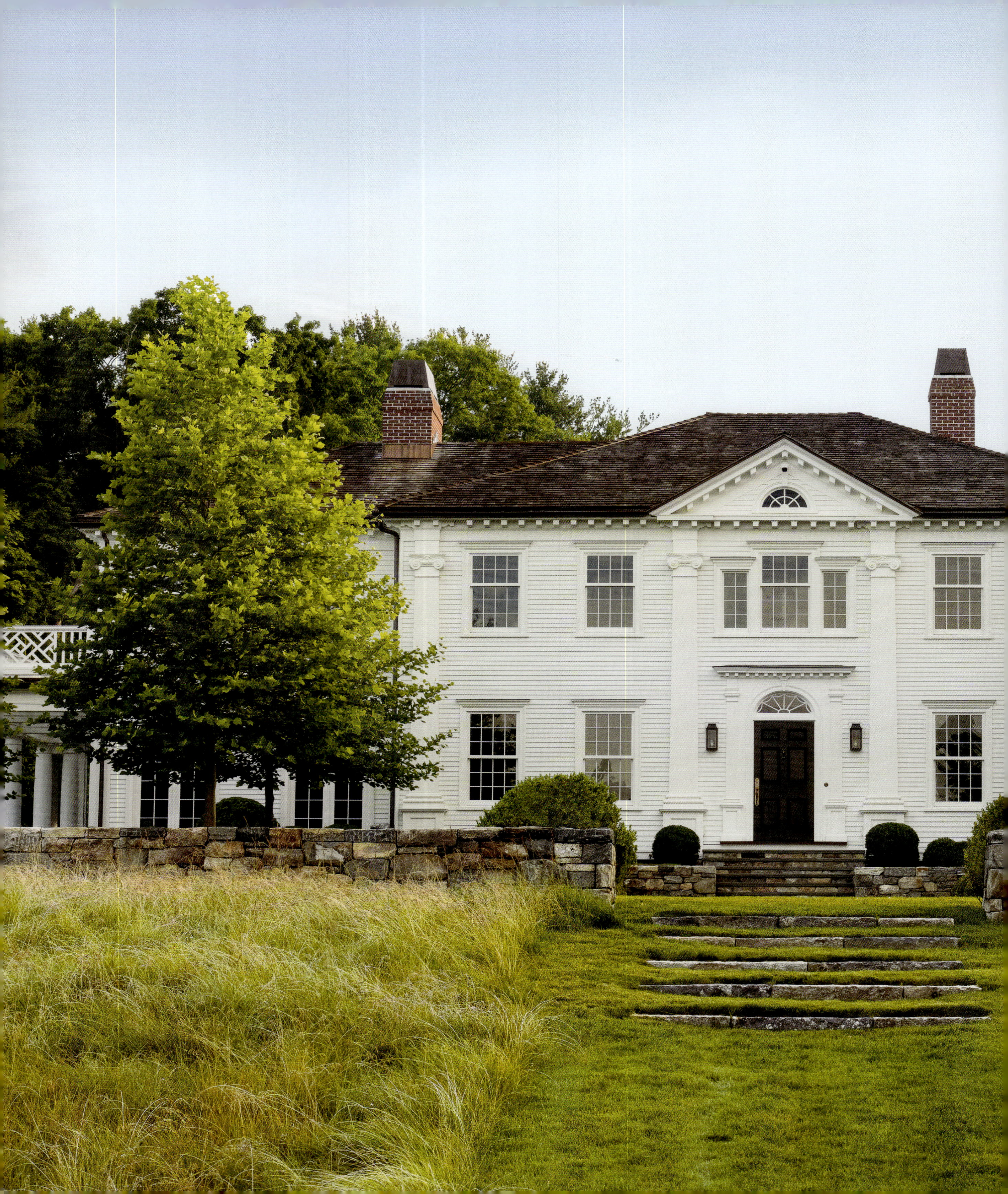

Poetic License

In the land of Emerson and Longfellow, Dan Gordon culls back an overgrown landscape, evoking its lyrical pedigree.

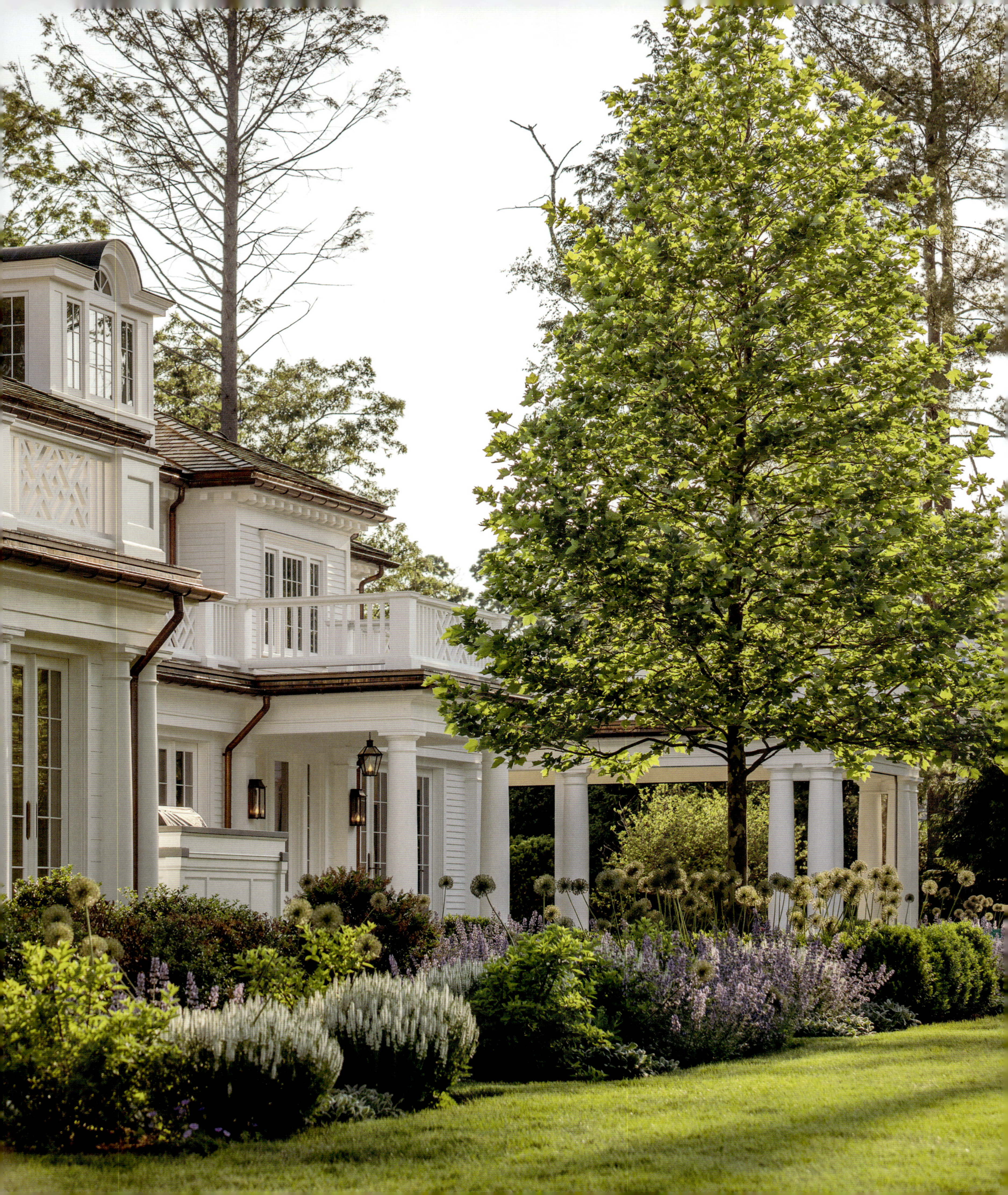

LEFT On the crest of Concord, Massachusetts's Authors' Ridge, landscape architect Dan Gordon reworked the overgrown grounds, reinstating a sense of order and grandeur befitting the classic Georgian Revival house. Mounded boxwoods and an allée of London plane trees frames the entrance and spotlights the architecture.

PAGES 44-45 A backyard lawn gives way to a grassy meadow, inviting a soft transition to the "rural nature of the surrounding landscape," says Gordon. He introduced a stone retaining wall to add definition and create quiet contrasts of form.

LEFT Closer to the home, white salvia, catmint, and allium puff balls embrace a backyard bluestone walkway, creating a more intimate, and fragrant, contrast to the six acres of expansive lawn and meadow.

RIGHT Attuned to the sensory lyricism of a garden—visual, olfactory, and auditory—Gordon added a fountain engulfed by white hydrangea. "It's always lovely to hear a water feature from a porch," he says.

ROOTED IN THE PAST 47

On the Hunt

Preserving Bunny Mellon's estate in Virginia means paying heed to horses and exquisite pastoral vistas.

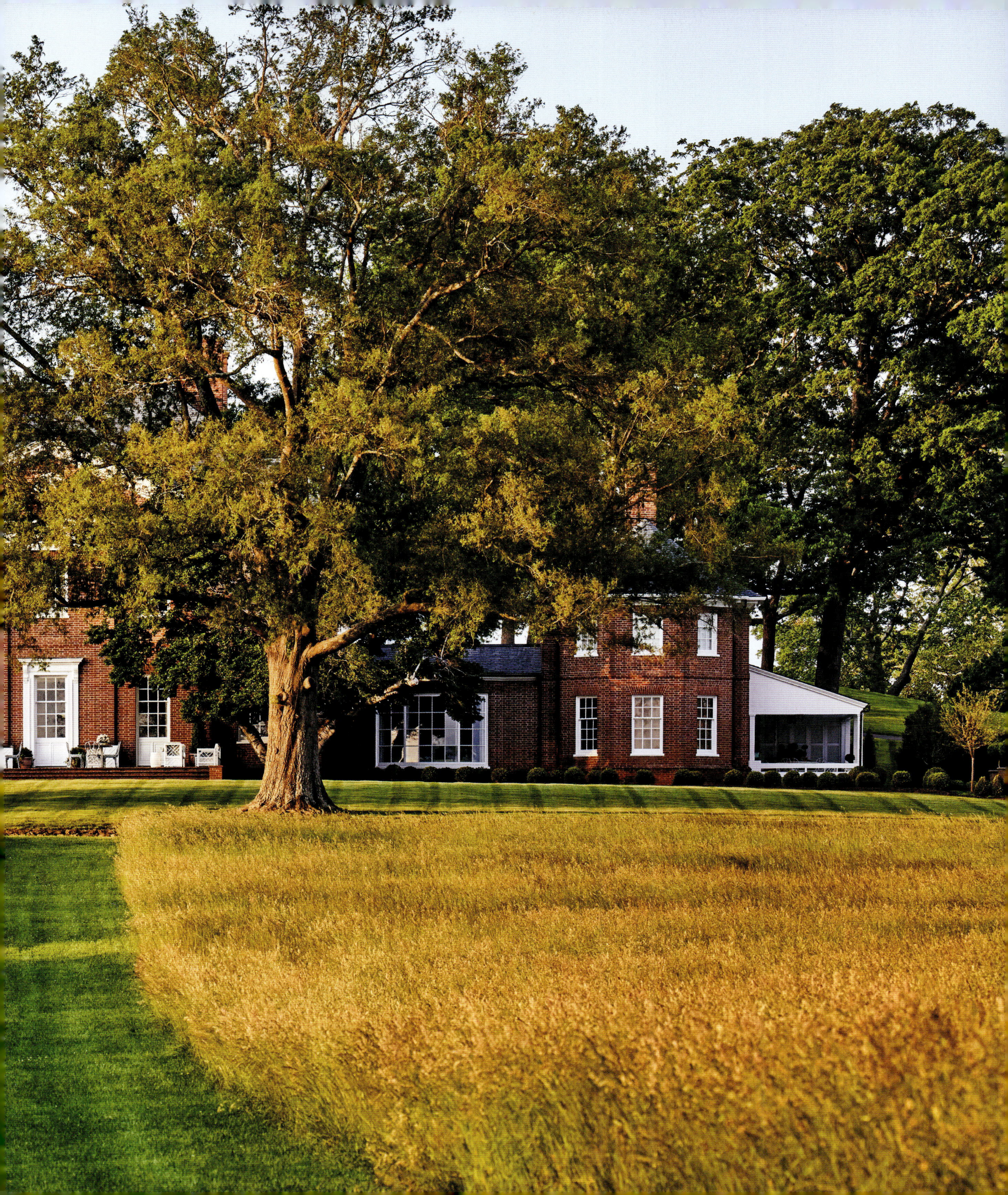

PAGES 49-50 The late Paul and Rachel "Bunny" Mellon's estate has been the starting place of the nation's oldest fox hunt since 1840. The current owners have preserved the legacy and Mrs. Mellon's gardens.

ABOVE Landscape designer Charles Stick and garden designer Bridget Wilson insisted that the gardens pay homage to the original Delano & Aldrich design. Red brick walls and walkways match the neo-Georgian-style main house.

RIGHT A resident peacock patrols the side gardens consisting of three tiered spaces leading down to Bunny Mellon's famous Serpentine garden. In the background, rolling horse pastures and hills for riding stretch for miles.

ENCHANTING GARDENS

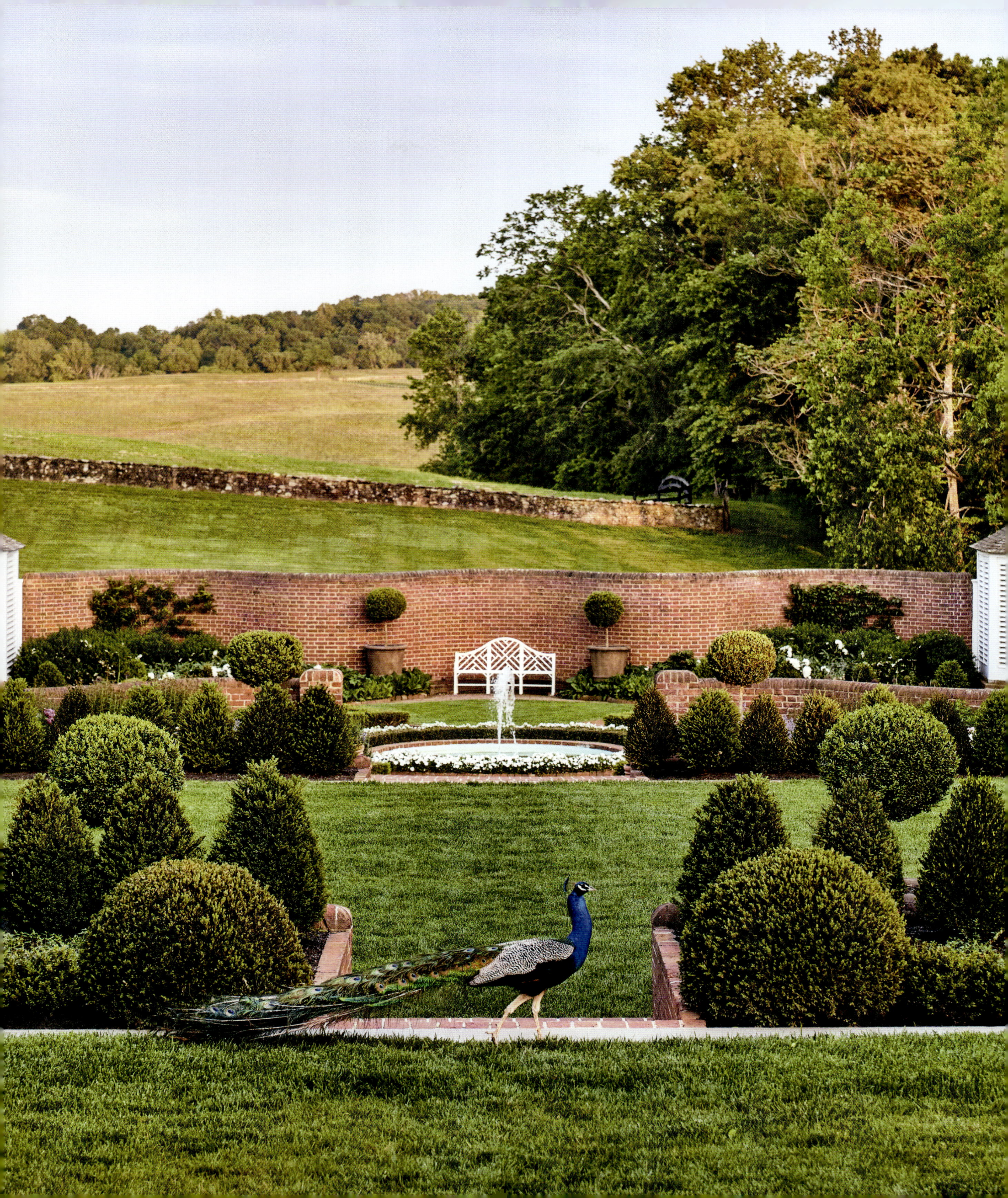

RIGHT Wilson reimagined a sloping lawn behind the house with Green Mountain boxwood parterres accented with spherical topiaries, spirals, and columns. Espaliered magnolia trees reach and stretch along the brick wall.

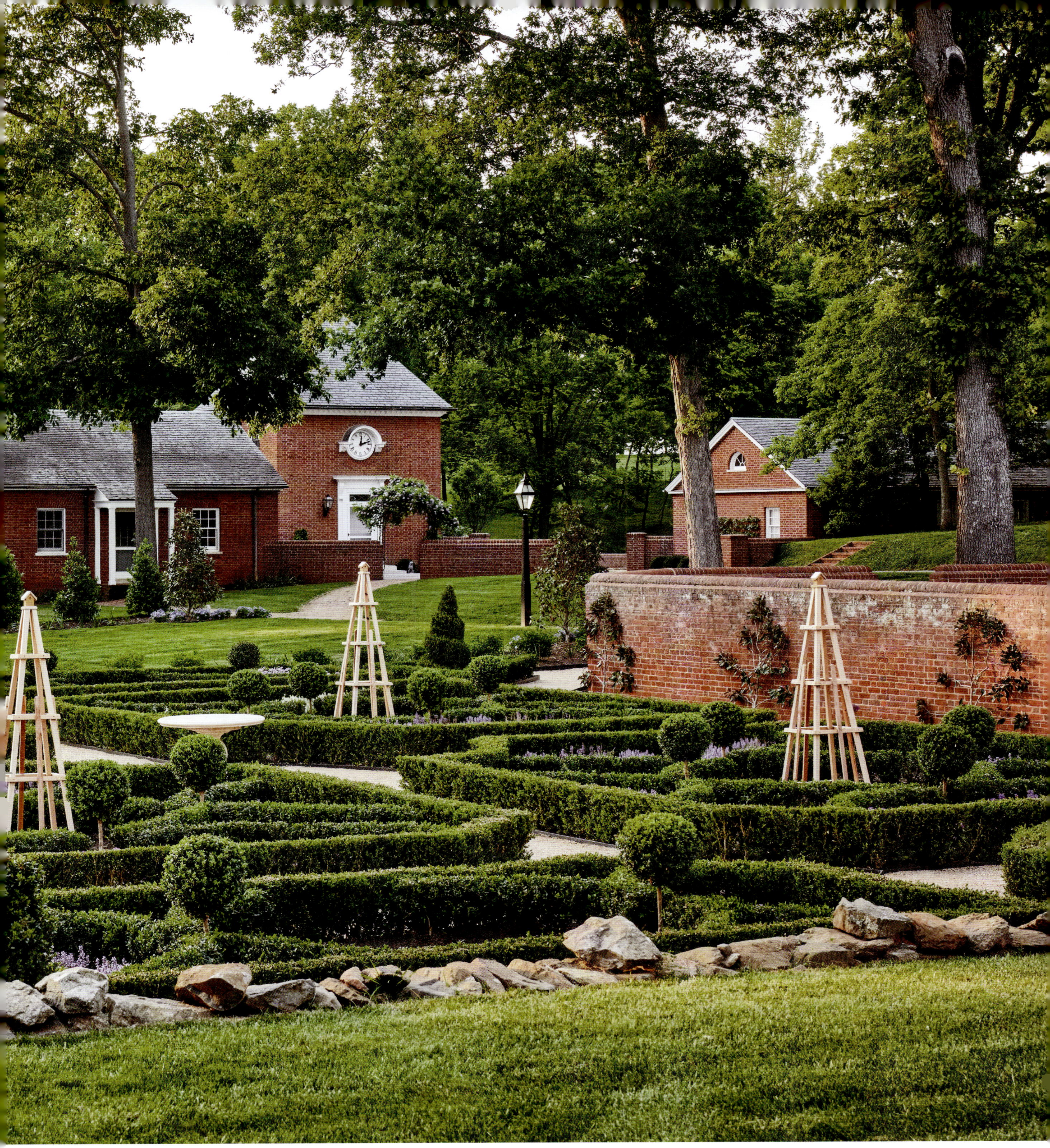

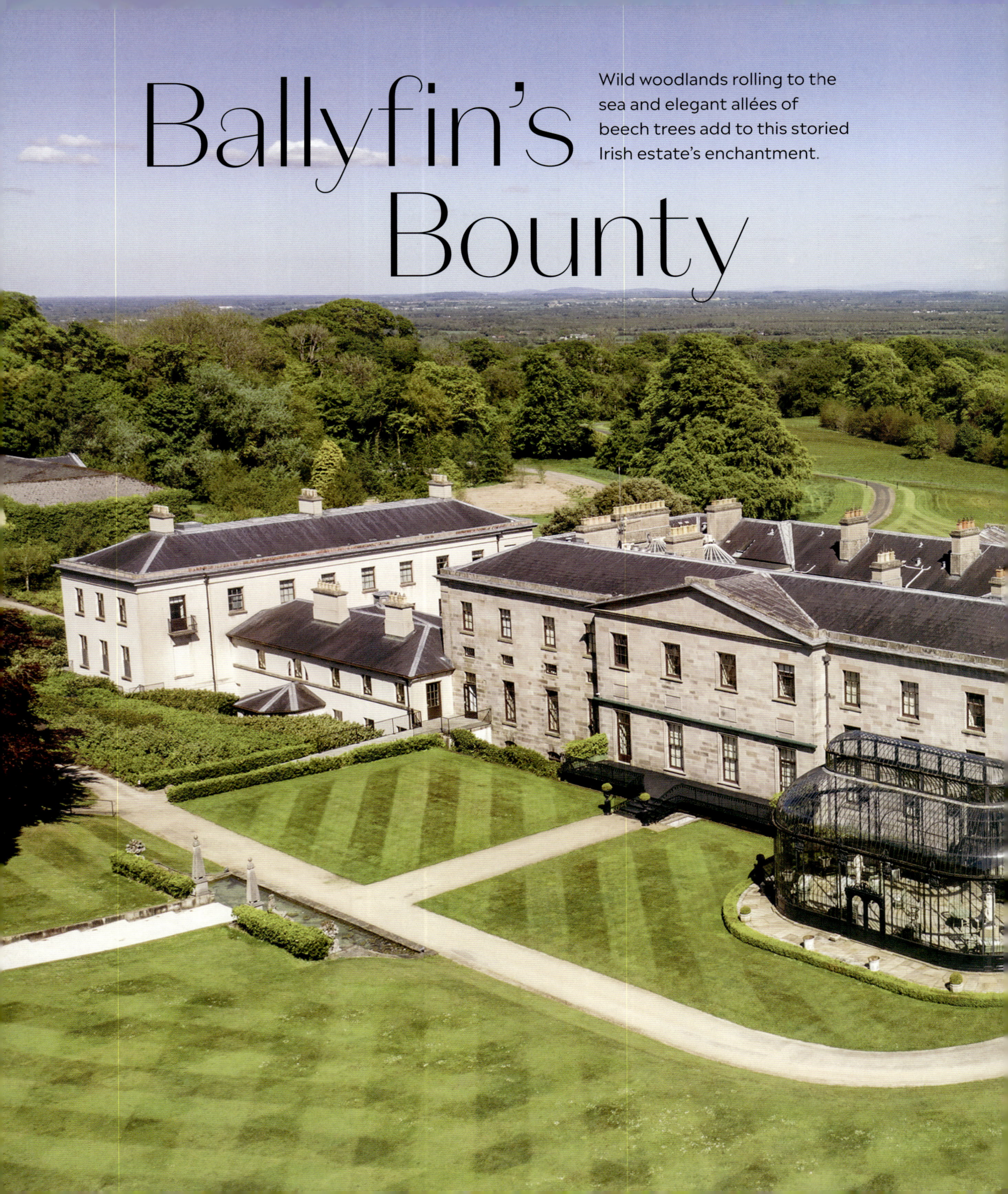

Ballyfin's Bounty

Wild woodlands rolling to the sea and elegant allées of beech trees add to this storied Irish estate's enchantment.

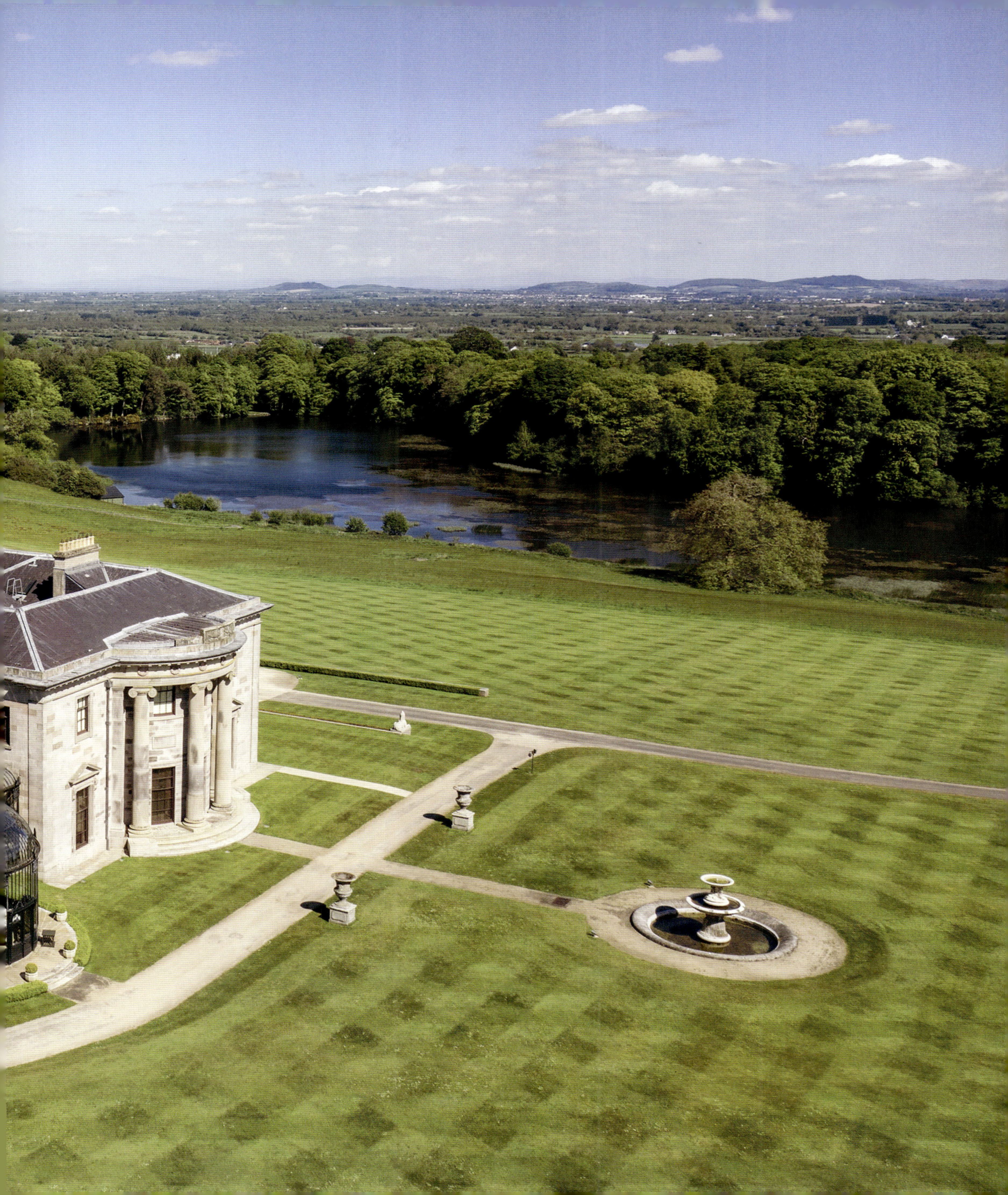

56   ENCHANTING GARDENS

PAGES 54-55 Ballyfin Demesne's 1820s neoclassical country house and grounds were restored by American businessman Fred Krehbiel, who reopened the property in 2011 as a five-star hotel.

LEFT A fountain cascades from a Doric temple at the house's rear, designed by landscape architect Jim Reynolds with architect John O'Connell. The 1,260-acre estate also has a quercetum, "home to 85 taxa of oak with plans to become the largest collection in Ireland," says Dublin-based forester and arborist Joe Codd.

ABOVE Ballyfin's epic orangery, designed by 1850s glass house star Richard Turner of London's Palm House fame, has been recently restored as a conservatory dining room and now stars as a shimmering jewel on this notable property.

ROOTED IN THE PAST 57

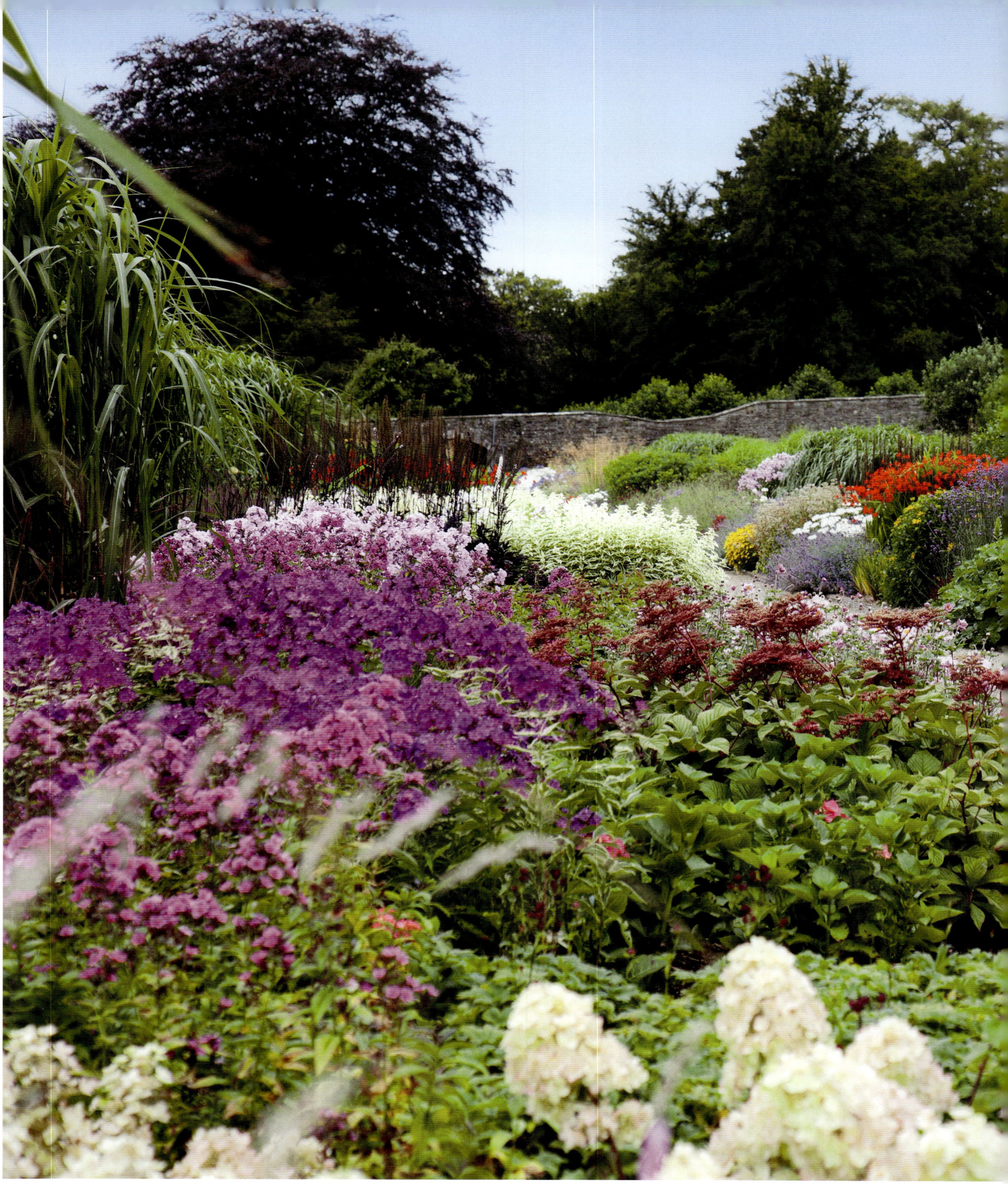

LEFT Centuries-old apple trees flank the lower walled garden, where vivid herbaceous borders of Phantom hydrangeas, Purple Flame phlox, tulips, and nepeta mingle with lettuces, sweet corn, and other vegetables. The pollinator bonanza is beneficial for insects and natural pest control.

ROOTED IN THE PAST 59

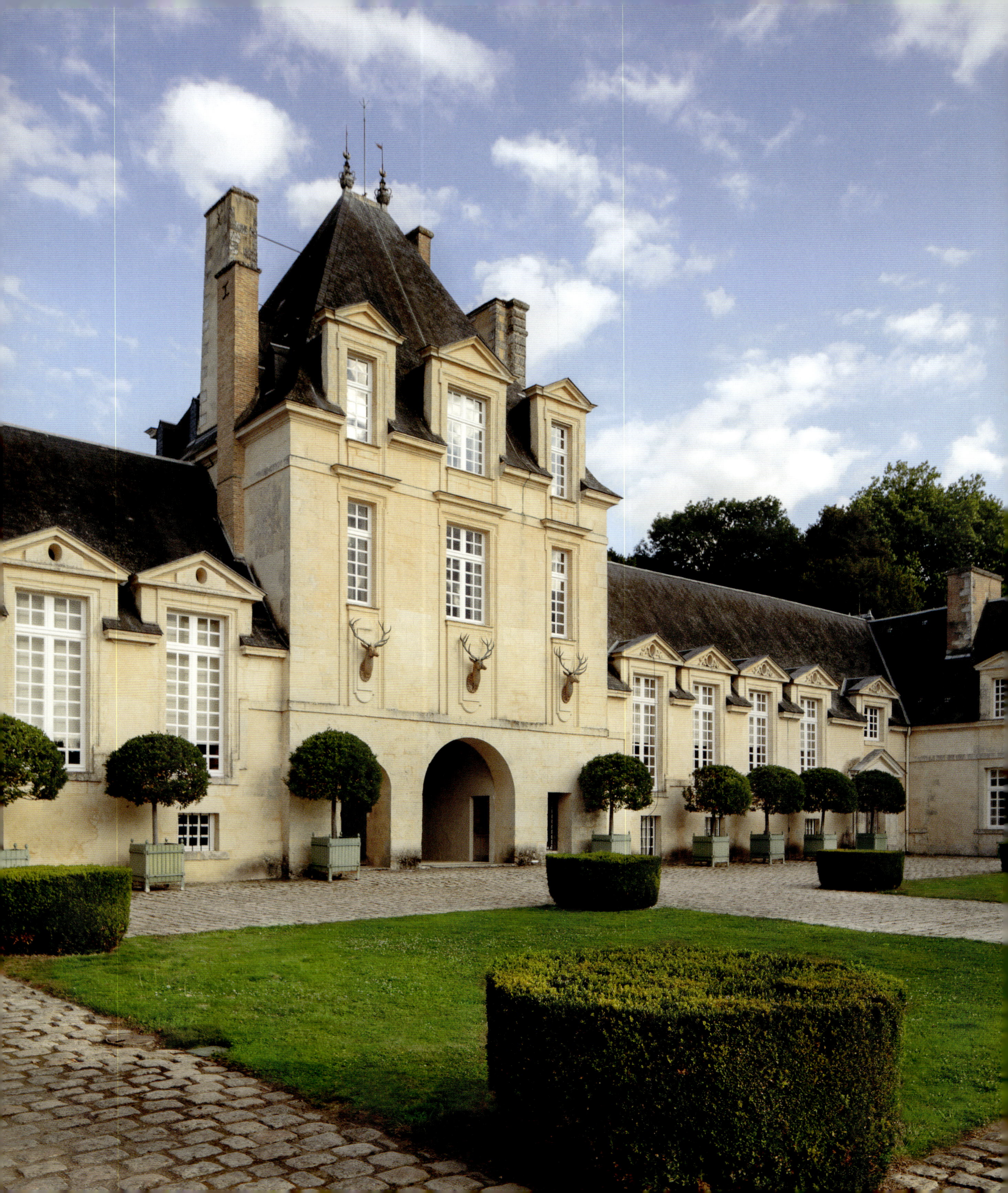

Estate of Grace

Zoë de Givenchy embraces intimate garden nooks and grand inspiration at Le Jonchet, her family's 16th-century manor in the French countryside.

LEFT Zoë and Olivier de Givenchy and their young family are now the residents at Le Jonchet. The grand manor outside of Paris once belonged to design icon Hubert de Givenchy, Olivier's late uncle. Hubert collaborated with his friend and designer Bunny Mellon in planning the estate's grounds, which Zoë, who grew up gardening alongside her mother, now tends.

RIGHT Afternoon picnics by the lake harken to days of yore. "It's a heady mix, as you might imagine," says Zoë. "This mythical place and the legacy of a great man—the sheer beauty of it, the gardens, the parterre, the lake, those golden fields of wheat that stretch over the distant hills."

ROOTED IN THE PAST

LEFT In honor of Hubert's namesake saint—Saint Hubert, patron saint of the hunt—stags are a mascot of sorts at Le Jonchet, both here in statuesque form, peering out over the meticulously clipped boxwood hedges, and as trophy medallions (at right).

RIGHT "Everything Hubert did was immaculate, so it's hard to think one might improve on anything. We've kept everything as it was," says Zoë. "It still feels remarkable to me somehow, and very grown-up, to think we're now in charge of this spectacular place."

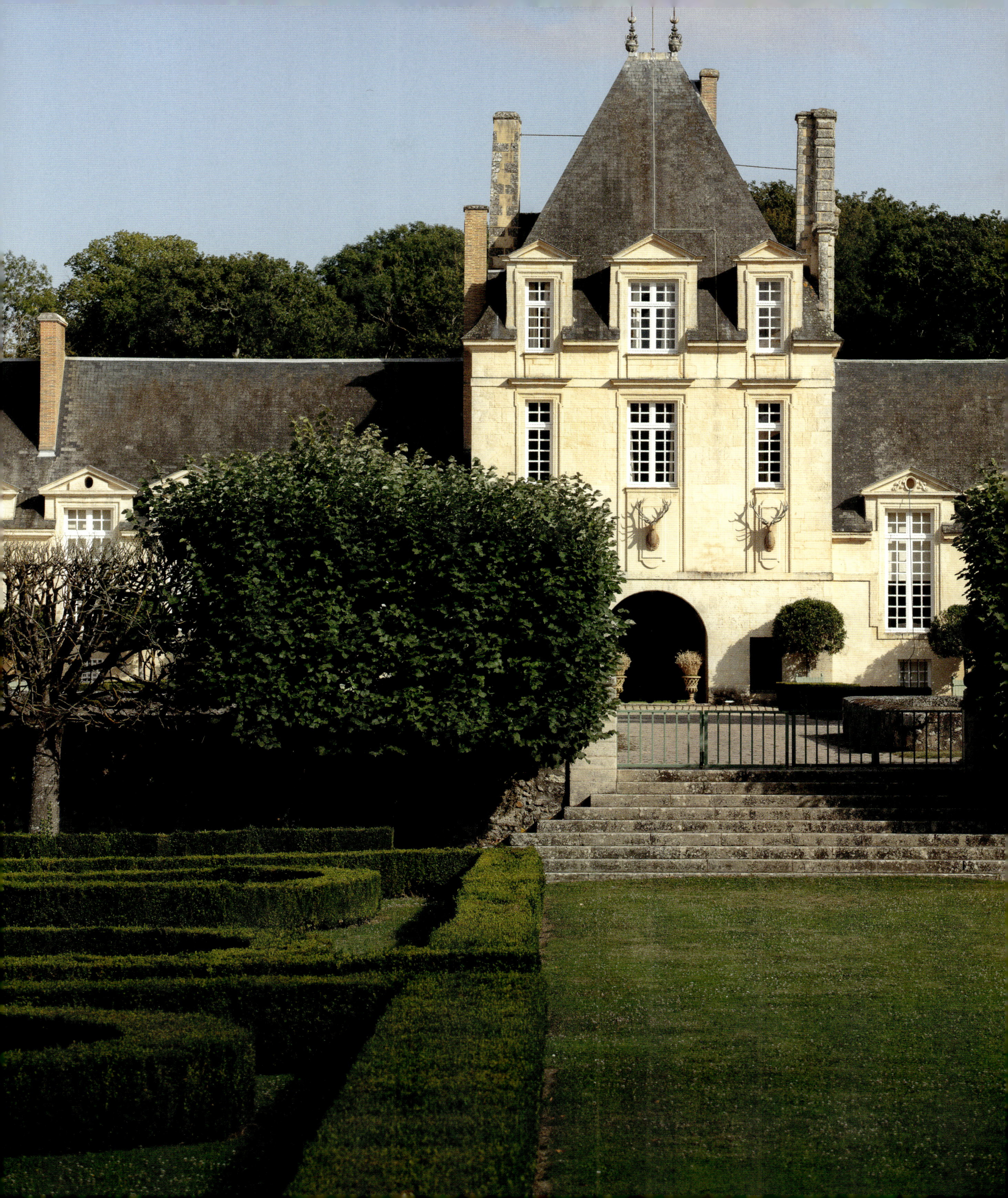

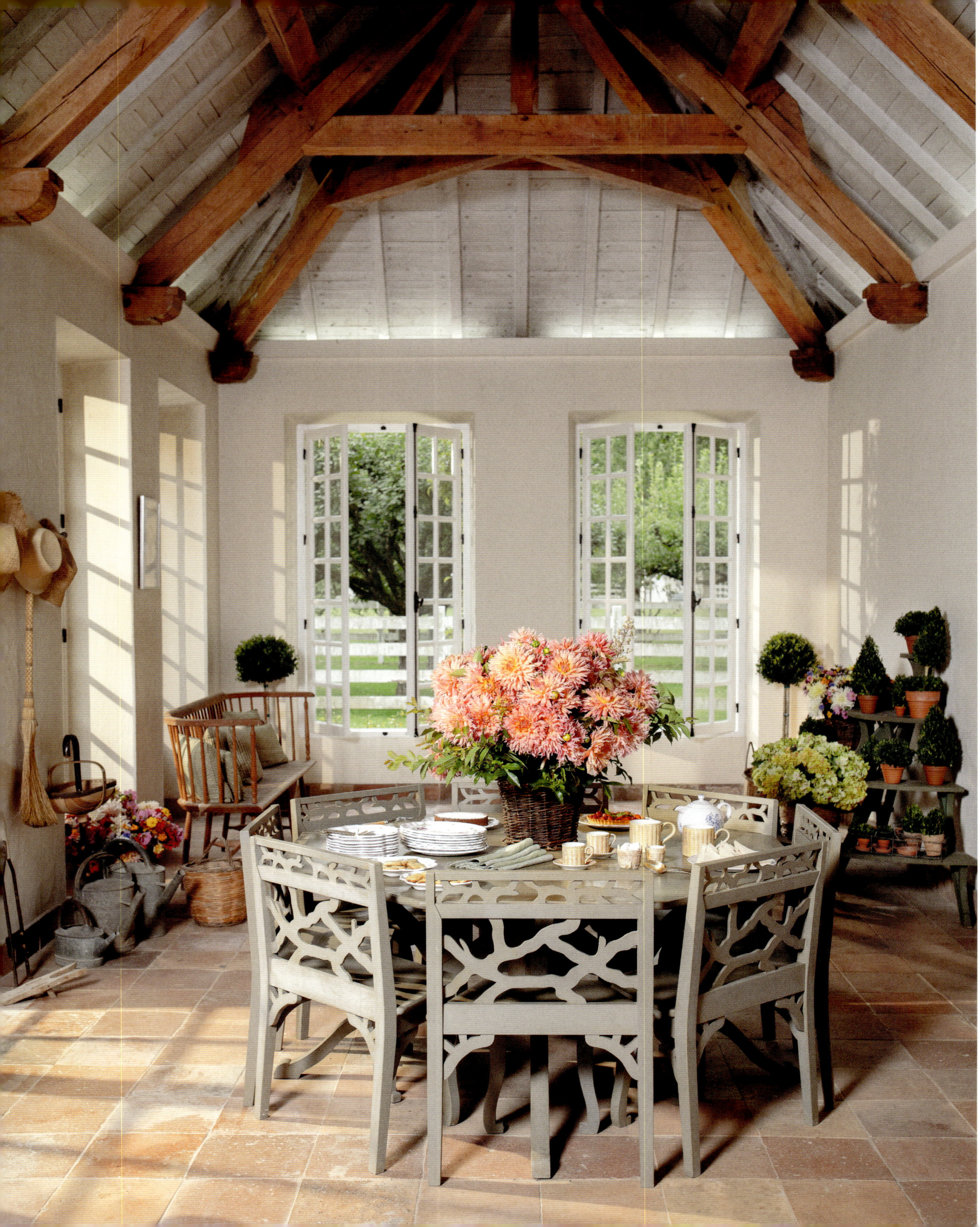

LEFT In the orangery, a central octagonal table designed by Hubert is surrounded by carved wood chairs that mirror the fruit trees visible through the windows. Hubert did everything with intention, notes Zoë. "Nothing was an accident."

RIGHT Espaliered pear trees climb the walls and windows of the orangery, where Zoë likes to host "long lunches or tea when the afternoon light is magical."

ROOTED IN THE PAST 65

LEFT "There's something so comforting about observing the repetition of the seasons on grounds with such long history," says Zoë. Le Jonchet is all about family and "authentic human connection," she adds— "coming together to share time and stories and long strolls with one another."

RIGHT Clipped miniature box hedges are the centerpiece for a luncheon in the parterre garden, "amid the joyful sounds of birds and sweeping views of the grounds," says Zoë, who sets the table with her own line of Z.d.G. tableware.

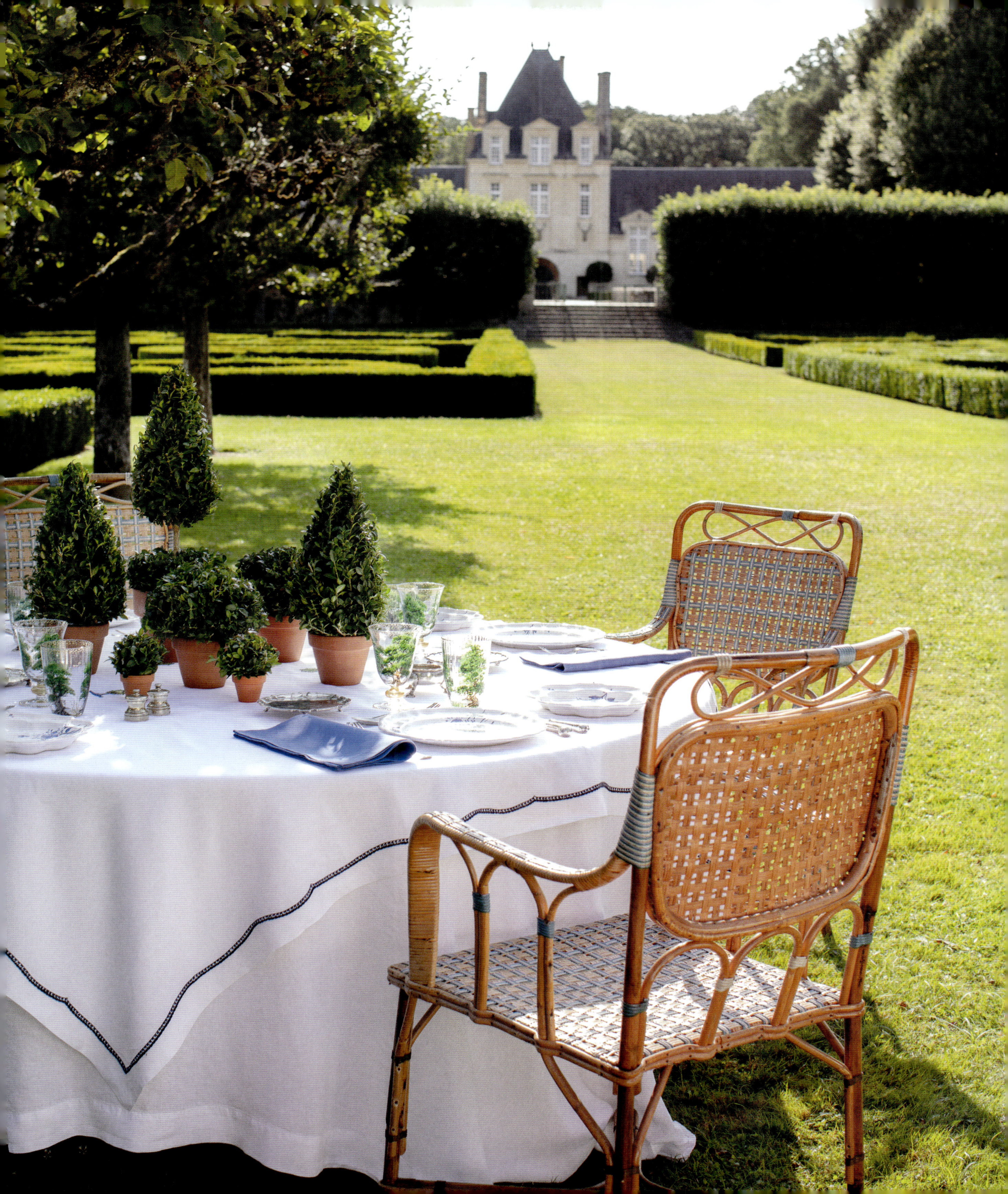

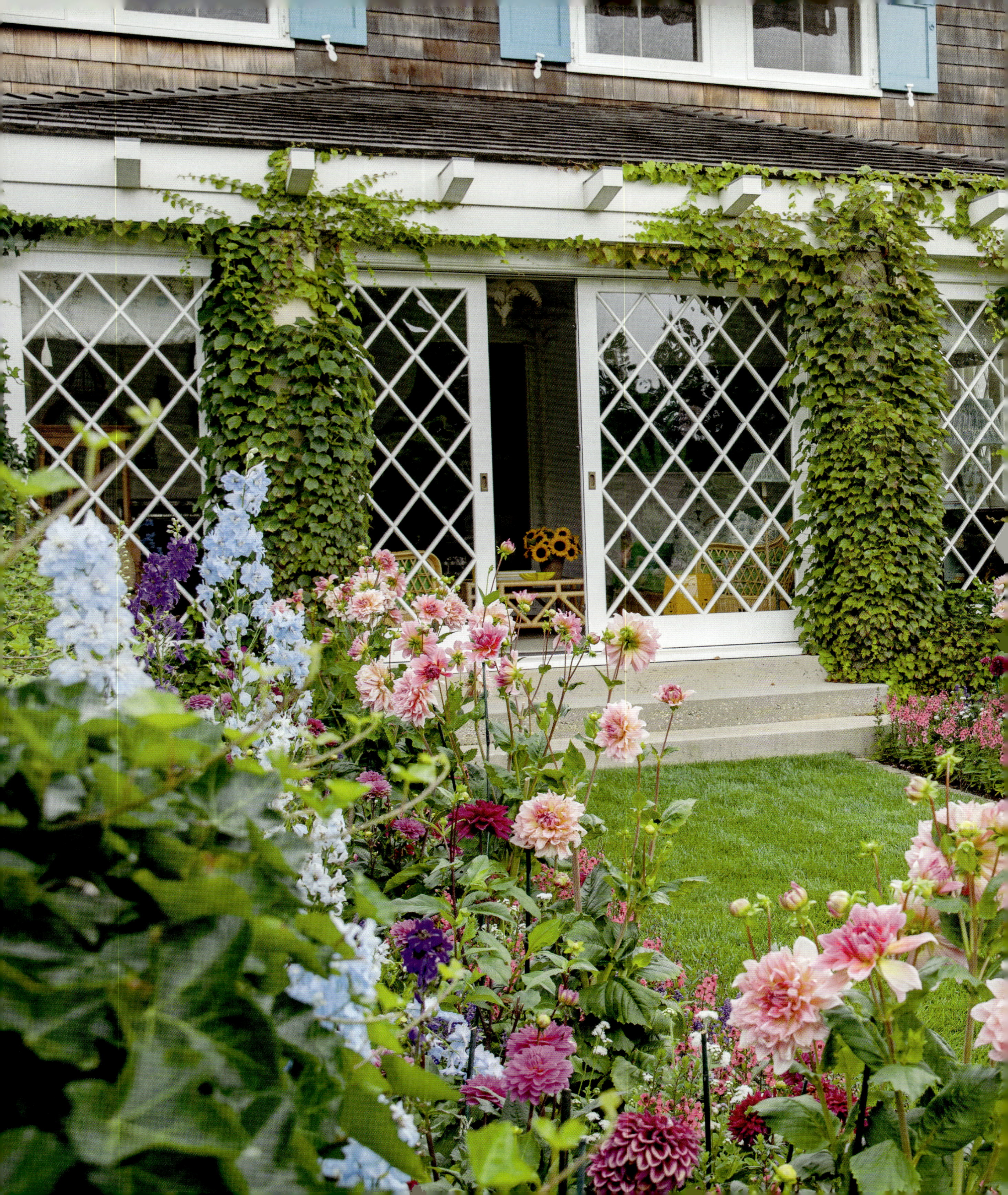

CHAPTER 2

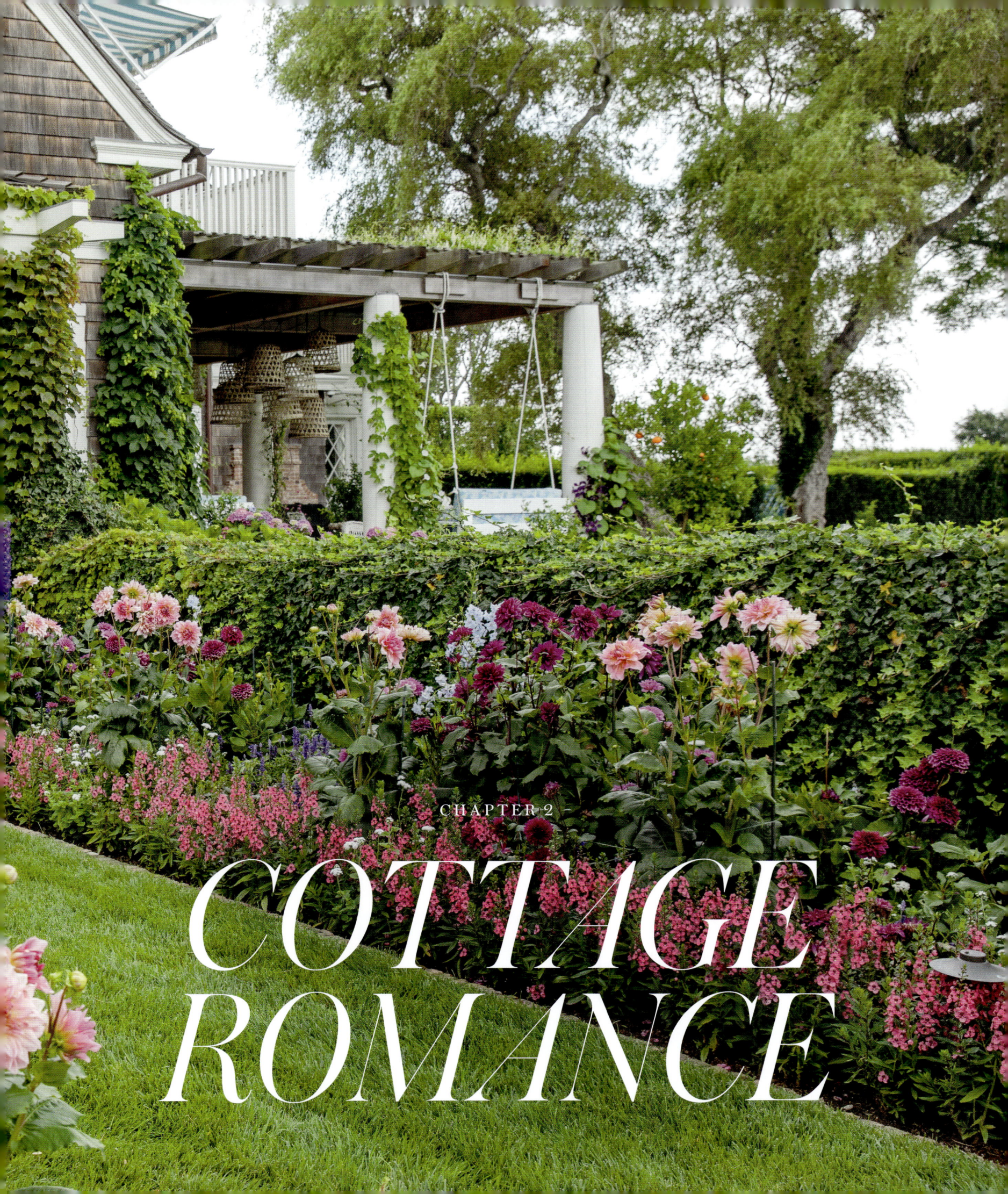

COTTAGE ROMANCE

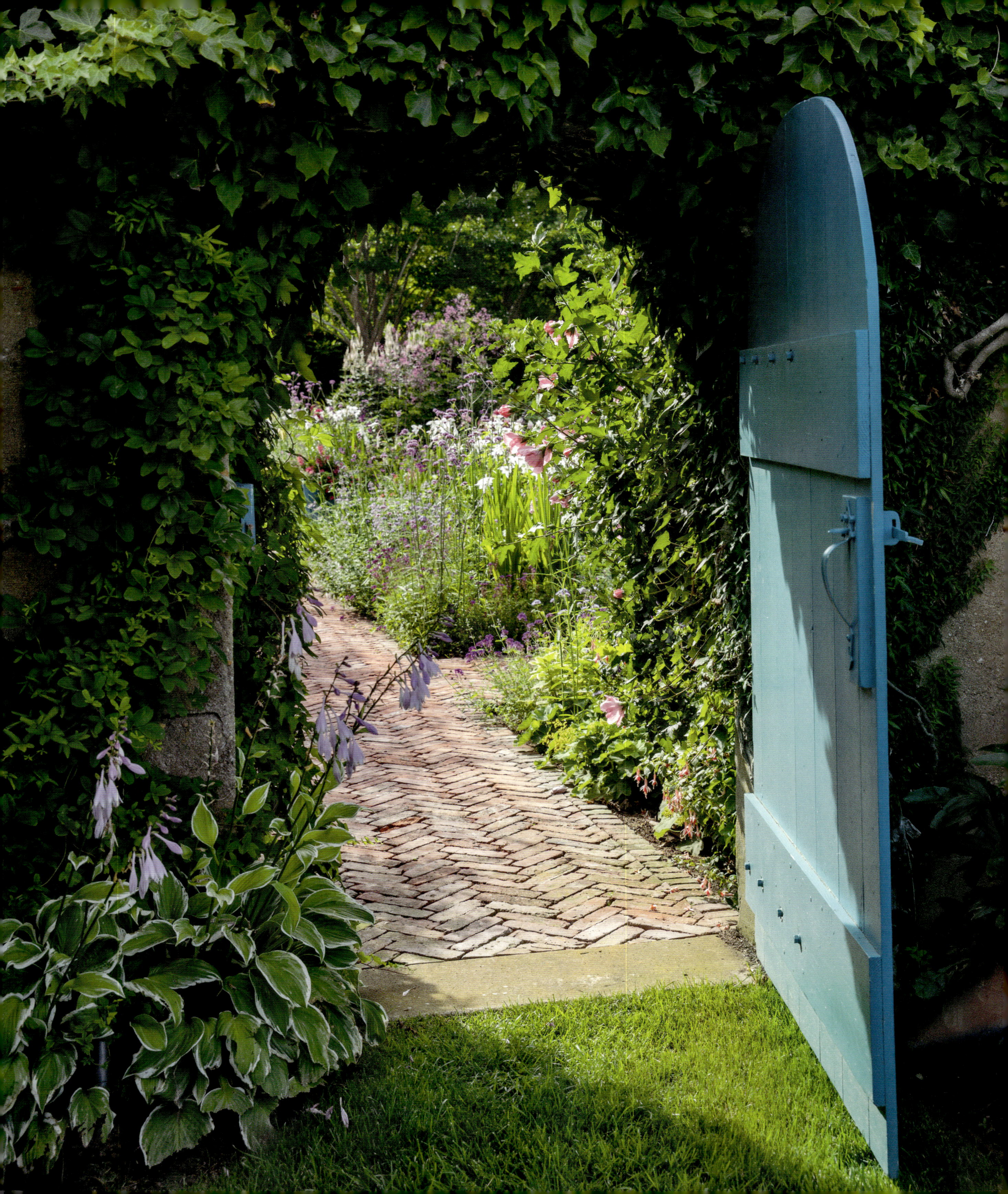

COTTAGE ROMANCE

gARDENS DELIGHT, ENTHRALL, AND NURTURE US, but they also reveal us. Are you formal or informal? A rule-following stickler or someone who daringly colors outside the lines? Do you prefer a librarian's sense of order or the jumbled box of books at a thrift sale? If a garden was given a Myers-Briggs assessment, the cottage garden would likely be an ENFJ (Extroverted, Intuitive, Feeling, Judging)— warm and gregarious, maybe a tad idealistic, focused more on the big picture than the minor details. We love a cottage garden's rumpled-hair charm, the way it revels in spontaneity and beguiles with nonchalance. A cottage garden is where secrets hide beneath layers and in between cracks, and where forgiveness, not perfection, is the name of the game.

But don't confuse the cottage garden's haphazard ease with assuming they're easy to pull off. As the designers featured in the following pages make clear, much thought and careful planning goes into a garden appearing slightly unplanned (the horticultural version of Dolly Parton's famous quote: "It takes a lot of money to look this cheap."). For Liz Lange, owner of the famed Grey Gardens in the Hamptons, achieving "that overgrown, wild feeling" for the cedar-shake cottage's grounds took three years of work with landscape architect Deborah Nevins. Whether in various corners of Bunny Williams's Connecticut garden, or beside a California poolside designed by Erica Timbrell, or on what's got to be the world's most fragrant farm, the classic elements of an English cottage garden—rampant color, roses gone haywire, a mash-up of height, texture, shape—are all present.

Cottage gardens romance us by sheer old-school flirting. A wink here, a whisper there, a glorious whiff of blooming perfection. They beckon with their casual, come-one-come-all openness. Nothing fussy or intimidating, just some happy dahlias, flashy foxgloves, and a smattering of friendly, slightly lazy ferns. There's most likely a little cottage garden gate you've been dying to open. Here's your chance; let's go explore.

LEFT Ivy-covered walls and a beckoning blue gate lead to one of many garden rooms on the restored grounds of the iconic Grey Gardens cottage in the Hamptons.

PAGES 68-69 Landscape architect Deborah Nevins layered dahlias and delphinium, among other perennials, for a riot of cheerful cottage garden blossoms.

Going Grey

Grey Gardens, the iconic East Hampton property with a colorful past, reblooms after a thoughtful revival by owner Liz Lange and landscape architect Deborah Nevins.

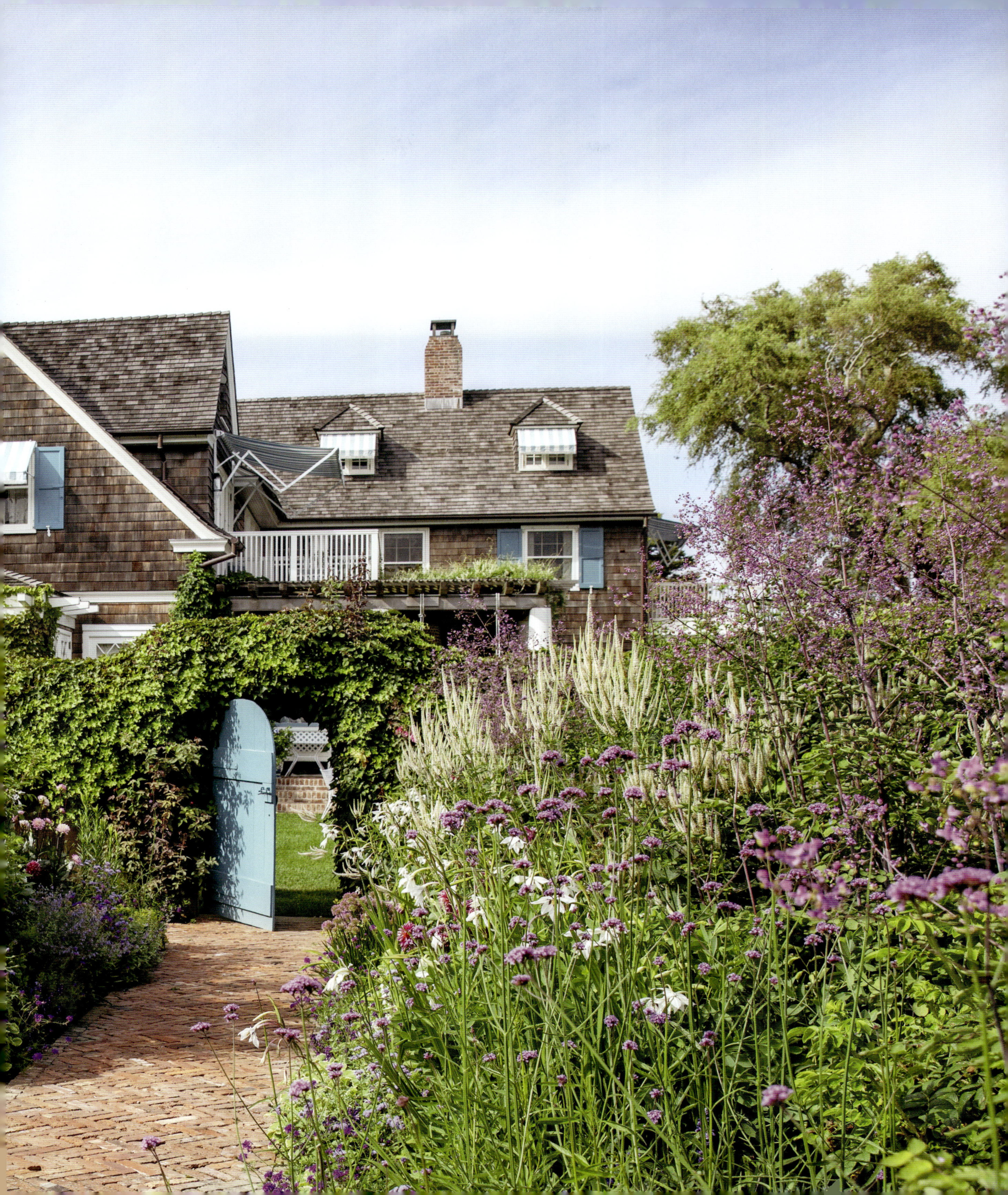

PAGES 72-73 "We wanted an English garden with an overgrown, wild feeling, but not so wild that it felt like Grey Gardens from the movie," says Lange, who was inspired by the gardens at Sissinghurst and Babington House in England. The walled garden with a herringbone brick walkway hosts a rambunctious array of leggy perennials at varying heights.

ABOVE Lange and Nevins worked to invoke and honor the property's past while making it "our own," says Lange, who added the octagonal fountain, for example. Aqua blue wooden planters and garden gates match the house shutters.

RIGHT The restored pergola offers a shady spot for a meal or cocktail, while benches invite a place to rest and savor the lushness of other garden rooms. "There's almost a quietness, and you feel like you don't even know where you are," says Lange. "The garden has this strangely magical, peaceful, beautiful atmosphere."

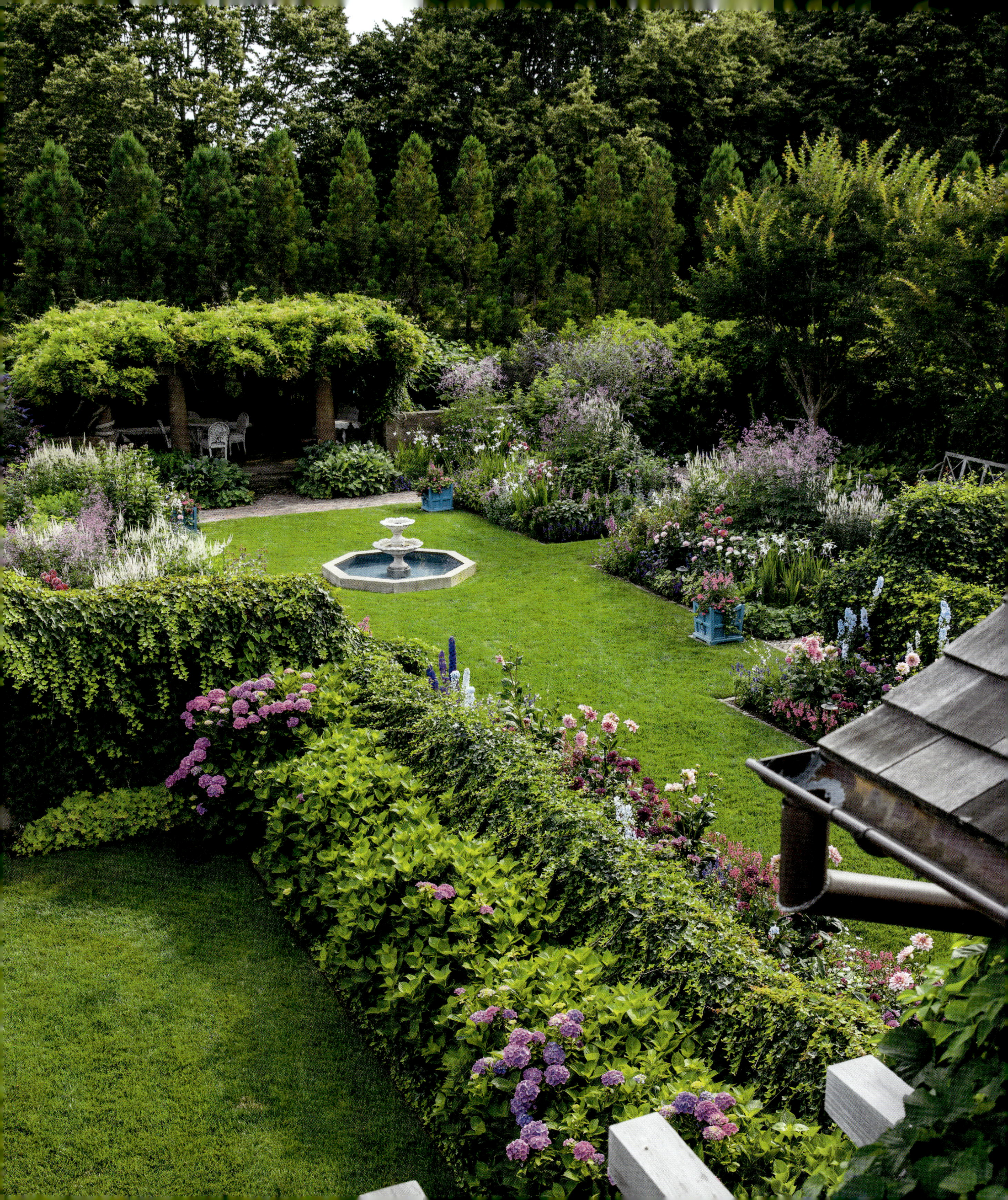

RIGHT On the east side of the house, a custom fountain, planters, and urns anchor an entirely new garden space added by Lange and Nevins. The garden decor was made in India, all inspired by a set of blue Indian palace doors Lange had found. A wall of white hydrangea adds a dramatic backdrop.

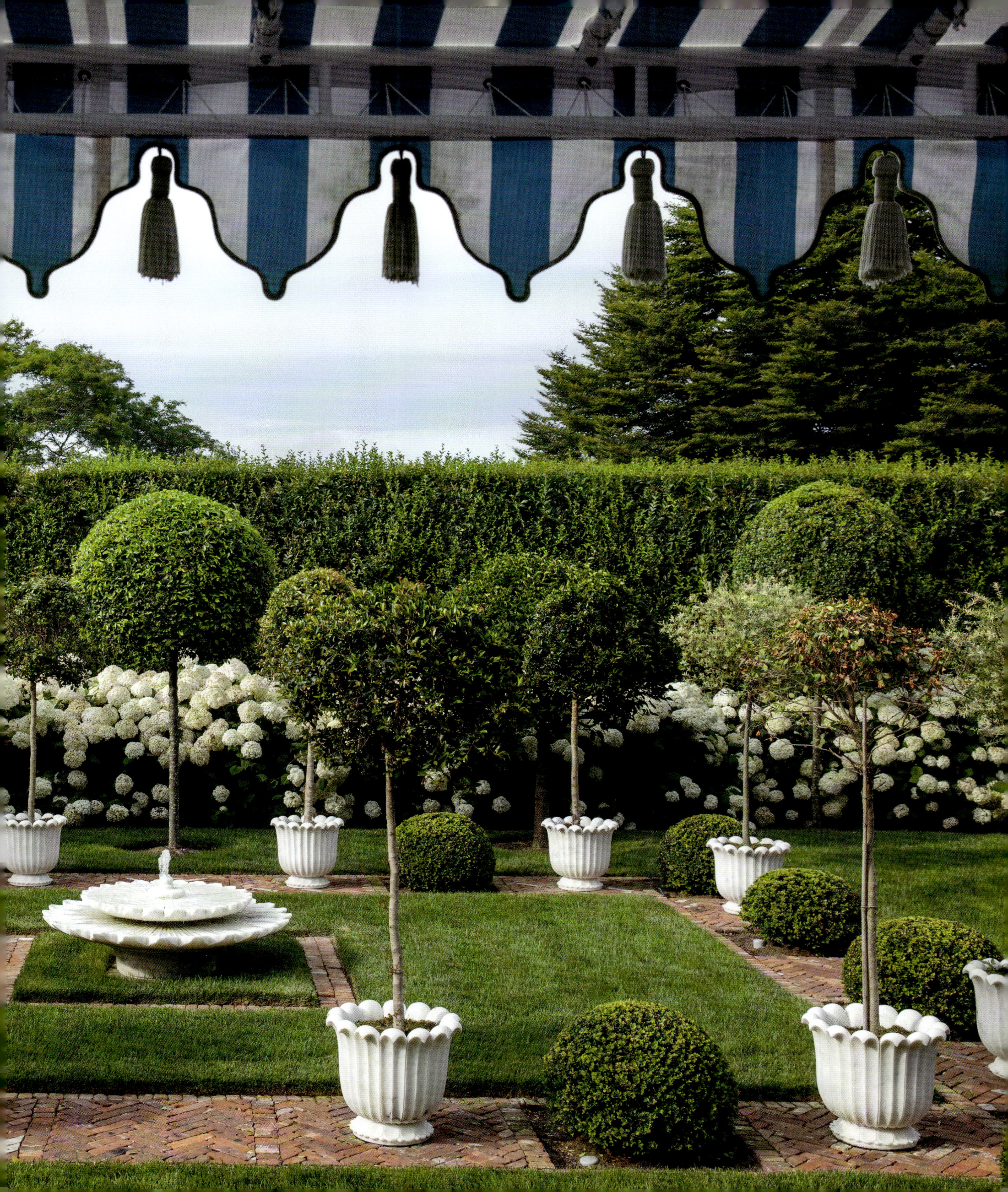

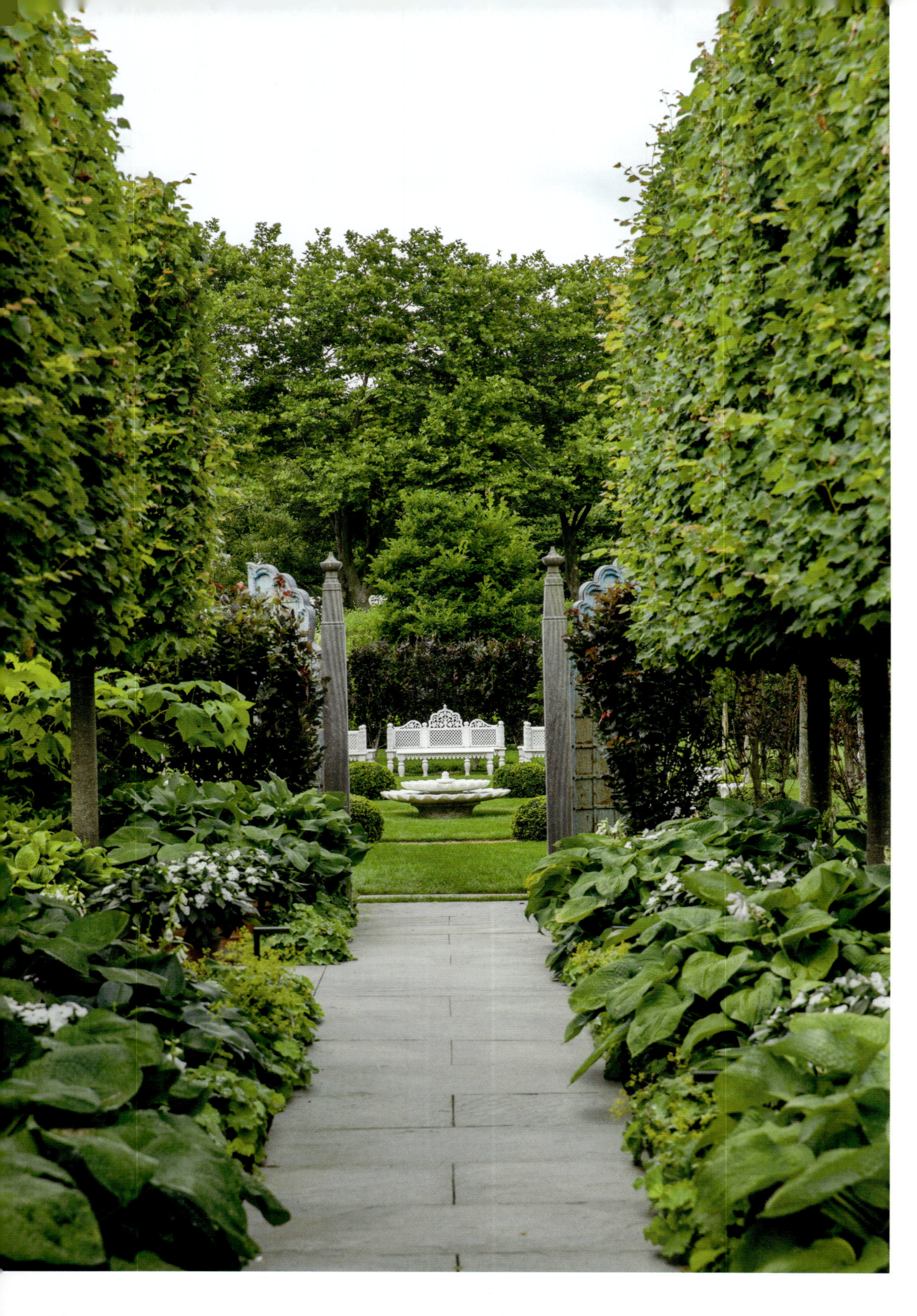

LEFT Connecting the back of the house to the Indian garden, a bluestone path lined with linden trees leads to the blue Indian palace gates, just visible behind the trees.

RIGHT To save the property's oldest tree, which had bent and grown in a direction that was perpendicular to the ground, Lange reworked the placement of the front driveway. She had vine-covered post added to support the heavy leaning branches, which now shade pink and purple hydrangeas.

PAGES 80-81 Nevins reinstated many elements, including the walled garden and a pergola. There's also a thatched garden hut that had been added by the property's second owner, the prominent horticulturalist and author Anna Gilman Hill—the first to name it "Grey Gardens." Garden paths use repurposed bricks from the house. "Nothing feels shiny or new," says Lange.

78   ENCHANTING GARDENS

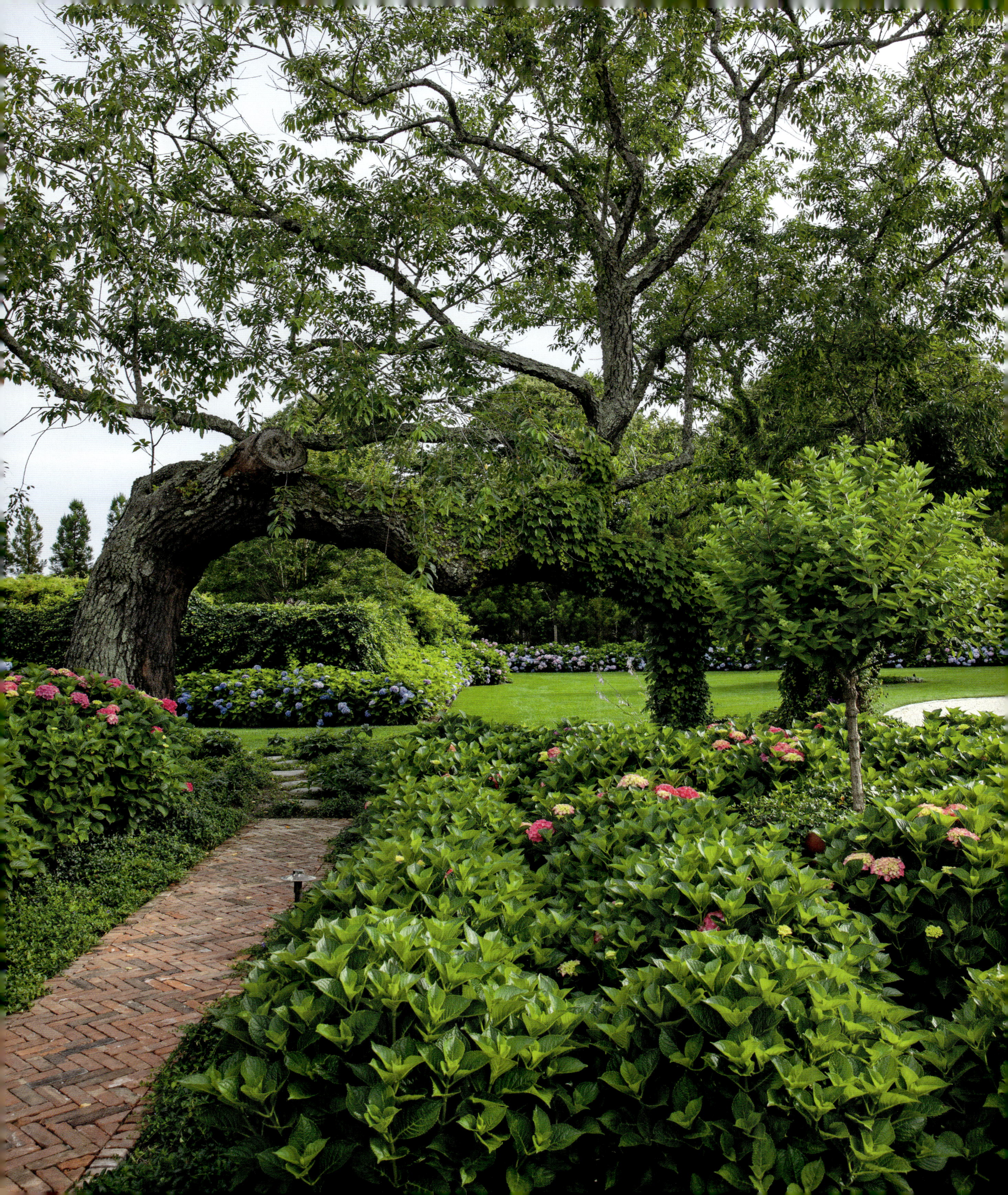

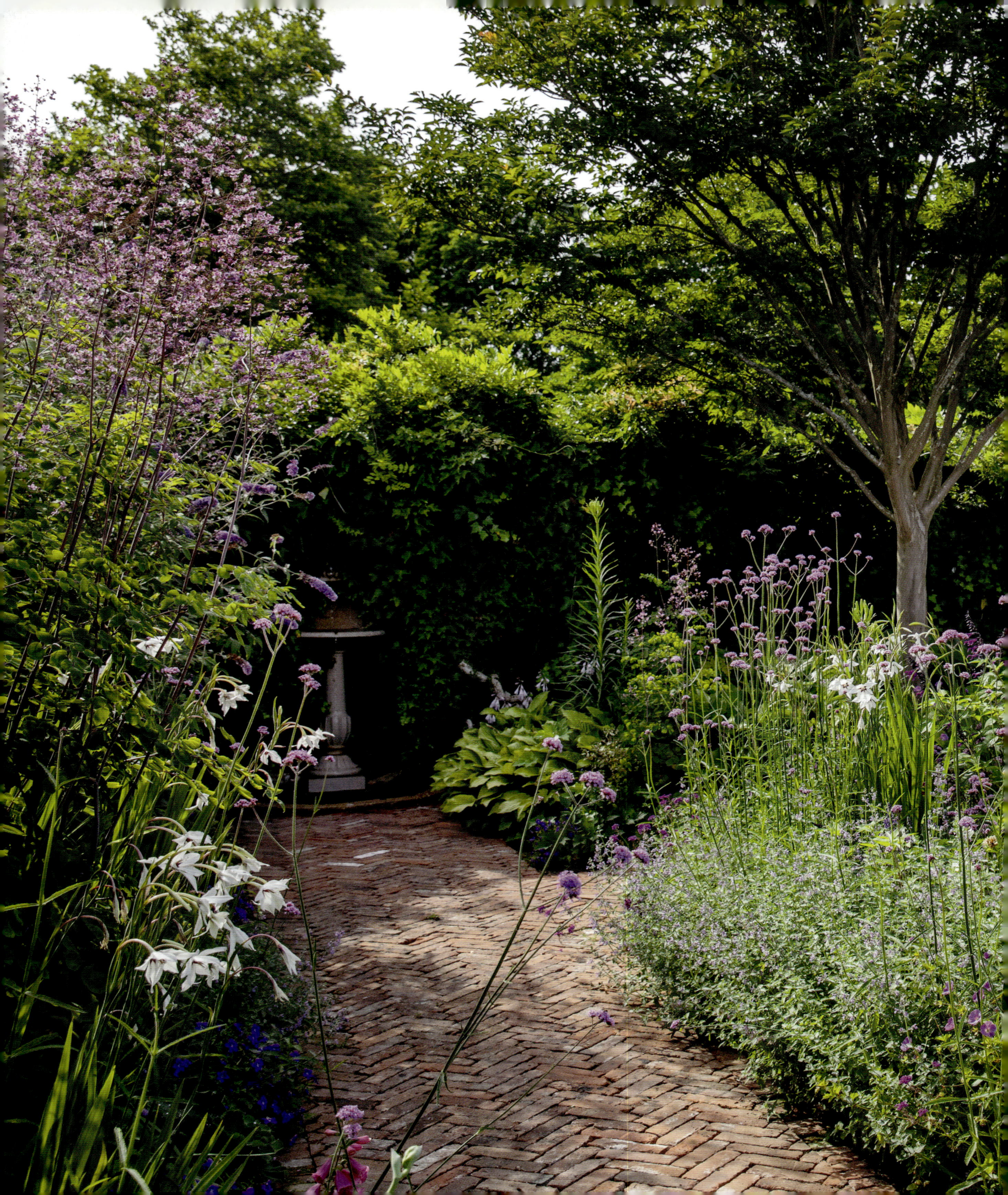

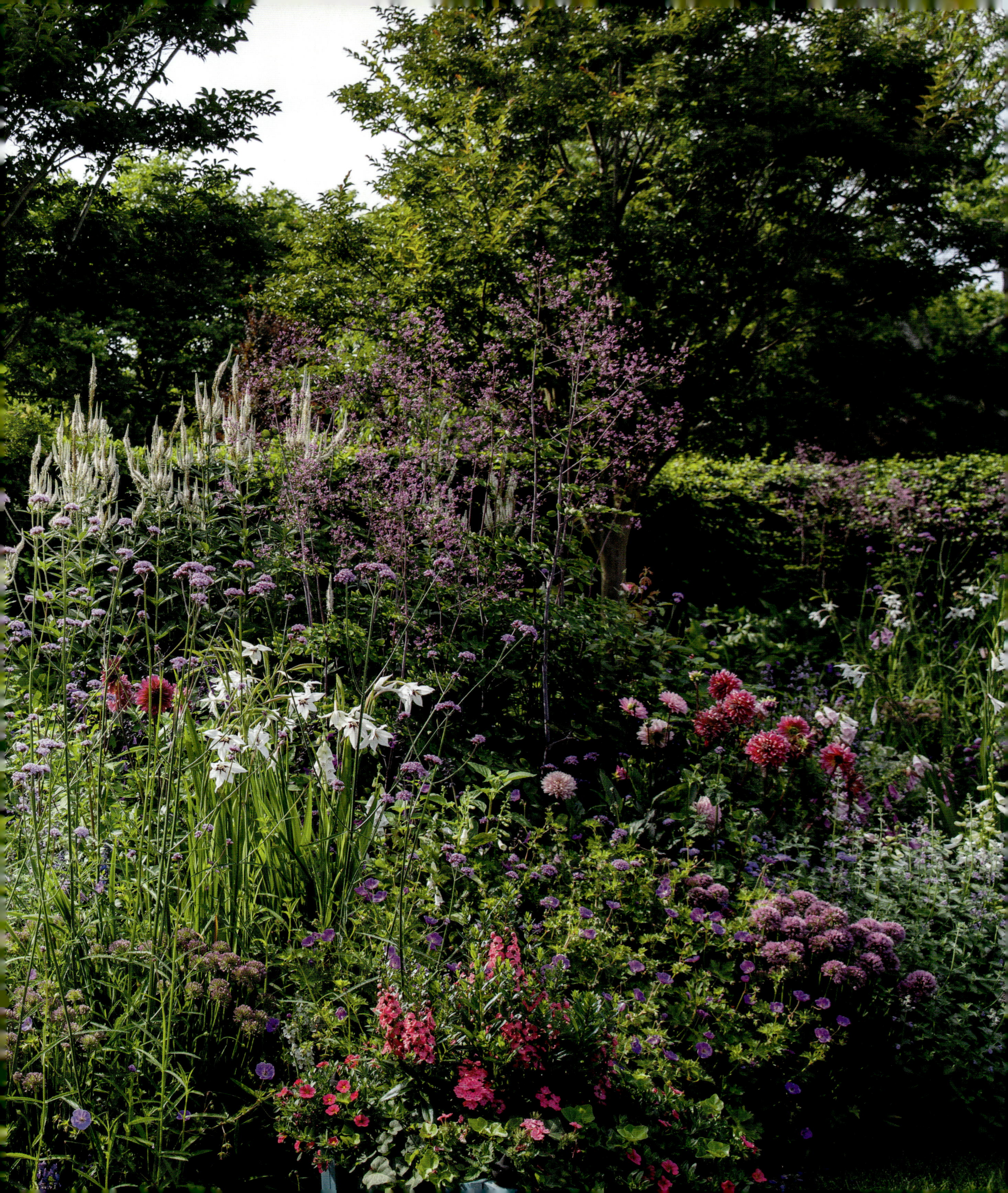

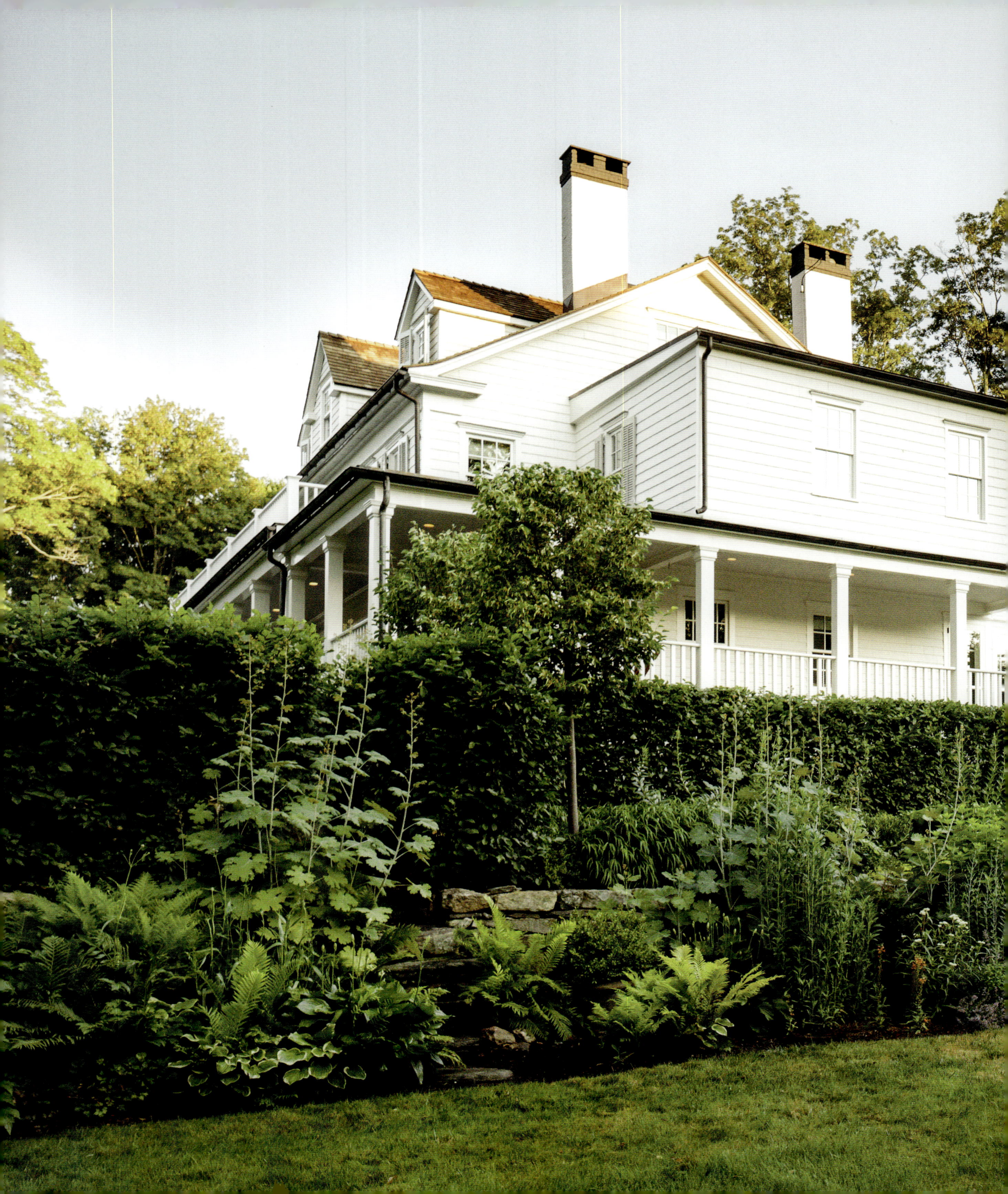

Greenwich Green

With loungey terraces and wispy garden paths, a Connecticut farmhouse rewards rambling and basking in the beautiful.

PAGES 82-83 A double herbaceous border filled to the brim with scarlet bee balm flowers, purple coneflowers, and Japanese anemone is punctuated by cubed linden trees. Hornbeam hedges frame the garden, providing structure and balance.

BELOW Tuteurs line up, waiting to support the top-heavy dahlias and peonies that bloom in the summer. Butterfly bush, giant scabious, and Japanese anemone are among other pollinators that draw bees and butterflies.

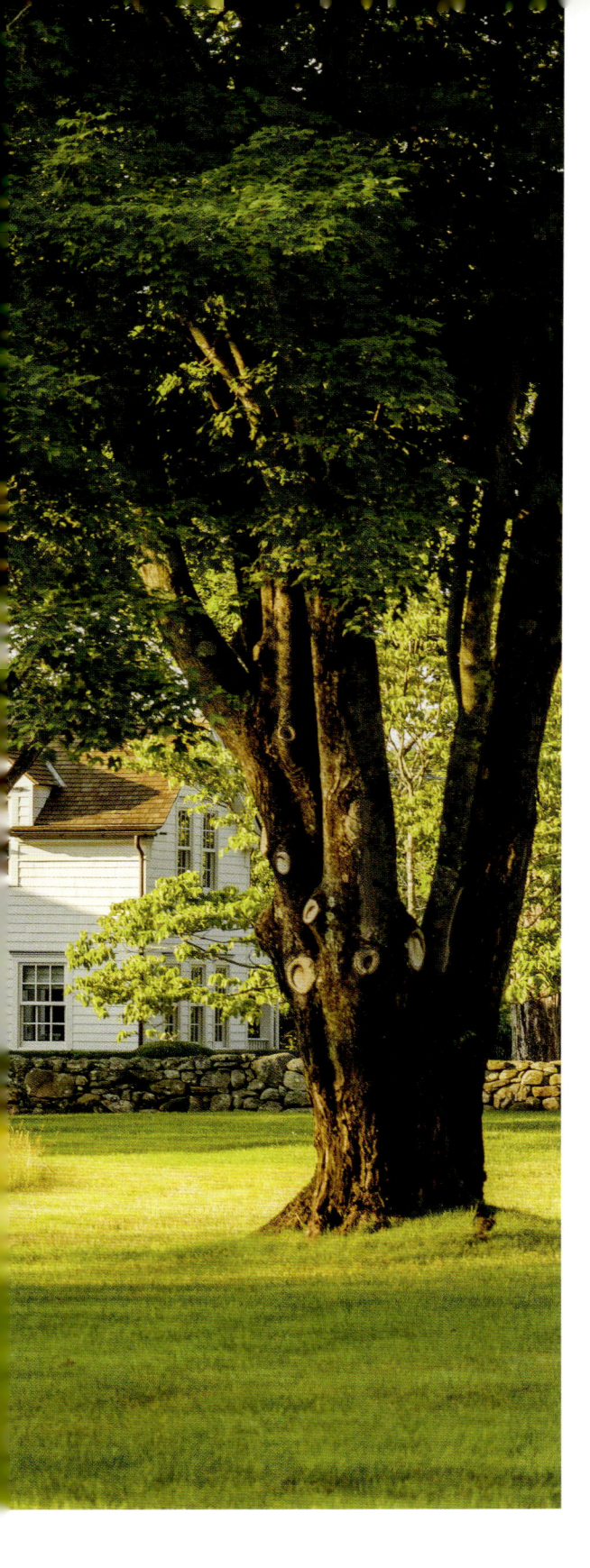

ABOVE When James Doyle and Matthew Willinger of James Doyle Design Associates first took in this pastoral six-acre New England property, it boasted regal, mature trees and a gently sloping topography with blowsy plantings of fescue overlooking a pond. "It lacked structured outdoor rooms and gardens," he says. Willinger and Doyle spent six years creating more cohesion and an overall ambiance that was appropriately "simple in form, but formal."

COTTAGE ROMANCE 85

ABOVE "We applied classic design principles, placing dressier rooms closer to the house, then progressing outward to looser styles," says Doyle, who used old stone for both garden walls and pathways. Billowy rows of Dropmore catmint add definition to an upper allée garden.

BELOW Stacked stone pillars and mounds of lamb's ears mark the exit from the border garden and frame the view to an original cabin on the property. The juxtaposition of more formal spaces with looser lawn areas and meadows gives the garden a graceful balance.

BELOW A roughly 80-year-old sugar maple stands sentry near private terraces along the side of the farmhouse and overlooking the pond. A large swath of native plants including blue flag irises in May and June attracts "so many bullfrogs, and their sounds fully absorb you," says Doyle.

COTTAGE ROMANCE 87

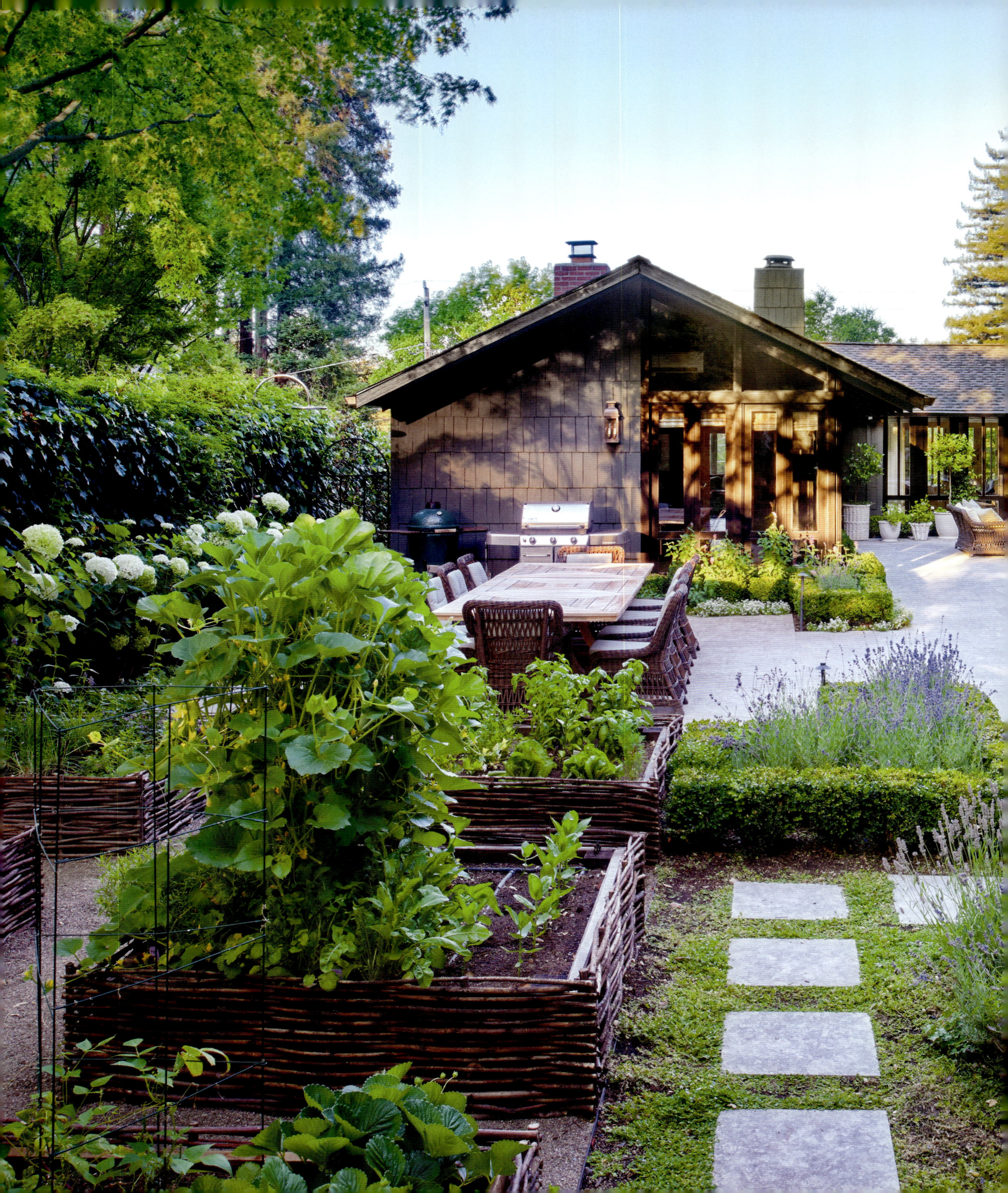

An Open (Air) Invitation

Erica Timbrell dreams up a garden for cocktails and conviviality in Northern California, complete with willow-wattled raised beds and other delights.

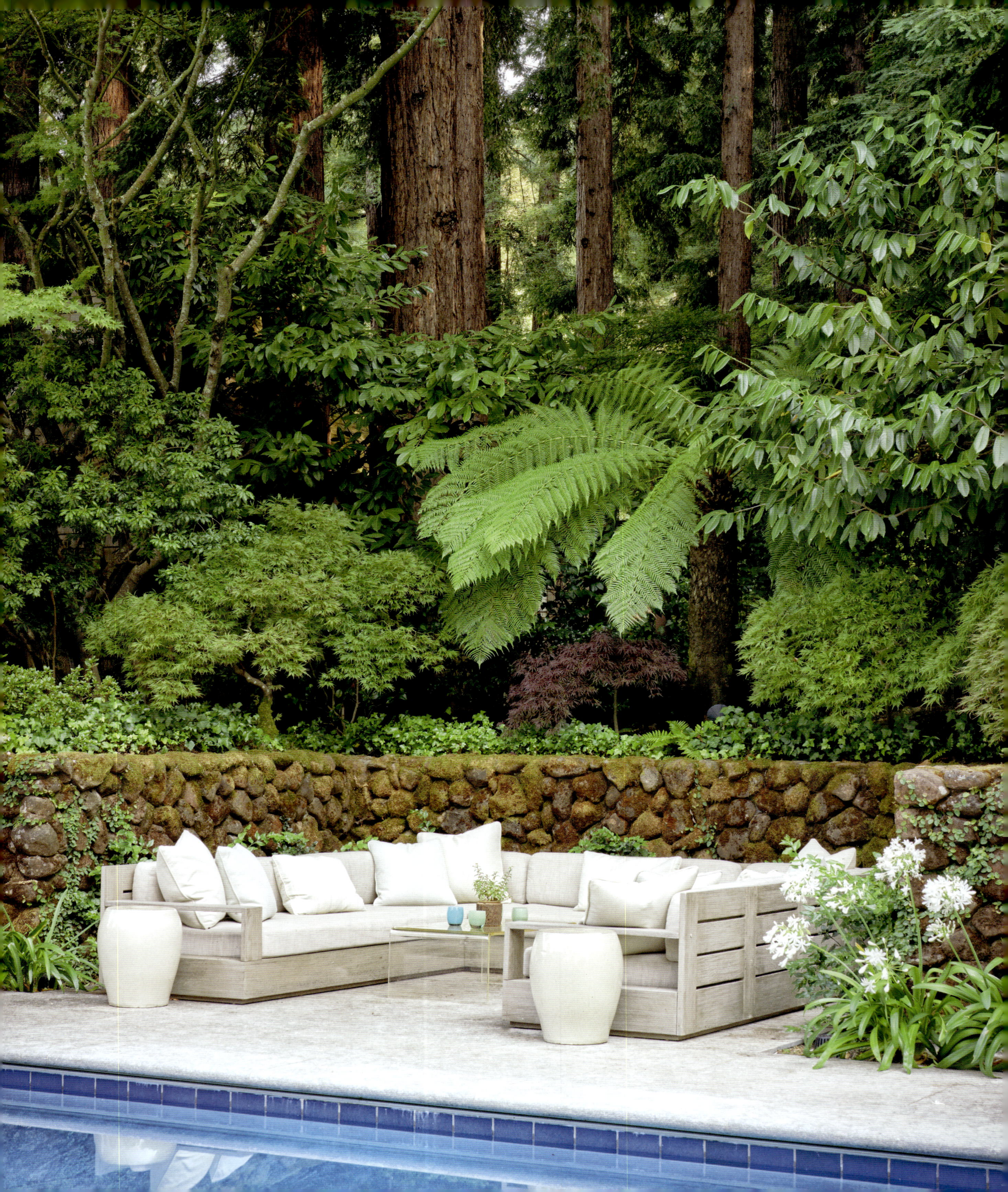

LEFT In this Bay Area cottage garden designed as a young family's primary living area, landscape designer Erica Timbrell nestled a poolside teak sectional in a stone-wrapped alcove graced by a leafy woodland backdrop of California redwoods and tree palms.

RIGHT The back entry opens to wicker seating and fragrant whiffs of citrus, thanks to potted bay laurel, gardenias, and lemon and dwarf lemon trees. Timbrell chose gray limestone pavers to unite the patio living area with the pool deck.

PAGES 88-89 Big white hydrangea may be the garden showstoppers, but raised beds are equally eye-catching. "Vegetable beds are typically messy, not something you want front and center," says Timbrell. She tidied these up with large-scale willow panels. "It's a creative way to dress up less-predictable plantings." Aligning the kitchen garden with the dining table means "you know just where to go when you need an extra sprig of mint for a mojito," she adds.

COTTAGE ROMANCE 91

Rosy Revival

Danielle Dall'Armi and Bill Hahn harvest a fragrant fantasy: transforming their California lemon and avocado farm into a wonderland of romantic roses—130 varieties of them.

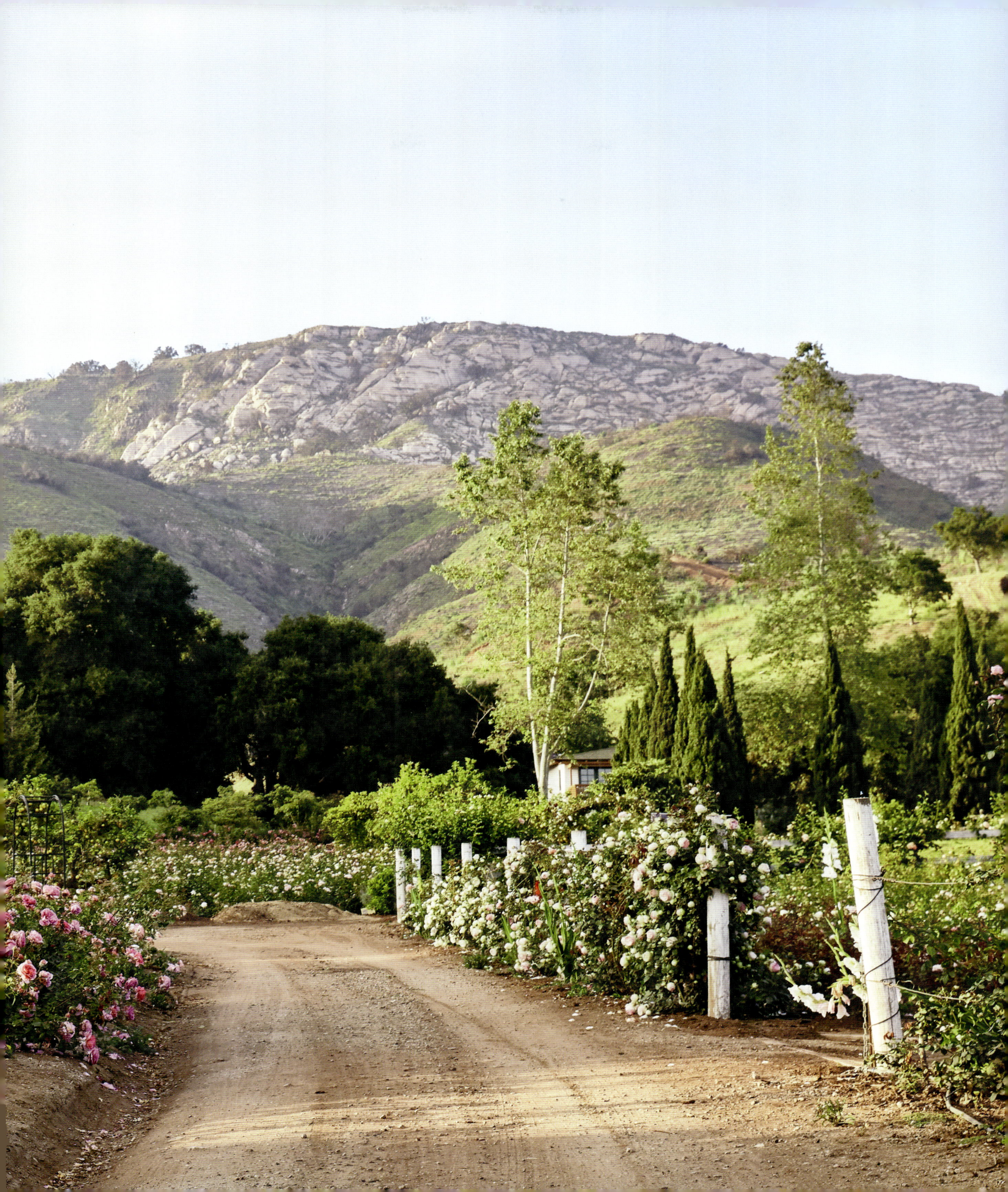

LEFT Danielle Dall'Armi and her husband, Bill Hahn, transformed a half-acre avocado and lemon farm in California's Carpinteria Valley into a 15-acre paradise where life is…rosy. A former 1930s Spanish colonial barn is now the Rose Story Farm office.

RIGHT Rose Story Farm specializes in the "big, voluptuous, wildly fragrant pre-1950s French and English roses," says Dall'Armi. Fragrant Cloud, the large coral bloom shown here, was a James Alexander Gamble Fragrance Award winner.

PAGES 92-93 Dall'Armi and Hahn grow some 130 varieties of English, French, Italian, and some old American roses, all chosen for their beautiful aroma. "There are roughly 10 families of rose fragrance, ranging from nutmeg and clove to citrus," explains Dall'Armi.

94 ENCHANTING GARDENS

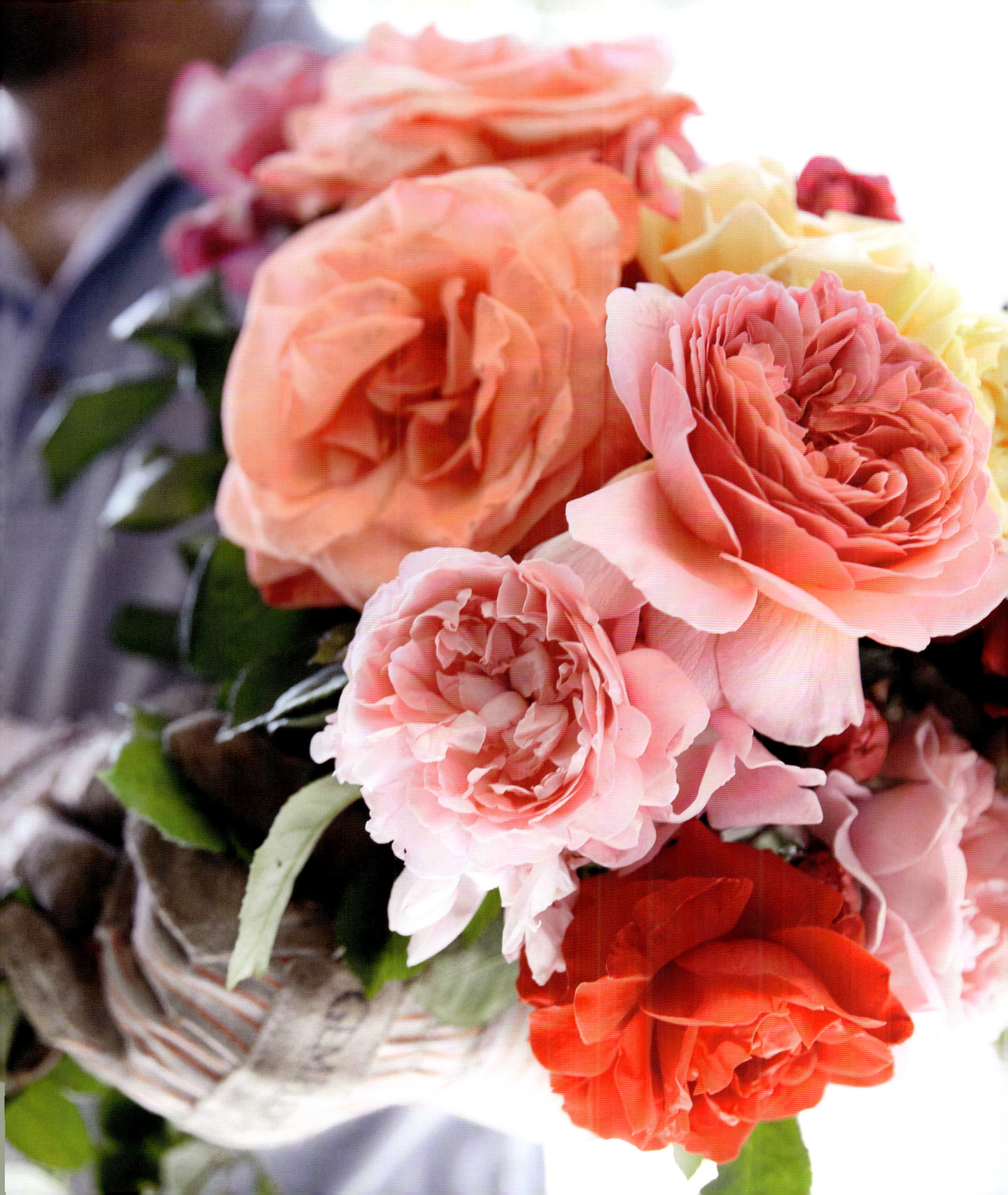

ABOVE An arrangement of some of Rose Story Farms' most fragrant blossoms, including the award-winning Secret hybrid tea rose, shine in the dappled California sunshine. The family both lives and works on the farm, where they still grow some citrus today.

RIGHT Princess Alexandra of Kent roses, an exceptionally large David Austin variety, thrive. "We both grew up in gardening families, with grandmothers on each side who were rosarians," says Dall'Armi. "Memories of my grandmother's fragrant roses were my inspiration."

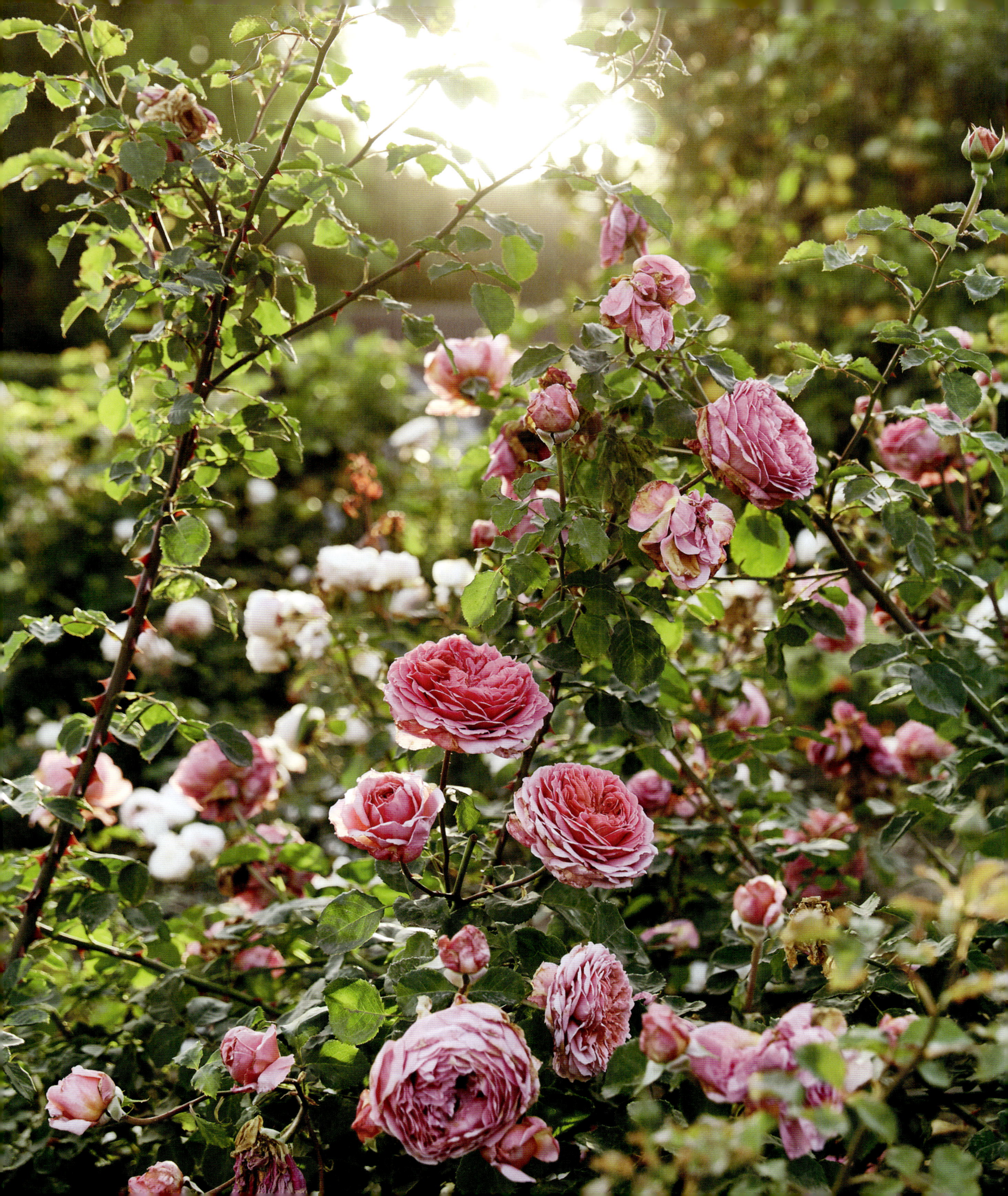

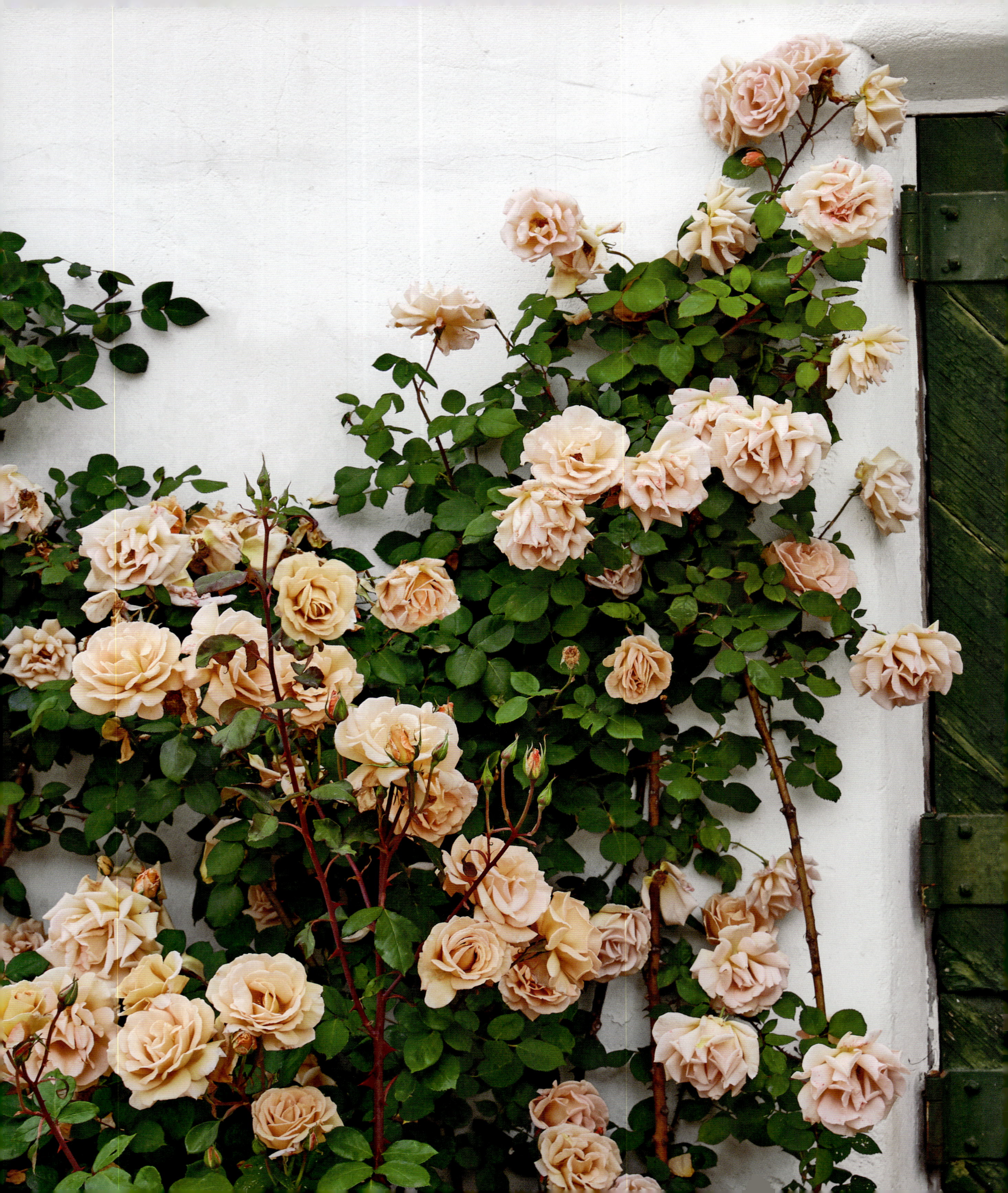

LEFT At Rose Story Farm, roses are not just relegated to the fields. Climbing Butterscotch roses ramble up the side of an old Spanish Colonial barn.

ABOVE "Our top criteria isn't perfection—holes and brown spots are all part of [the roses'] beauty. They just have to be fragrant," says Dall'Armi, who was honored in 2014 with the Great Rosarians of the World award. These Memorial Day hybrid tea roses fit the bill as "extremely aromatic," she adds.

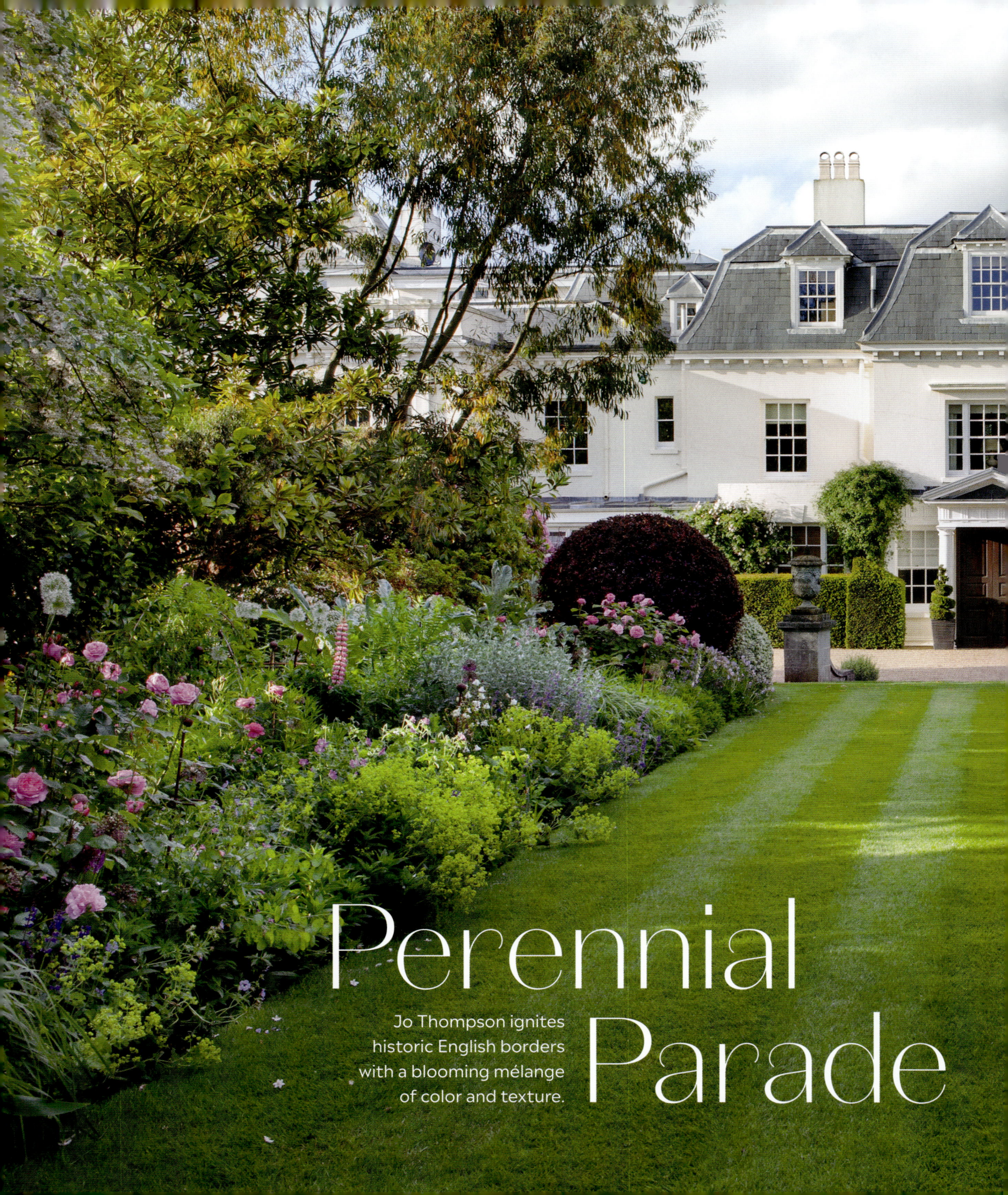

Perennial Parade

Jo Thompson ignites historic English borders with a blooming mélange of color and texture.

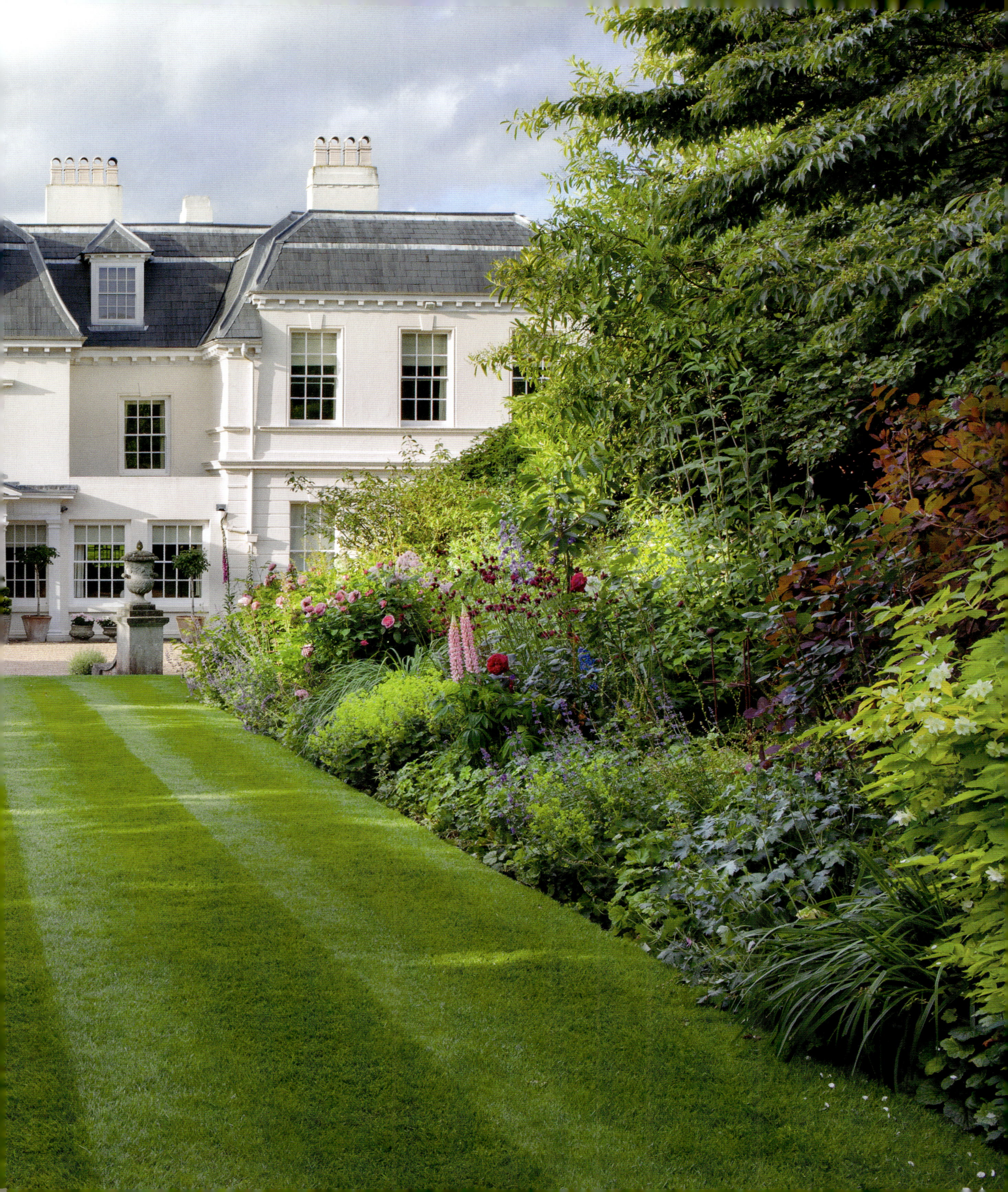

102 ENCHANTING GARDENS

LEFT While the 19th-century Italianate Ladham House in Southeast England isn't exactly a cottage, its lush and herbaceous borders designed by landscape designer Jo Thompson evoke the informal abundance of an English cottage garden. Amid perennial blue, lilac, and pink plantings, a modern globe sculpture by David Harber echoes the shapes of cloud-pruned topiary and alliums. Beyond, the eye is drawn to the ancient forests of the Weald.

ABOVE In a previously unused part of the garden, Thompson designed a sunken terrace of reclaimed York flagstone, where manicured hedges of yew, hornbeam, and boxwood create a cloistered effect, contrasting with bursts of white Annabelle hydrangea.

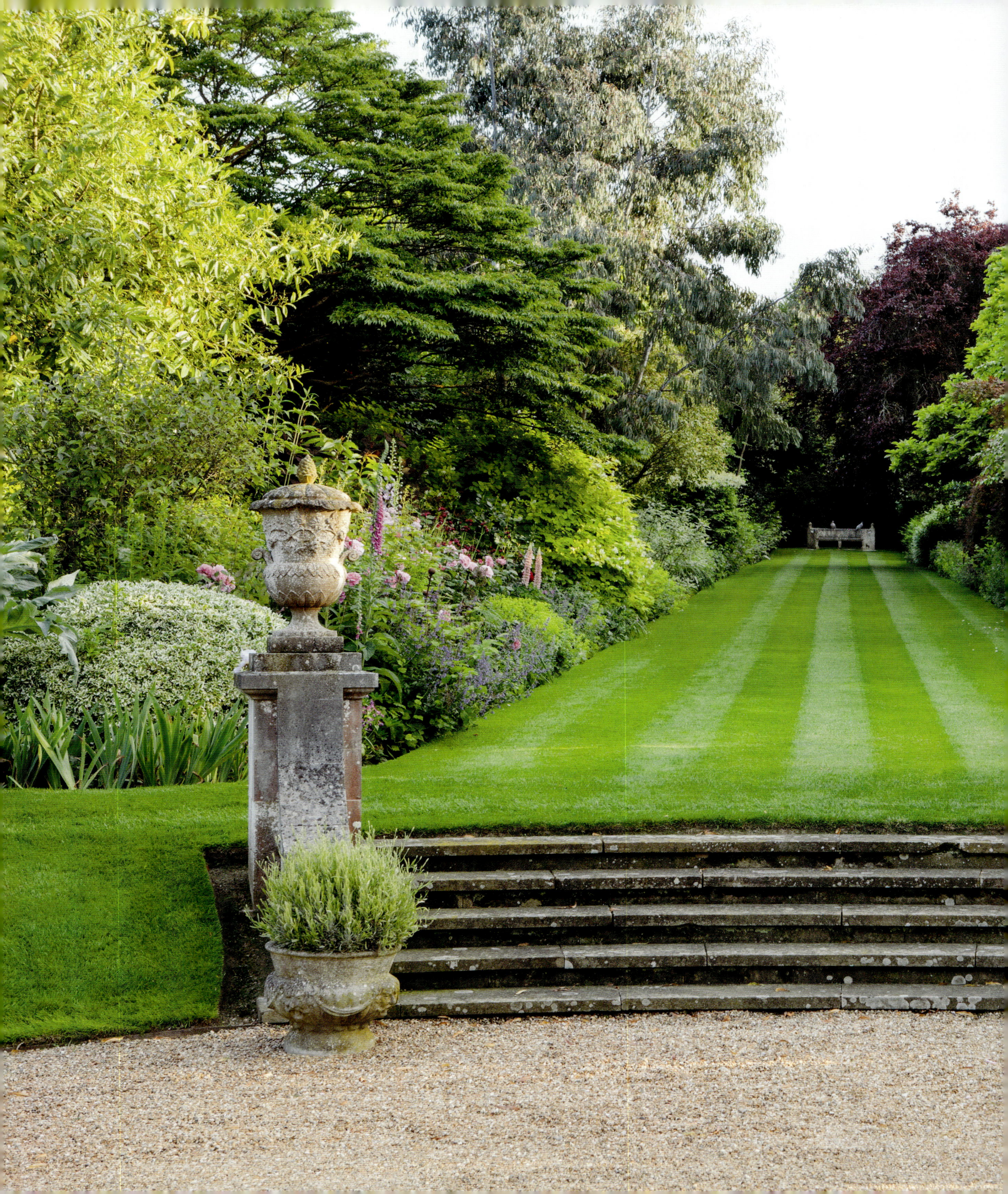

PAGES 100-101 AND LEFT
By infusing a gentle zigzagging rhythm of mixed-height perennials and pink roses—"such a British thing," Thompson says—she relaxed the formality of the 260-foot-long borders framed by "extraordinary" magnolias and other mature trees. "Instead of starting over, we regenerated what was there," says Thompson.

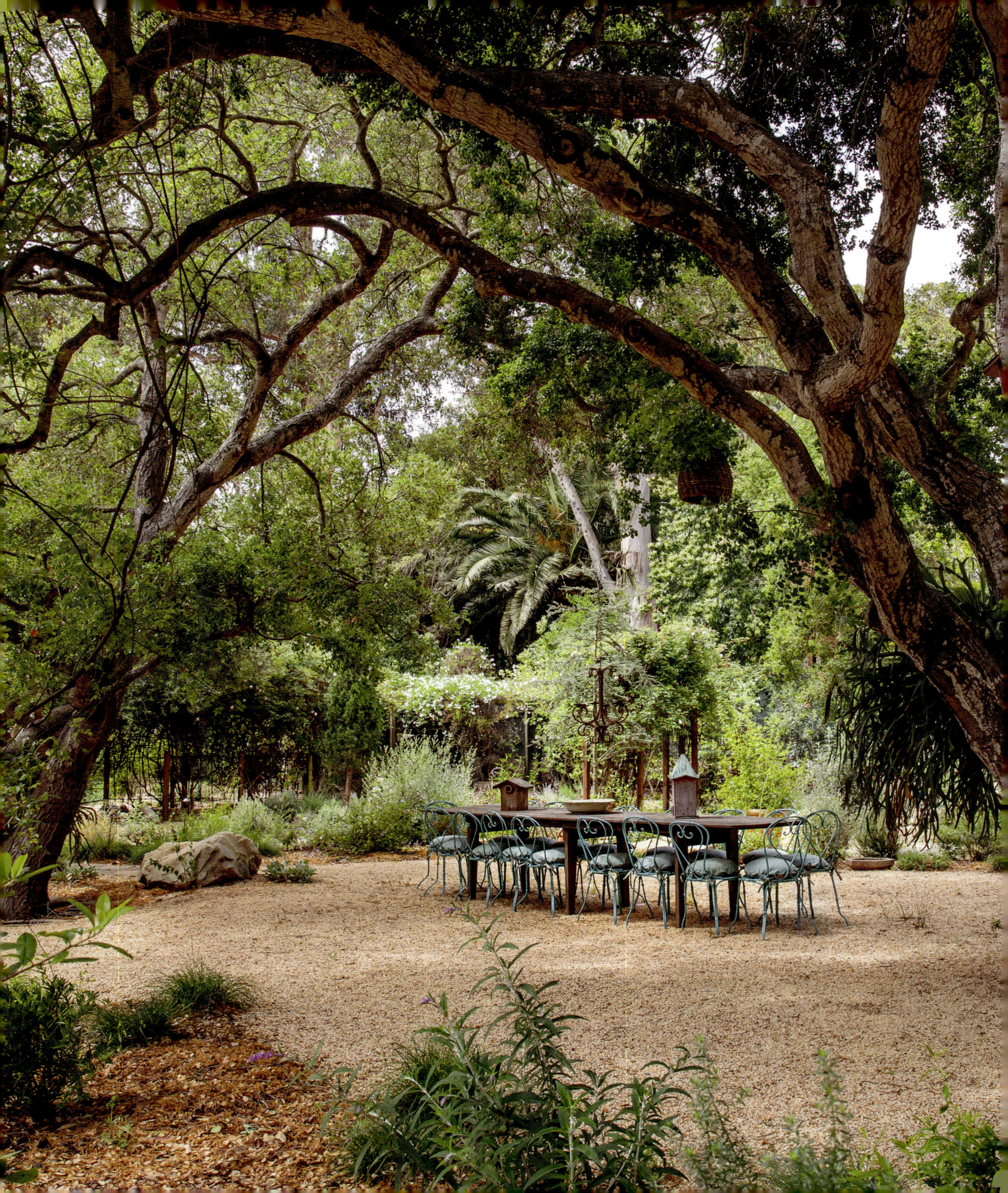

Embrace of Nature

Following a disastrous California mudflow, Margie Grace reckoned with the power of nature, embracing the wild.

LEFT After this Montecito garden was wiped out by mudslides, landscape designer Grace incorporated the sludge into a new garden plan, including a new hill planted with sycamores. She was thrilled to discover the sediment was wildly fertile. A Coast live oak shades a rustic dining terrace behind the main house, while a neighboring nature preserve offers a backdrop of towering palms and oaks.

RIGHT "Everything was wiped out…plants, fences, animals. We learned the absolute power of nature," says Grace. Yet they discovered nature's resilience, too, after the ducks and wildlife came right back, meandering amid new plantings of nasturtium and blue fescue.

COTTAGE ROMANCE

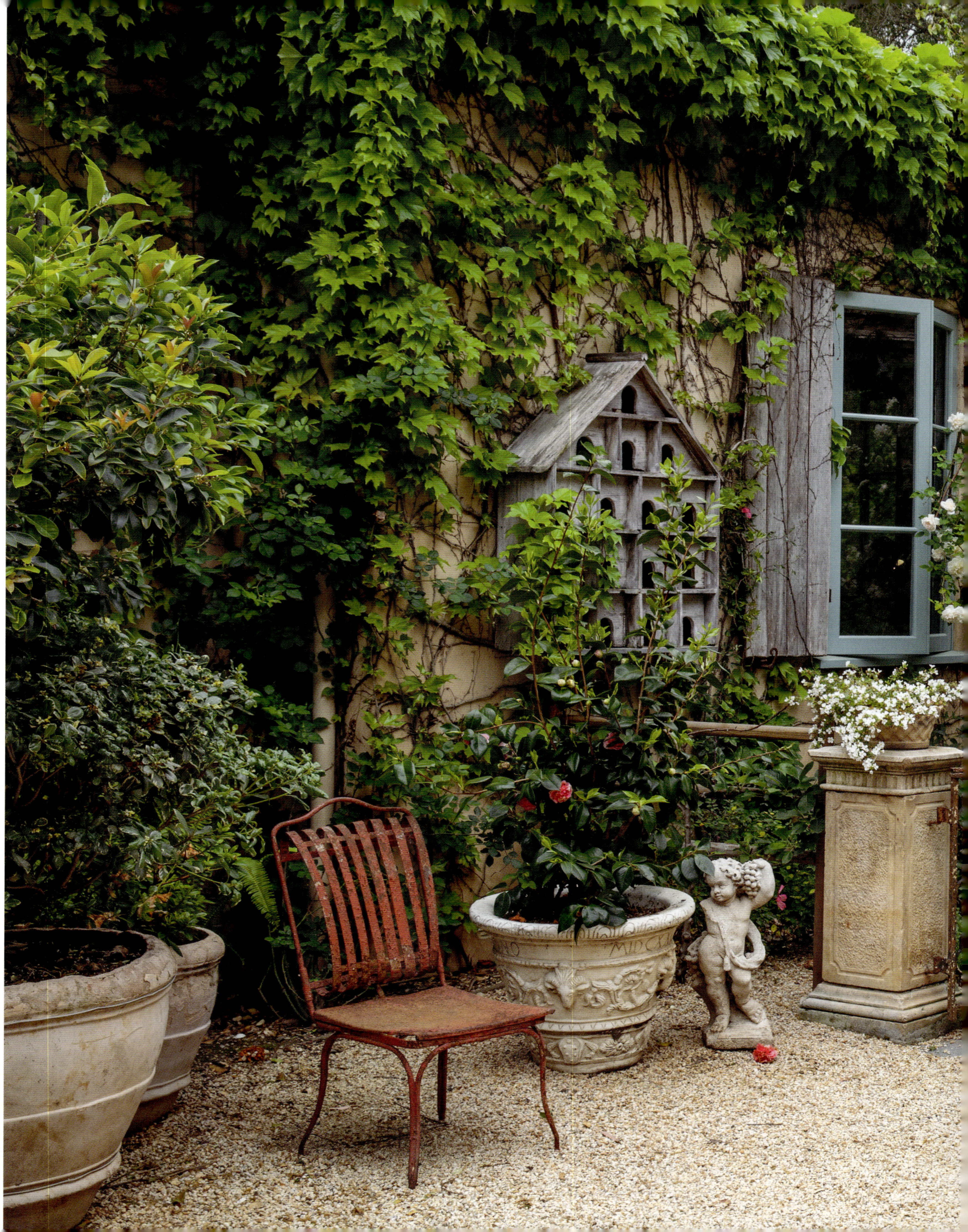

109

PAGES 108-109 Coated in mud, the Boston ivy on the main house and guesthouse was cleaned up, and "the roots just started sprouting again," says Grace, who filled the courtyard with planters of camelias and big blue lilyturf. Inside a rustic gate, climbing white roses have full, fertile leeway.

ABOVE The pond, which borders the neighboring 45-acre nature preserve, was an important water element needed for the ecosystem's health. An observation platform nestled by yellow iris is a great place for turtle watching. "Even great blue herons stop by from time to time," says Grace.

RIGHT Beyond a border of Wendy's Wish sage, an aged garden urn, one of several that had been swept across the property in the mudslide, was resurrected and returned to its former glory.

110 ENCHANTING GARDENS

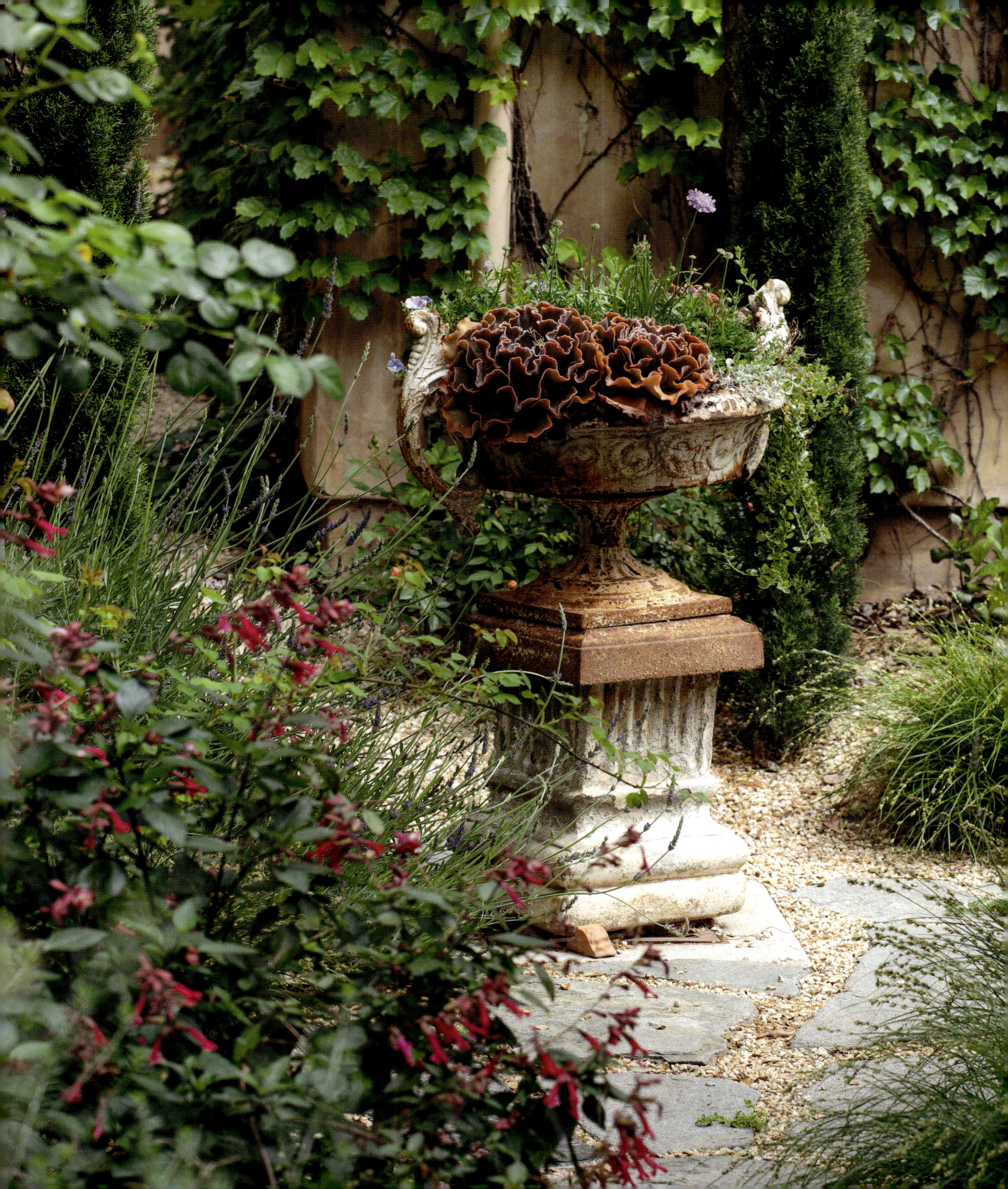

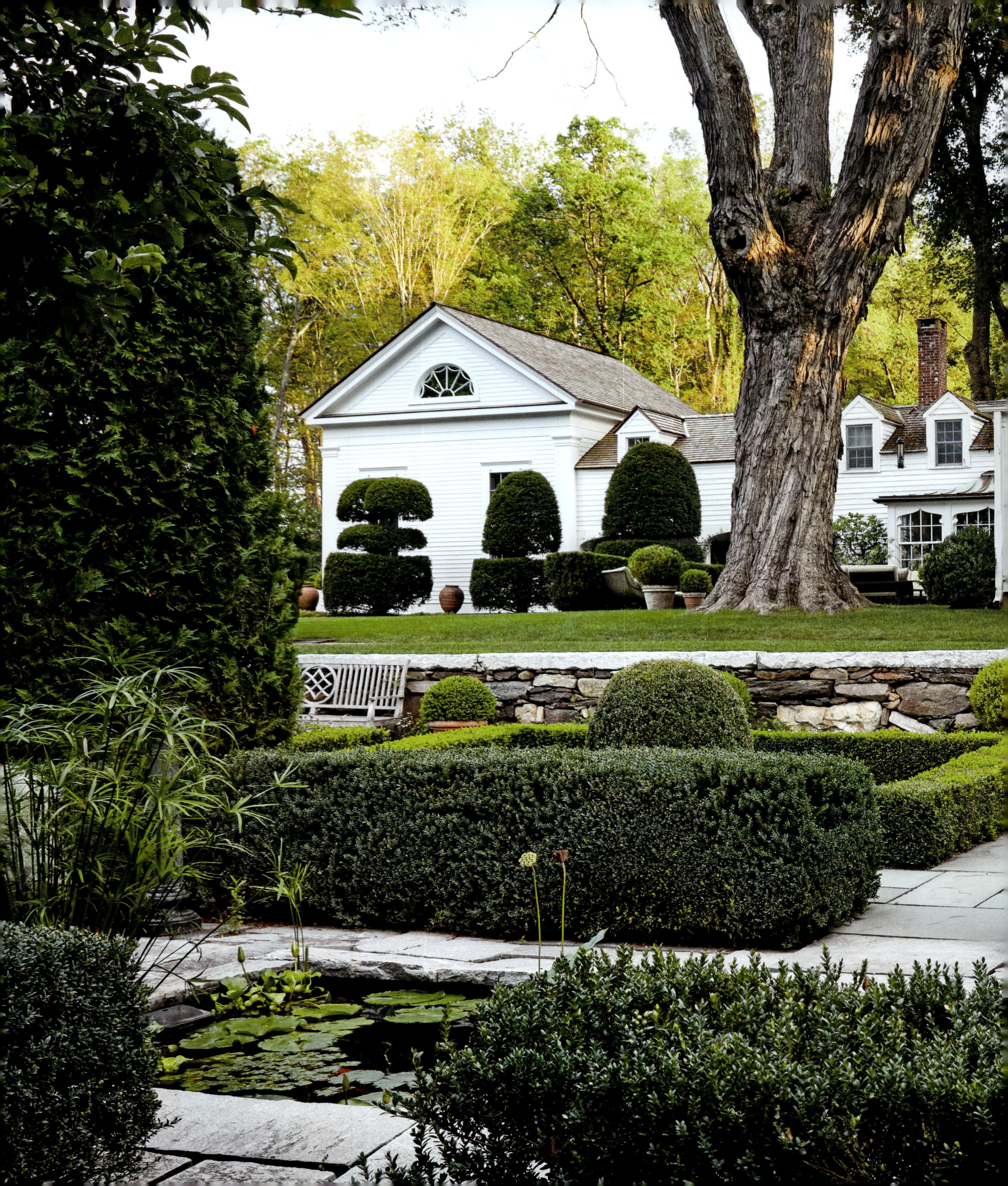

A Gardener's Sanctuary

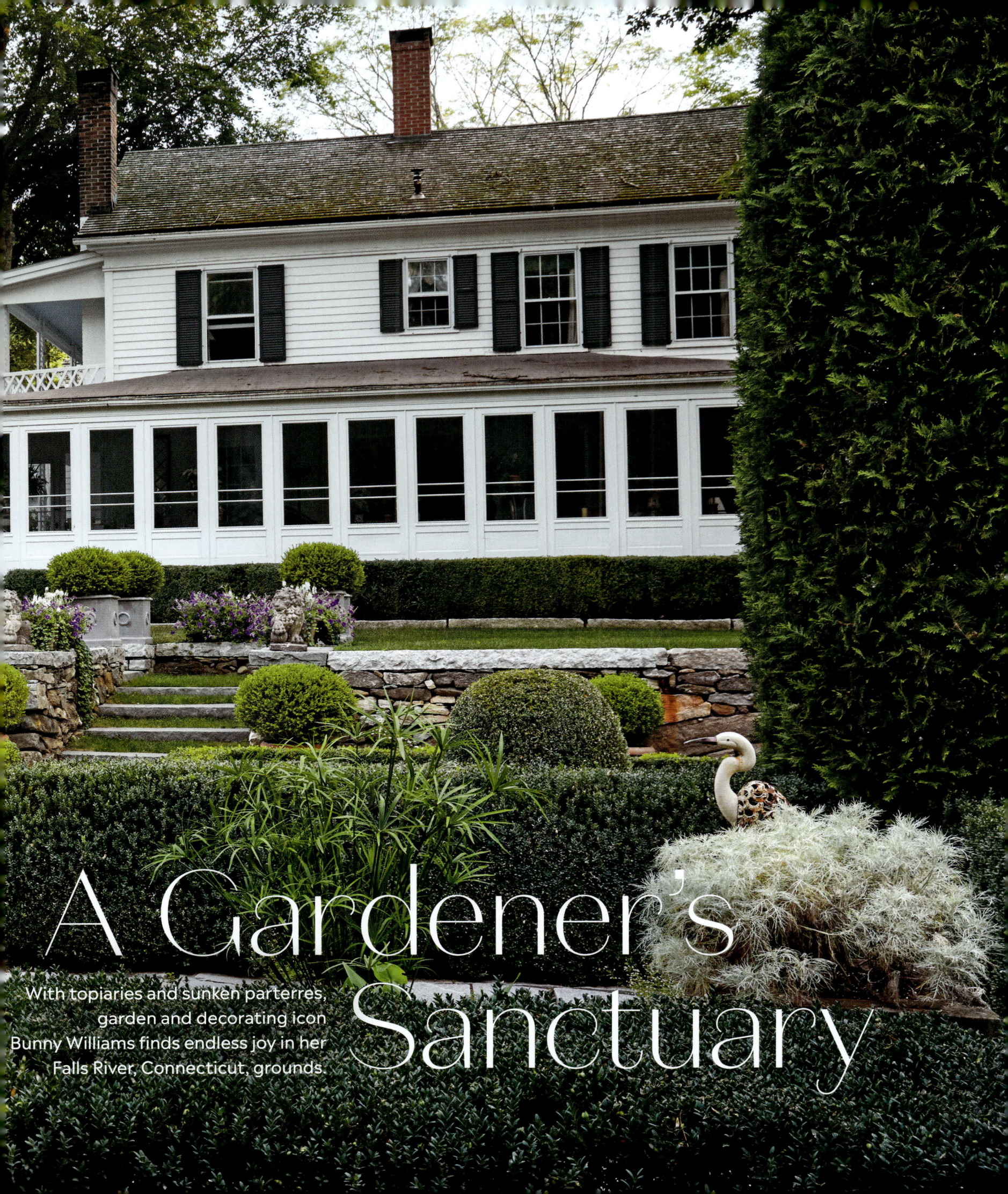

With topiaries and sunken parterres, garden and decorating icon Bunny Williams finds endless joy in her Falls River, Connecticut, grounds.

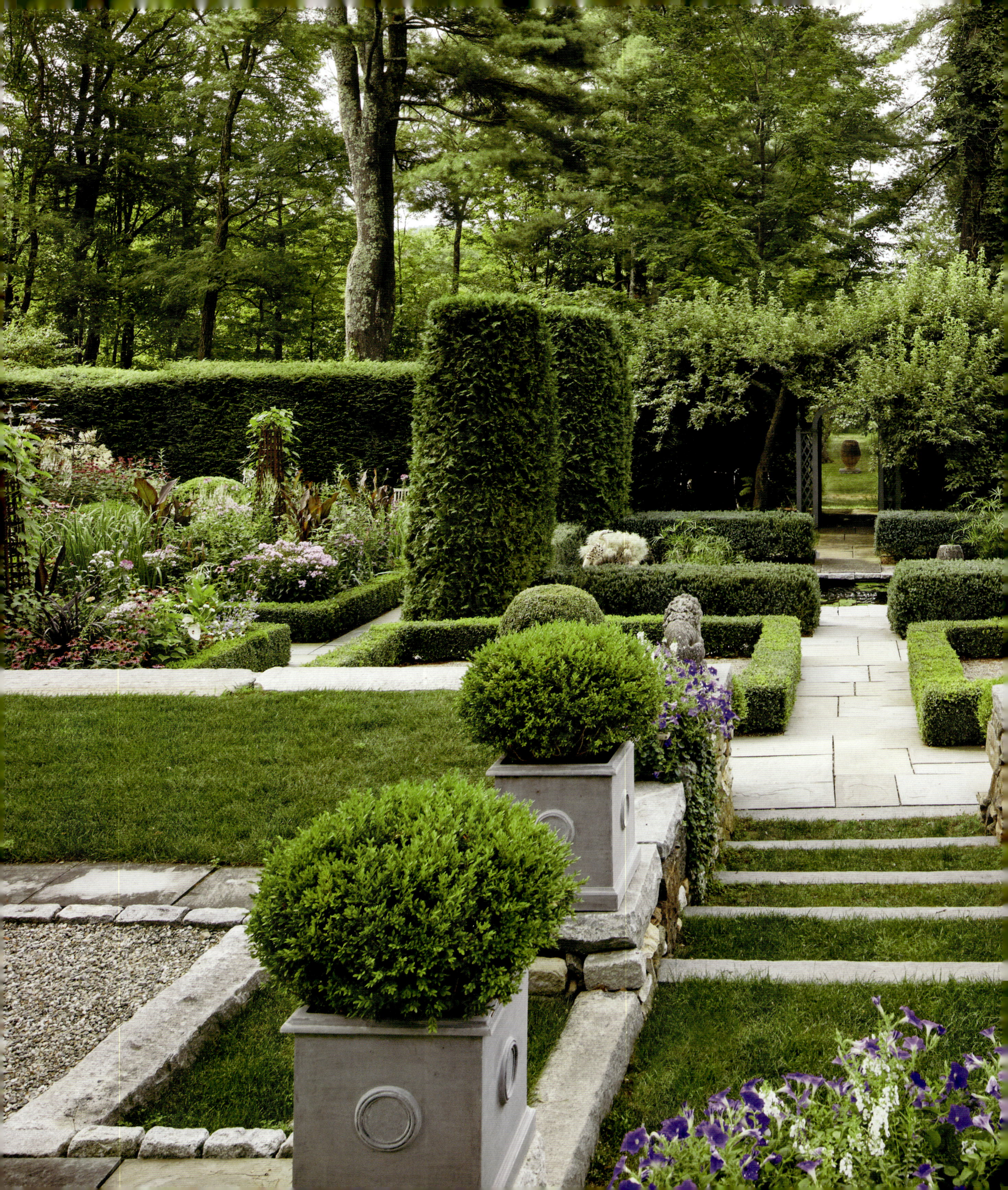

LEFT Tall, cylindrical arborvitae columns command the sunken garden, where Williams clips box hedges into a series of parterres, with lush perennial borders planted with a mix of bulbs and annuals. Through the aromatic archway lies a natural meadow sprouting a fanciful birdhouse collection.

PAGES 112-113 When adding a first-floor bedroom (far left) to her Connecticut home, Williams insisted it not disturb a path that links the parterre behind the barn to a formal sunken garden on the far side of the house, or encroach on three majestic 10-foot-high yew topiaries that she planted close to the house more than 35 years ago.

COTTAGE ROMANCE 115

RIGHT Williams approaches a garden with the same sensibility as she would an interior space, paying as much attention to the linkages and transitions as to the garden rooms they connect. Here an old brick path bordered by box hedges segues to looser gravel and a more open, airy passage beneath a curved arbor.

ABOVE The potting shed was moved to make room for the bedroom addition and is now positioned next to the greenhouse and the kitchen garden.

PAGES 118-119 A conservatory, where Williams often hosts dinner parties among the plants, opens to a green and white parterre garden, inspired by English gardener Rosemary Verey. Two potted Korean lilac trees punctuate the space.

ENCHANTING GARDENS

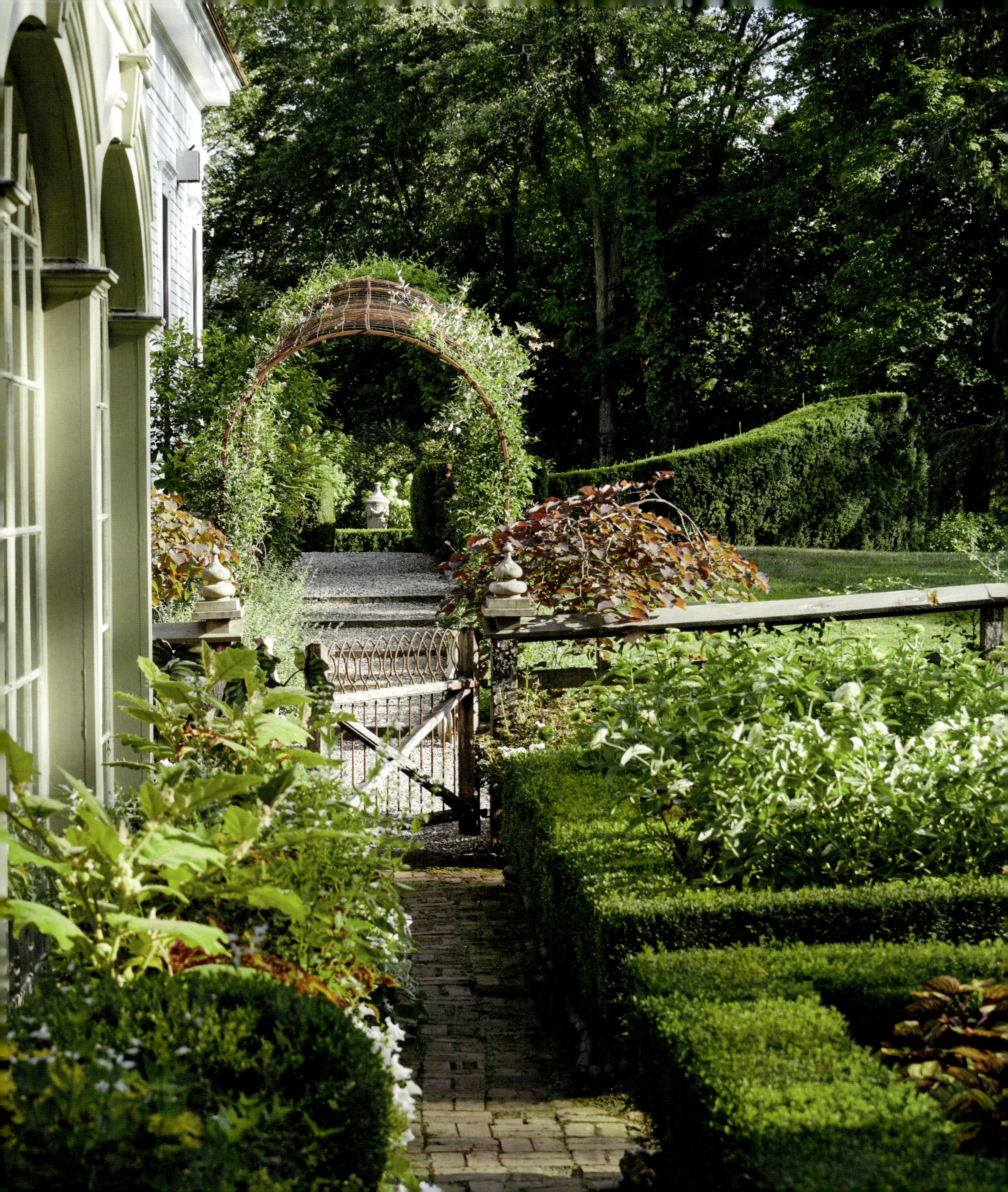

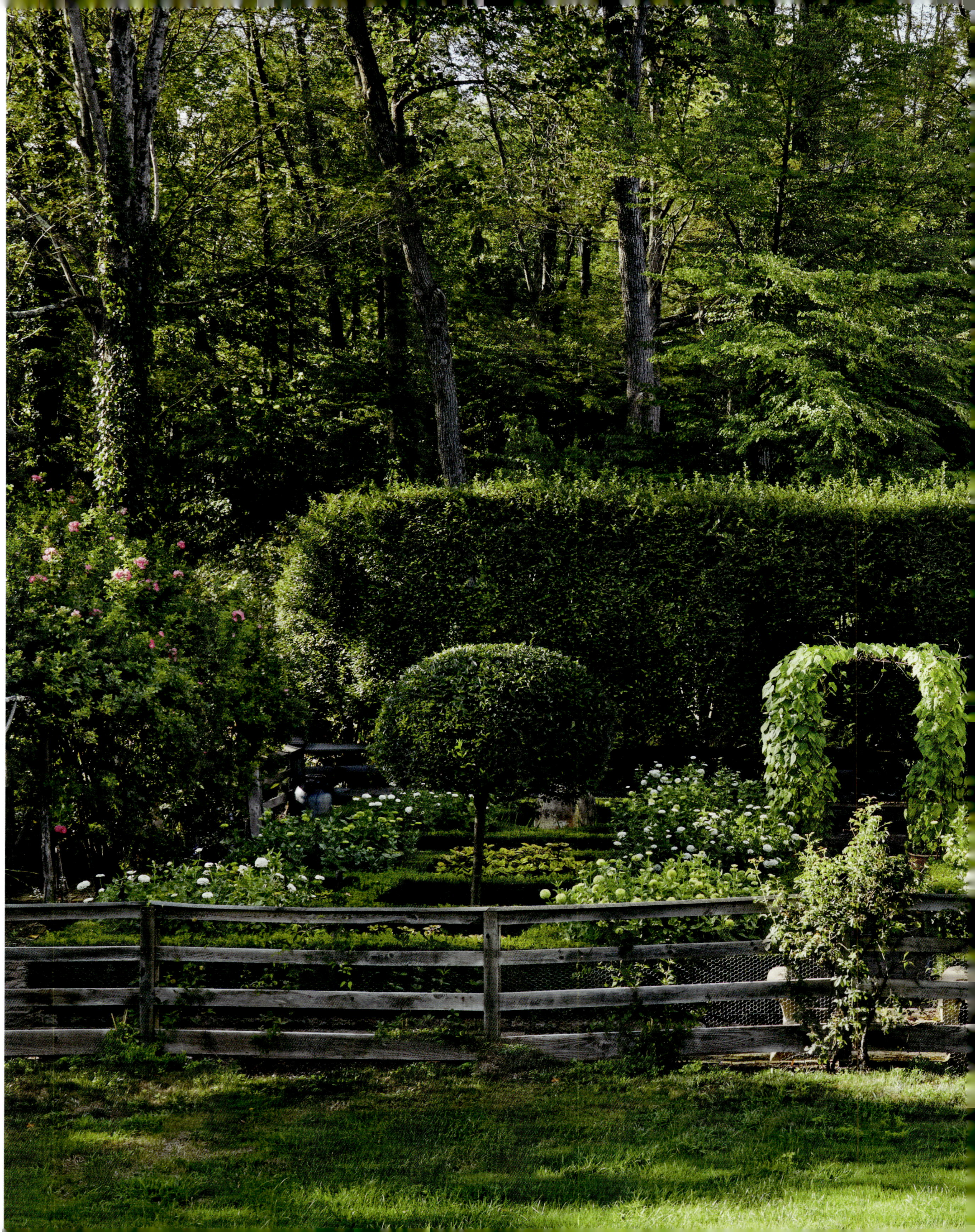

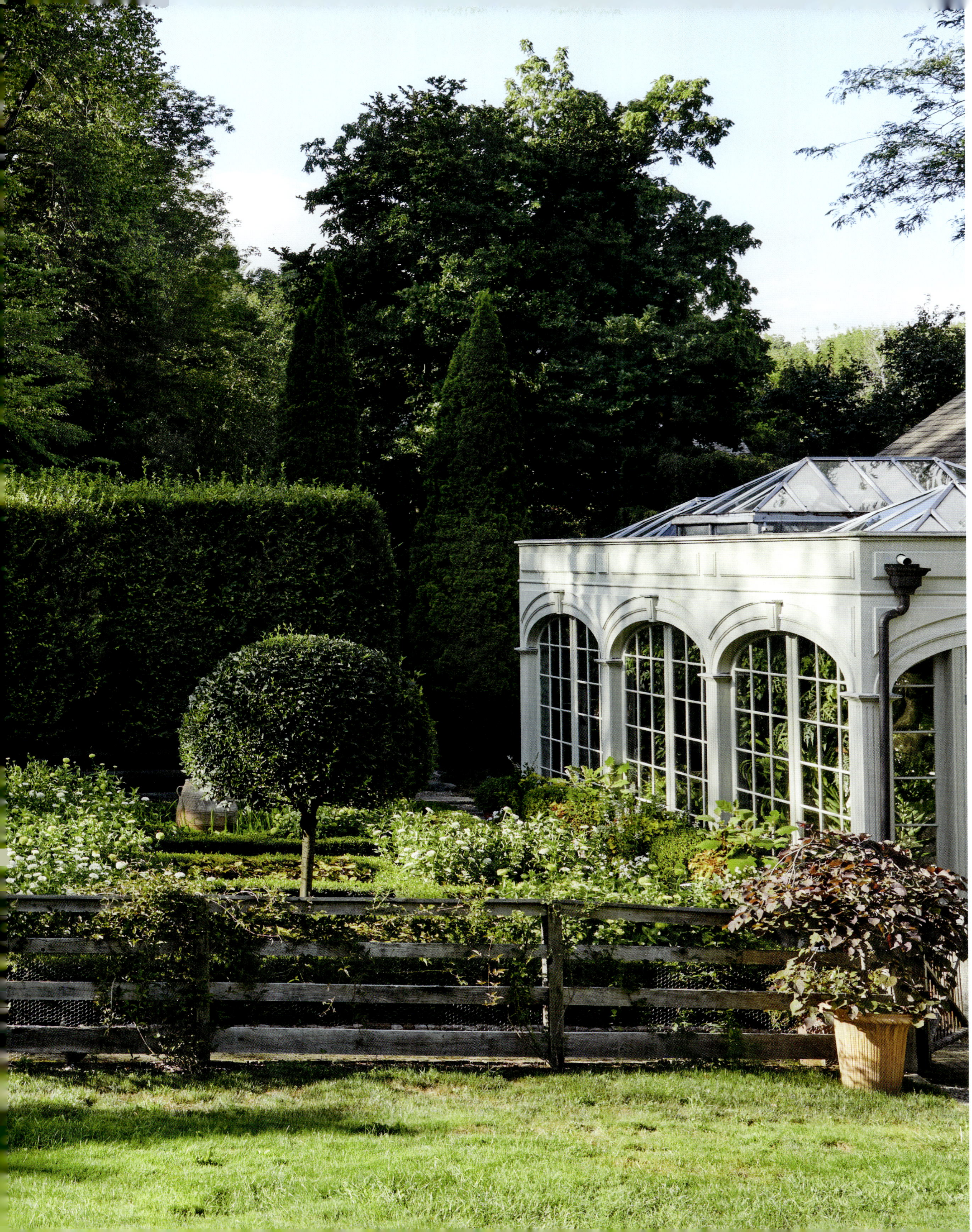

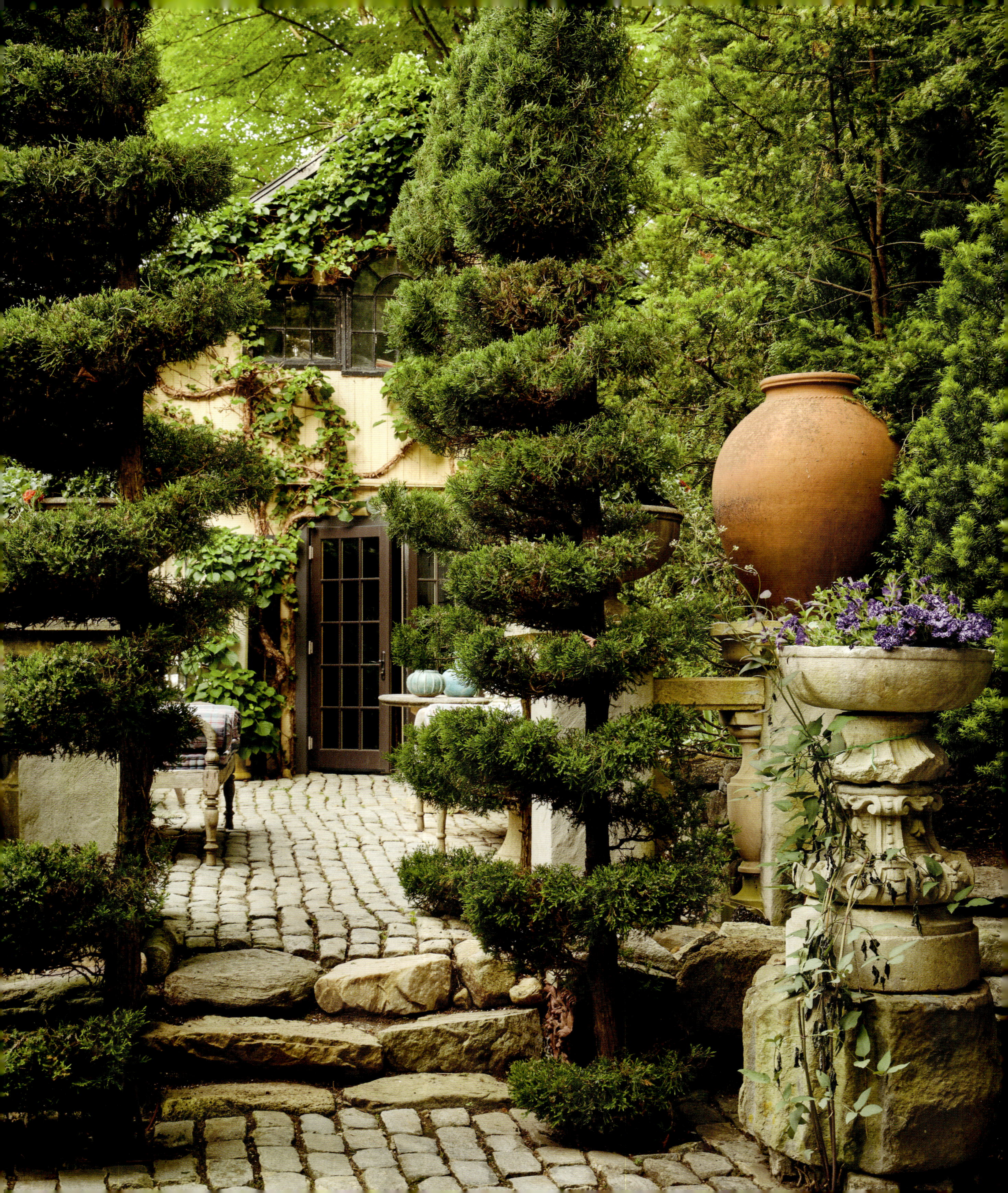

Ruins & Rarities

An English- and Italian-influenced Connecticut garden steps back in time, with architectural curiosities, salvaged stone, and a dreamy wisteria canopy.

LEFT Antique dealer Michael Trapp's Connecticut garden is a wonderland of classical whimsy. Terraced on two levels, cobblestone paths and hand-laid cobblestone steps lead past spiral juniper topiaries to fountains, a lap pool, a library, and even a grotto.

RIGHT A Dutch colonial bench that Trapp found in Jakarta is dressed in country plaid. Every touch is intentional: cobblestone pavers encourage mindful movement, and intimate spaces welcome conversation or quiet reflection.

COTTAGE ROMANCE

RIGHT "The collections, architectural salvage, the stonework—they all go together to tell the same story," Trapp explains. "Aged, romantic, otherworldly. It's not one specific place—and it's not Connecticut," he adds, noting his incorporation of hints from Italian, French, Spanish, and English gardens.

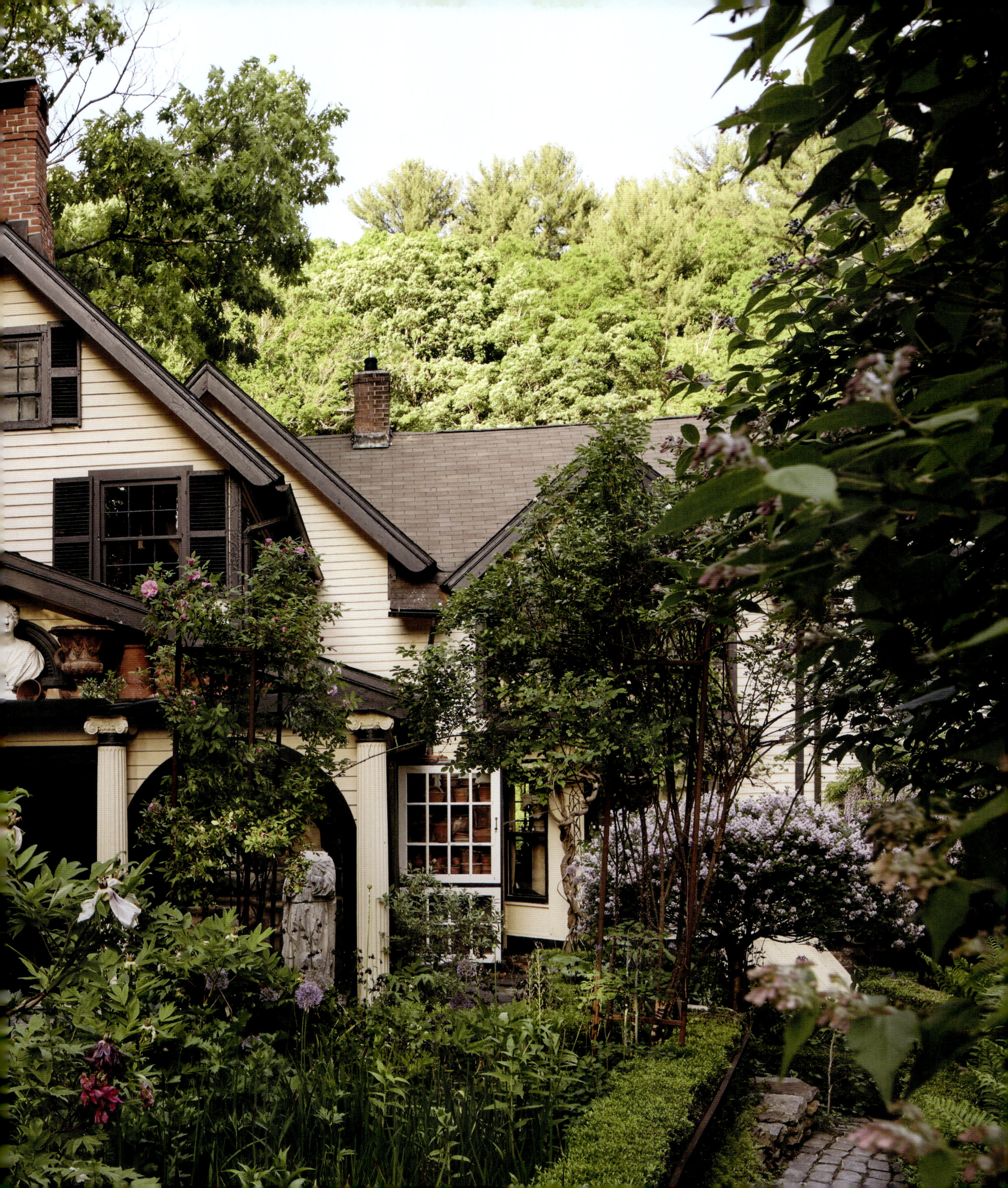

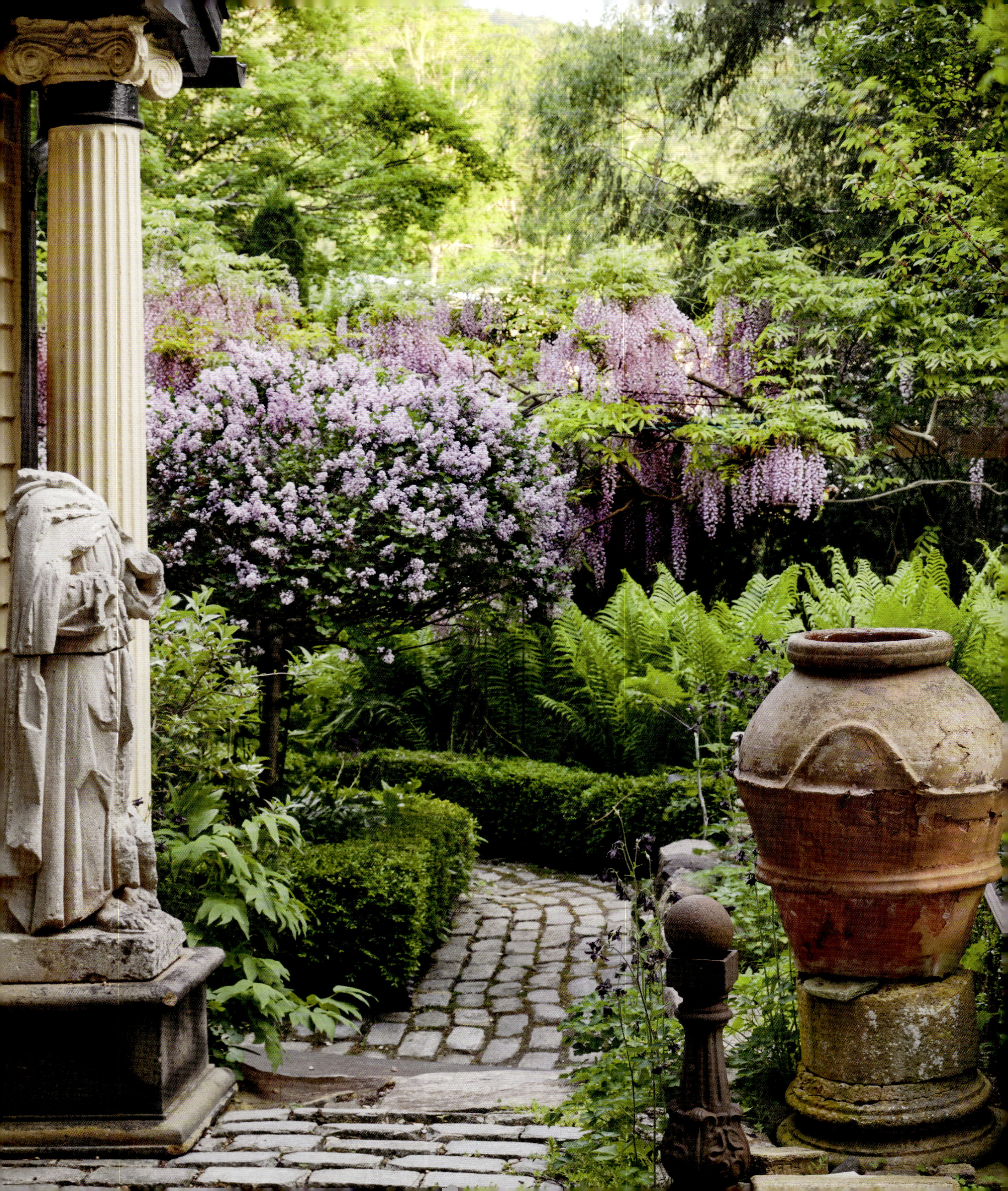

LEFT A headless 18th-century French limestone saint whispers welcome to the garden, while an early 19th-century Tuscan terra-cotta urn lends classical framework. Boxwood hedges give way to lively ferns and Miss Kim lilacs.

ABOVE The garden library, with its pediment populated with antlers, offers a quiet, tucked-away retreat for reading, writing, and garden pondering.

ABOVE Not surprising for an antiques aficionado, Trapp is all about the fanciful flourishes. A drystone wall, hand built from pieces of local granite, is crowned by a 19th-century Mississippi limestone corbel.

RIGHT A pink wisteria canopy is a showstopper, in spring. "Flowers are lovely," Trapp says. "But for a garden to look good all the time, it takes good bones. So even when the beds are a complete mess, it's all framed by classical architecture—a beautiful frame on a messy painting."

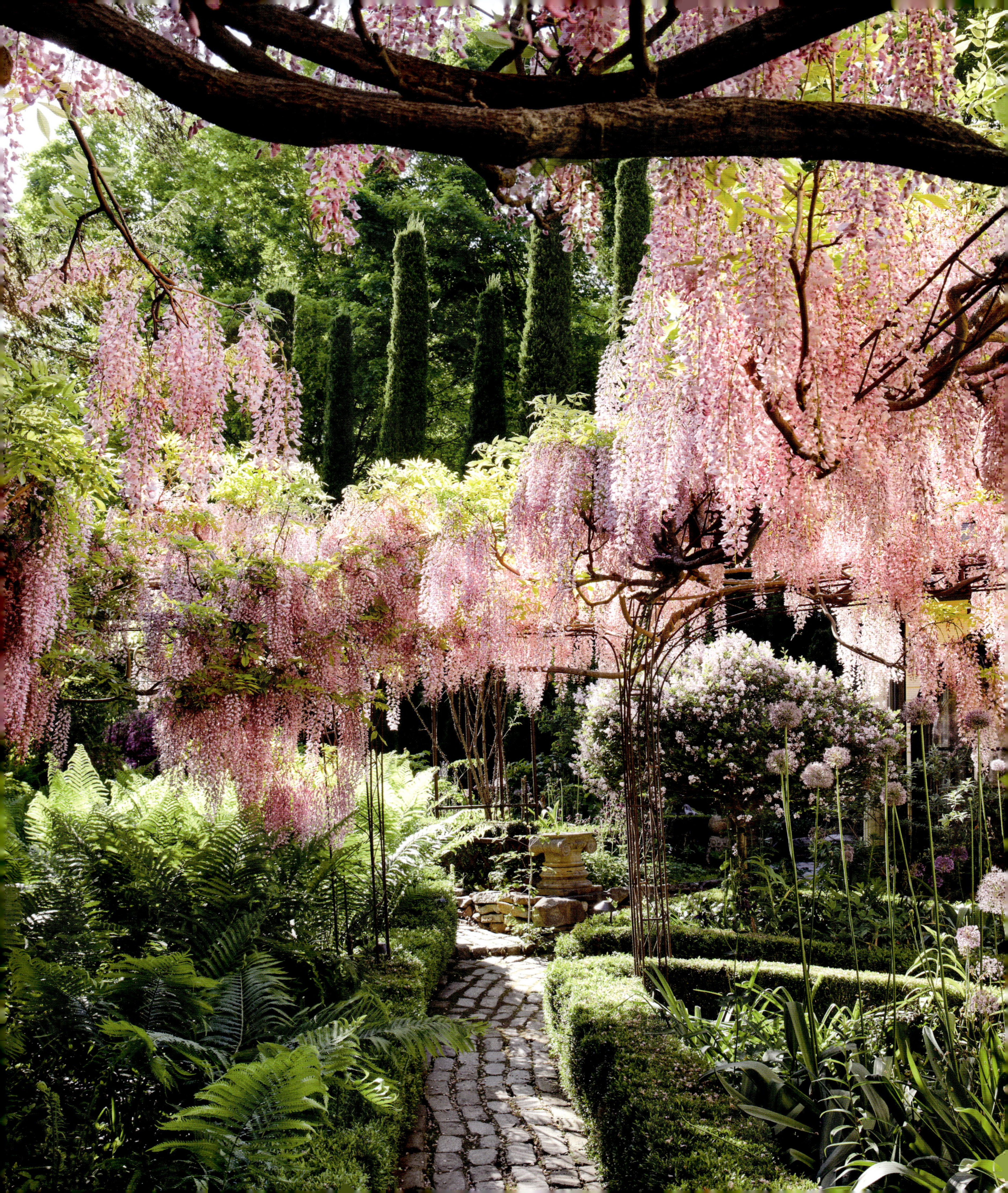

CHAPTER 3

COUNTRY ESCAPES

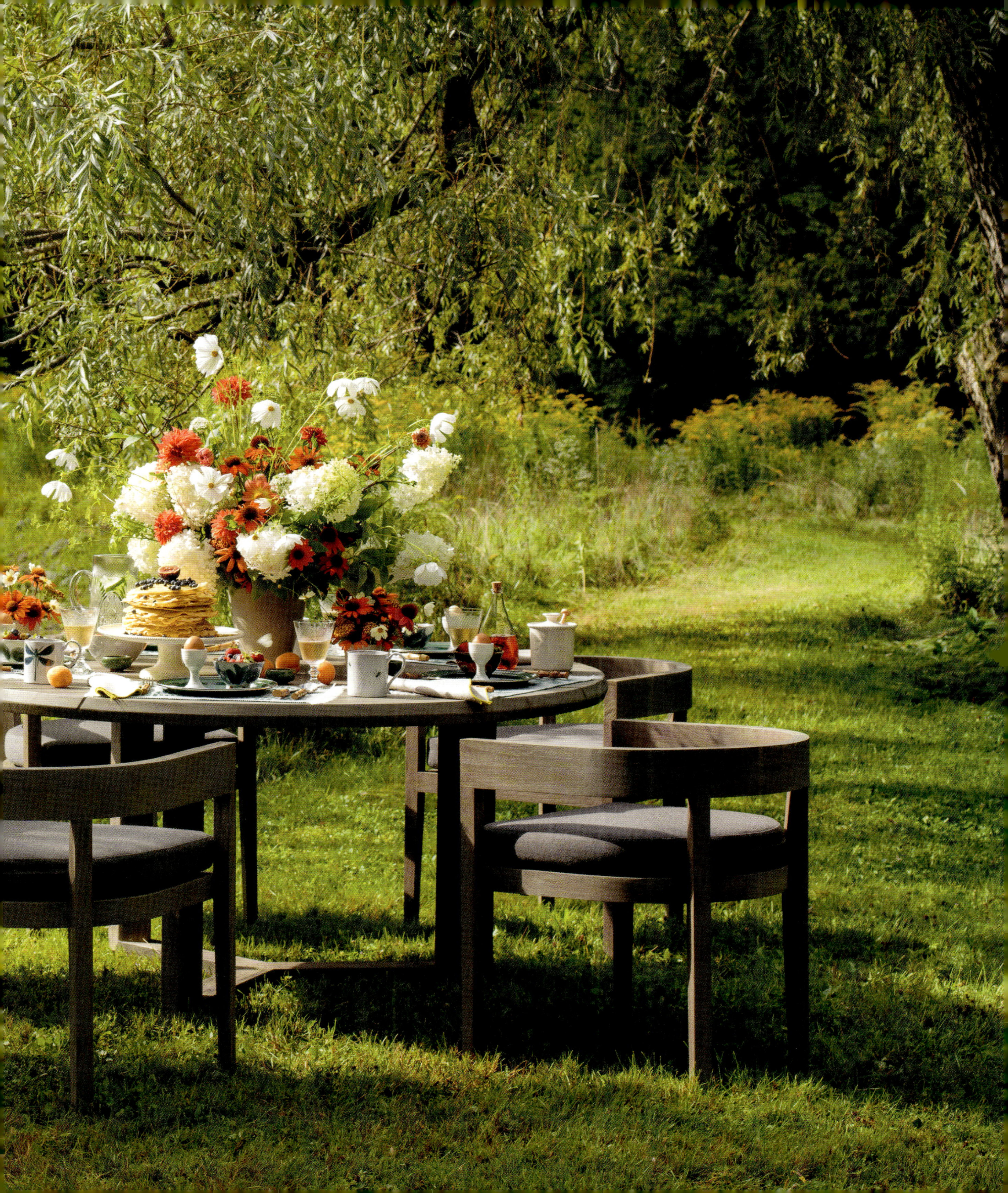

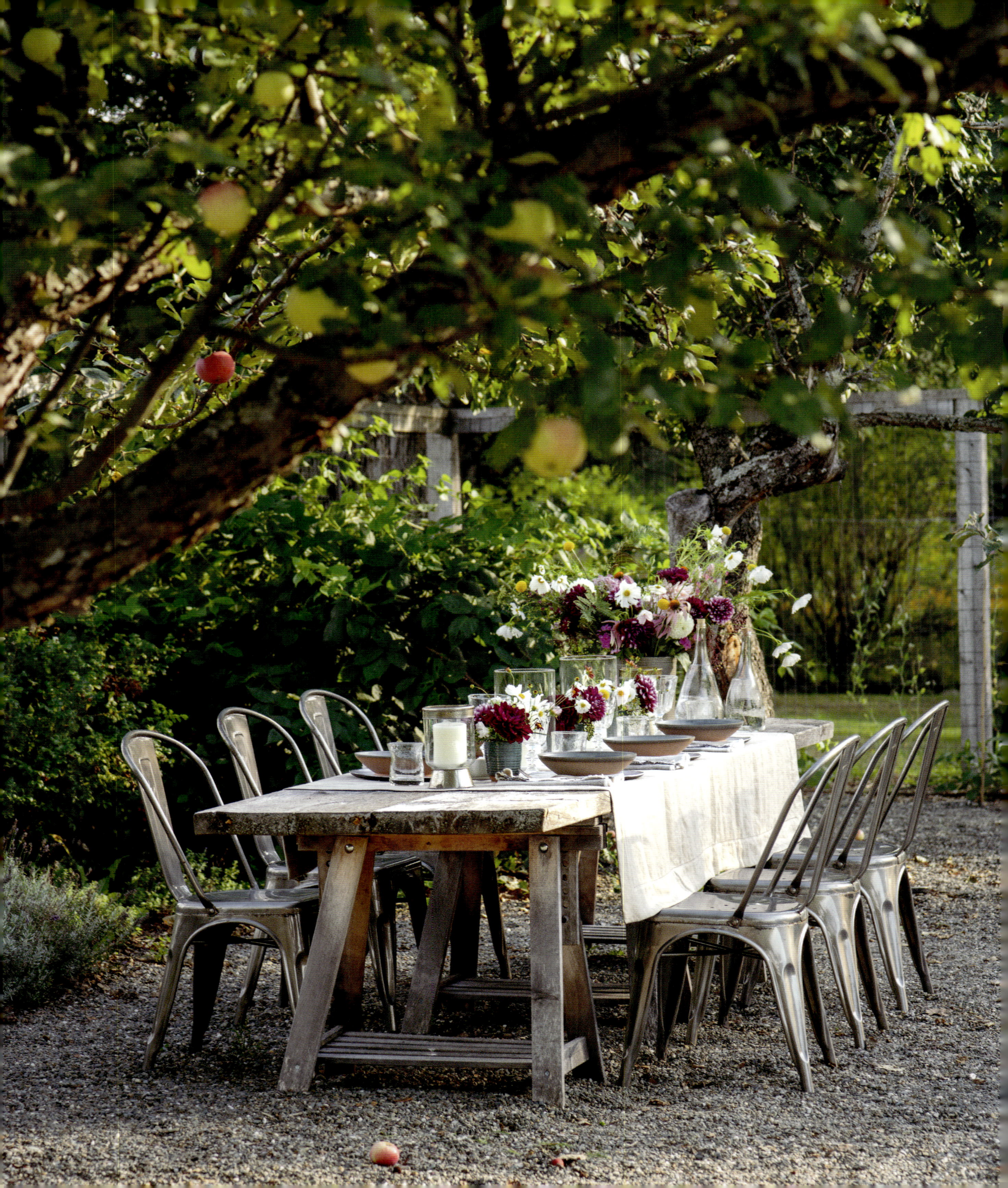

COUNTRY ESCAPES

y

OU KNOW THE MEME: "Shuts Laptop on Friday," and then…well, then, for many people, either in reality or in dream life, it's time to escape to the countryside. The lure of greener pastures tugs on many of us. It whispers to our souls—that promise of broader horizons, fresher air, louder birdsong, deeper breaths. "As soon as we turn off the autoroute and cross the bridge, life gets better," says designer Richard Ouellette, who knows the joy of escaping the urban bustle of Montreal. Most weekends, he retreats with his life and business partner, Maxime Vandal, to an old farm they bought about an hour outside the city. The "dose of nature grounds us," he says of the robust garden of cut flowers, organic vegetables, and fruit that they've created.

For Ouellette and Vandal, as for many who plant roots in rural areas, gardens in pastoral settings often seem less a container than a portal, a bridge to the landscape beyond. For property-owner and gardener Emma Burrill in East Sussex, that means creating a connected wildlife corridor to the woodlands beyond, for the sake of transforming an old horse pasture into a thriving biodiverse habitat. Not far away in the Dorset, England, countryside—an "Area of Outstanding Natural Beauty" as officially designated by the United Kingdom—landscape wizards Hugo Bugg and Charlotte Harris embrace meandering fields and rolling hills as central elements to link a garden to the surrounding dreamy woodlands. And for an expansive property along Connecticut's Greenwich Harbor, Kathryn Herman introduces a wild meadow reflective of the pastoral setting, an unfettered domain that she says is "unexpected and terribly romantic."

Whether castle grounds in Ireland or a resurrected farm in Quebec, a country garden understands that it need not claim center stage. It knows the power of place and context, of backdrop and belonging. "Having so much nature surrounding the garden enhances it somehow," says Rob Nestor of his rural Connecticut Eden, a true salute to the countryside, complete with a Greek temple.

LEFT Richard Ouellette and Maxime Vandal initially fell for the old apple trees on this 80-acre property outside of Montreal, where they have created Humminghill Farm, their retreat from city life. Vandal loves cooking from their kitchen garden for alfresco entertaining.

PAGES 128-129 A relaxed weekend brunch by the pond is a tradition on Humminghill Farm. A cake plate piled high with Quebecois homemade crepes almost steals the show from the centerpiece of dahlias, cosmos, and other blossoms from vast cutting garden.

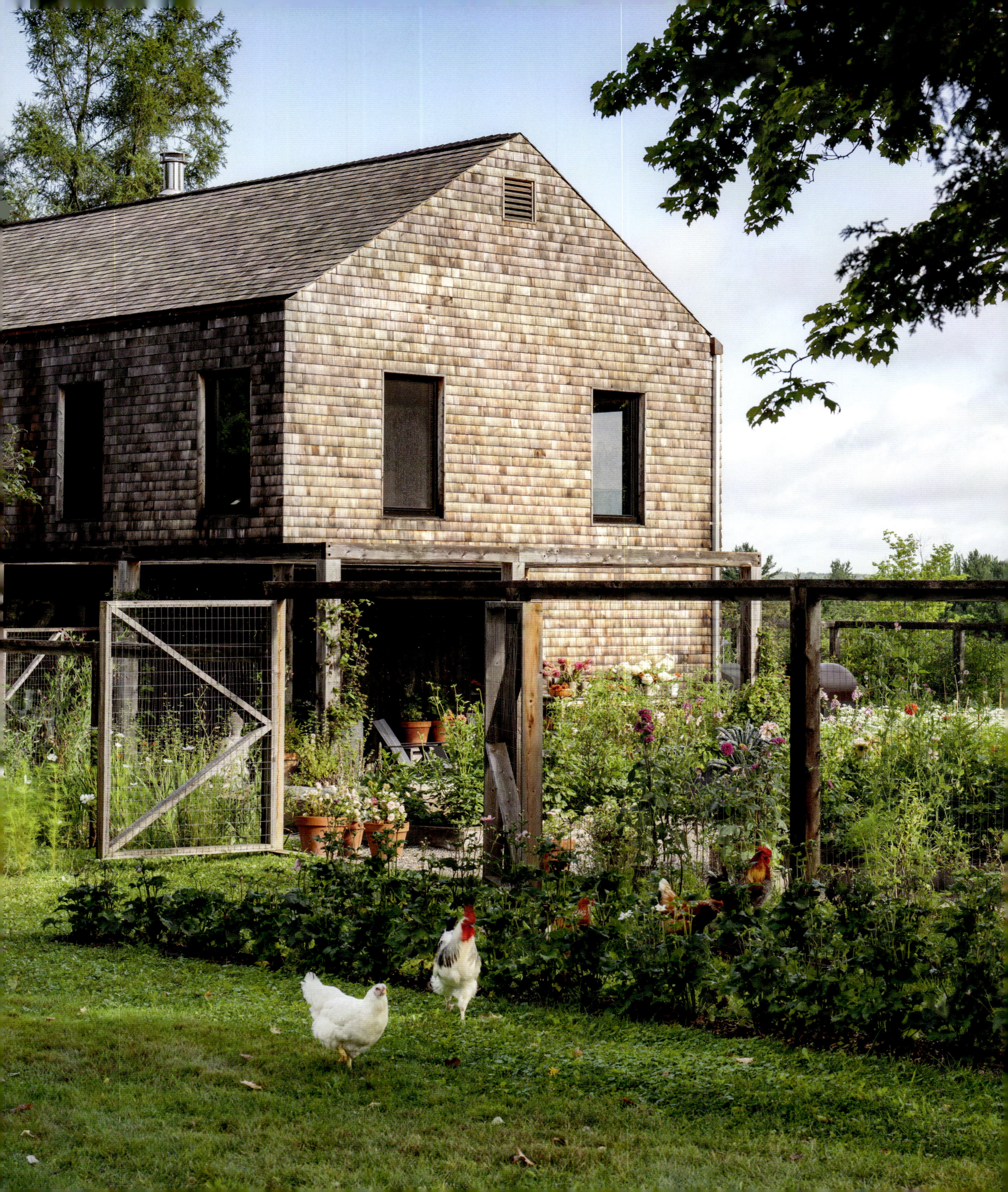

Rural Renaissance

On their farm on the outskirts of Montreal, Richard Ouellette and Maxime Vandal trade city bustle for cut flowers and beekeeping, and plenty of romping room for their pups.

LEFT Humminghill Farm, a nearly 80-acre property in West Bolton, about an hour from Montreal, has become an agri-adventure for design duo Maxime Vandal and Richard Ouellette. Vandal transformed a garage into a chic and functional cedar-shingle coach house by the parterre, with a ground-level kitchen that opens to the garden and living quarters above.

RIGHT Caesar, a light Sussex rooster, looks after the hens alongside the sunflower patch. In addition to the Chantecler chickens, Ouellette and Vandal have an apiary for pollination and honey.

COUNTRY ESCAPES 133

RIGHT Enchanted by noble apple trees, a grove of maples, acres of lush forest, and fields that had seen better days (but are now planted in hay), the couple began digging in and slowly transforming the property into a side hobby. On Saturday mornings they deliver cut flowers to neighbors and via La Ferme Humminghill, their shop that also sells homemade blended vinegars, honey, and other curated goods.

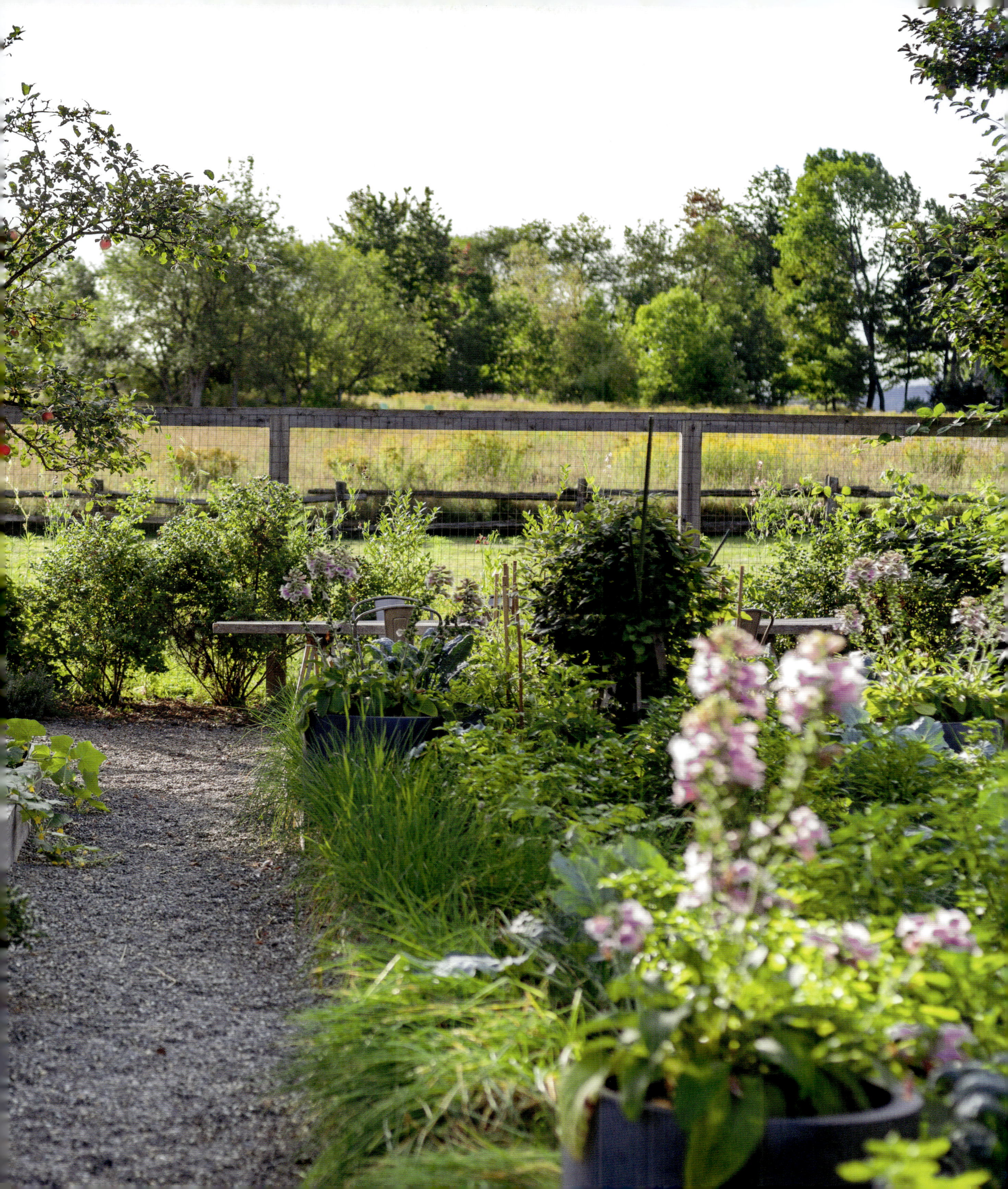

ABOVE Vandal cultivates a large vegetable garden of "almost inhuman scale," Ouellette says, laughing. Ouellette added beds of dahlias, cosmos, sunflowers, and zinnias to the mix. "If I was putting all this energy in the gardens, I wanted color and beauty," he says.

RIGHT A respite spot beneath the old apple trees offers reprieve from the endless farm chores. Working the land has reconnected the designers with the rhythms of the seasons, and they delight in sharing the bounty.

136   ENCHANTING GARDENS

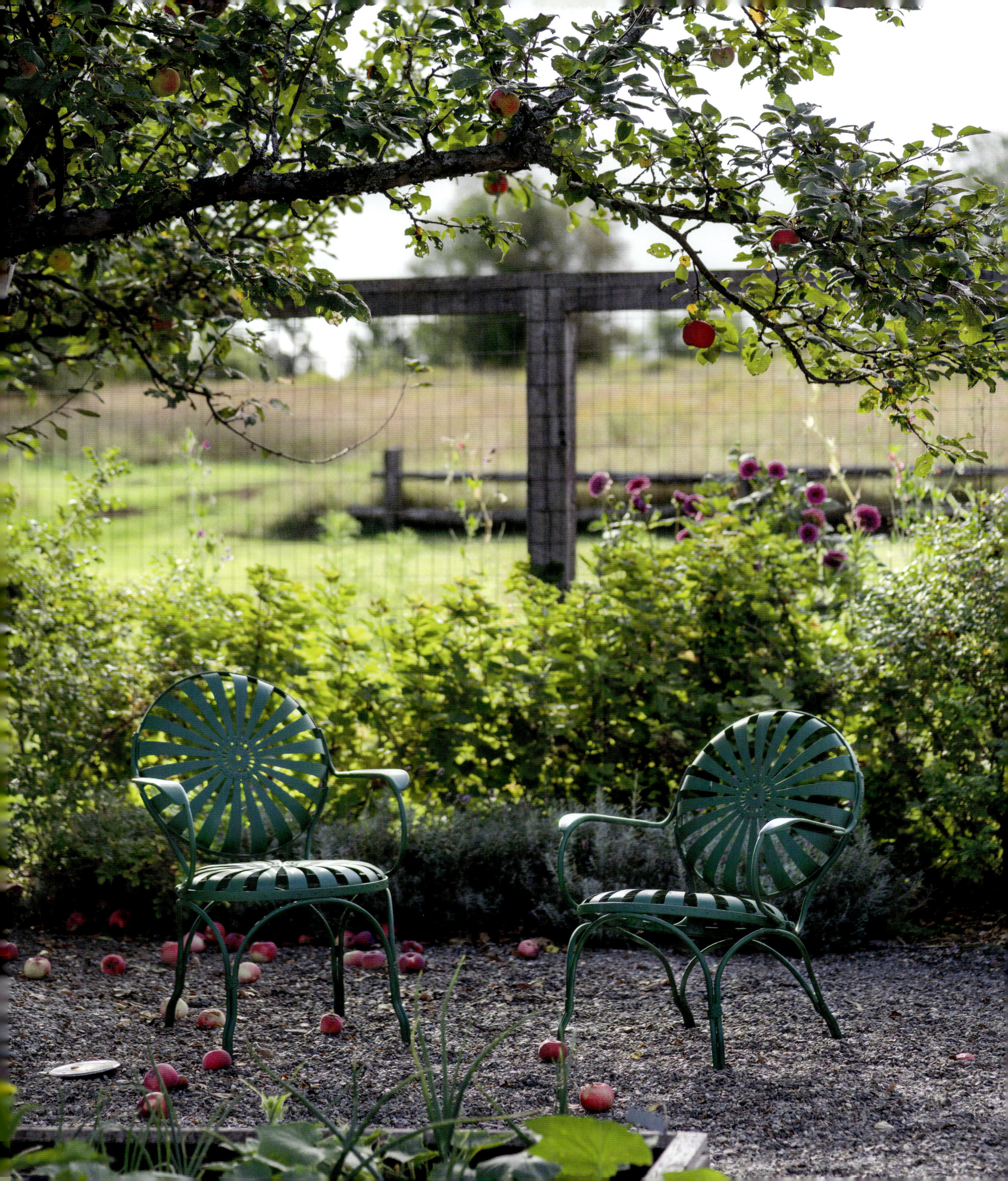

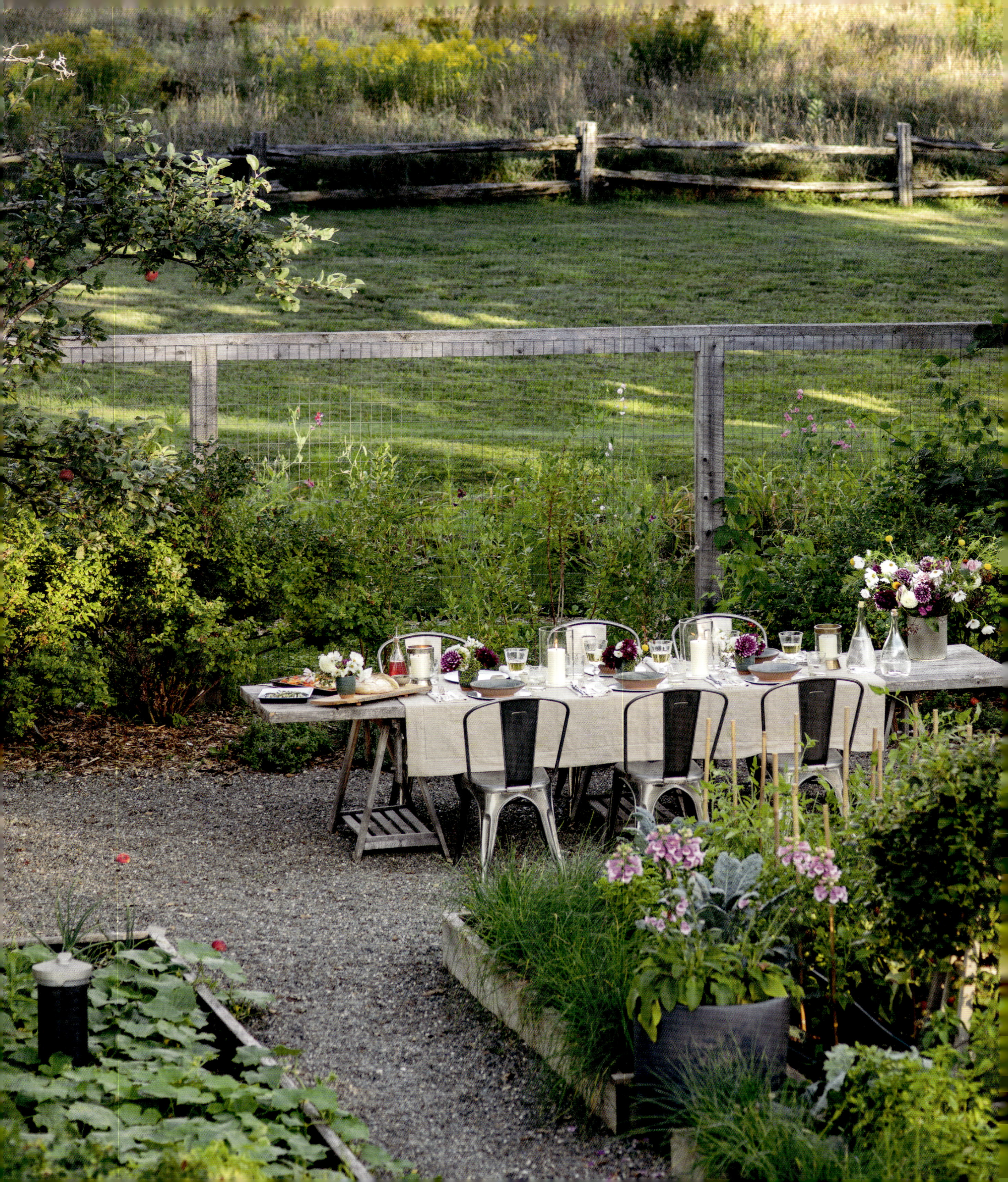

LEFT "Max loves to cook. As soon as we begin inviting friends, he starts his focaccia recipe—baking relaxes him, as does gardening. I prefer to do nothing and relax," says Ouellette. The two enjoy entertaining in the garden during Canada's delightful summer.

ABOVE While Vandal is the tireless baker, Ouellette makes his "never fail" sheet pan–roasted veggie dish and sets linen-draped tables in the garden and by the pond. They've befriended local artisans, and they enjoy showcasing their pottery, plateware, and linens.

COUNTRY ESCAPES 139

LEFT A bed of ornamental onion thrives in the sunshine. "It's a privilege to live here and repurpose this land in a sustainable way," says Vandal. "It changes our entire life on the weekdays to see this ahead of us, to come here and respond to the weather changing, to the chickens, who demand attention. We are connecting to a simplicity and a daily rhythm that's real and soulful."

RIGHT Farm-fresh eggs and a pile of crepes are the centerpiece for a Sunday garden brunch. It's not unusual for guests to bring their gardening gloves along. "We don't ask them to work," says Ouellette. "They want to join in!"

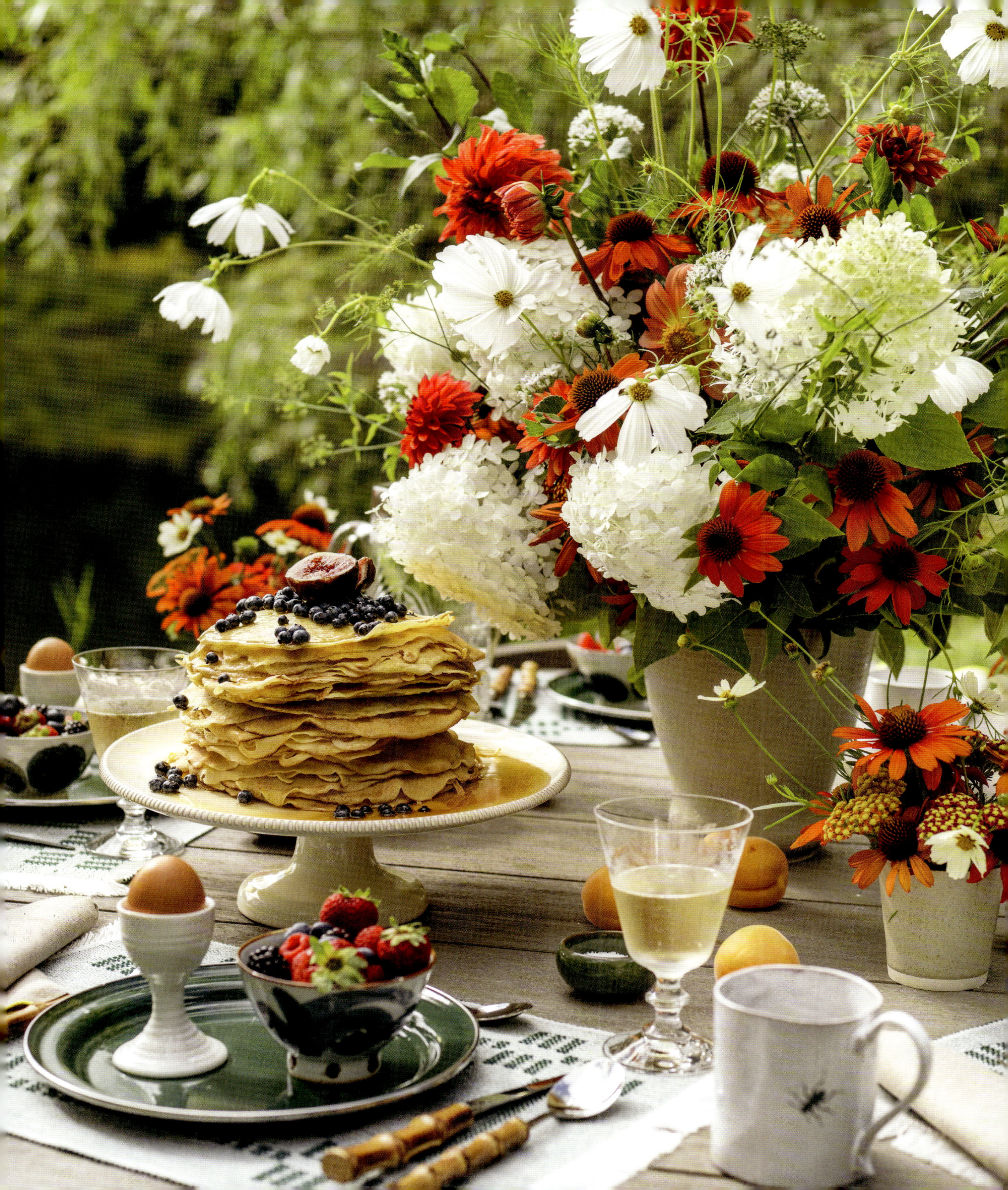

Slow & Steady

With equal parts playfulness and patience, Emma Burrill untames a former horse pasture, transforming it into a grassy haven for biodiversity.

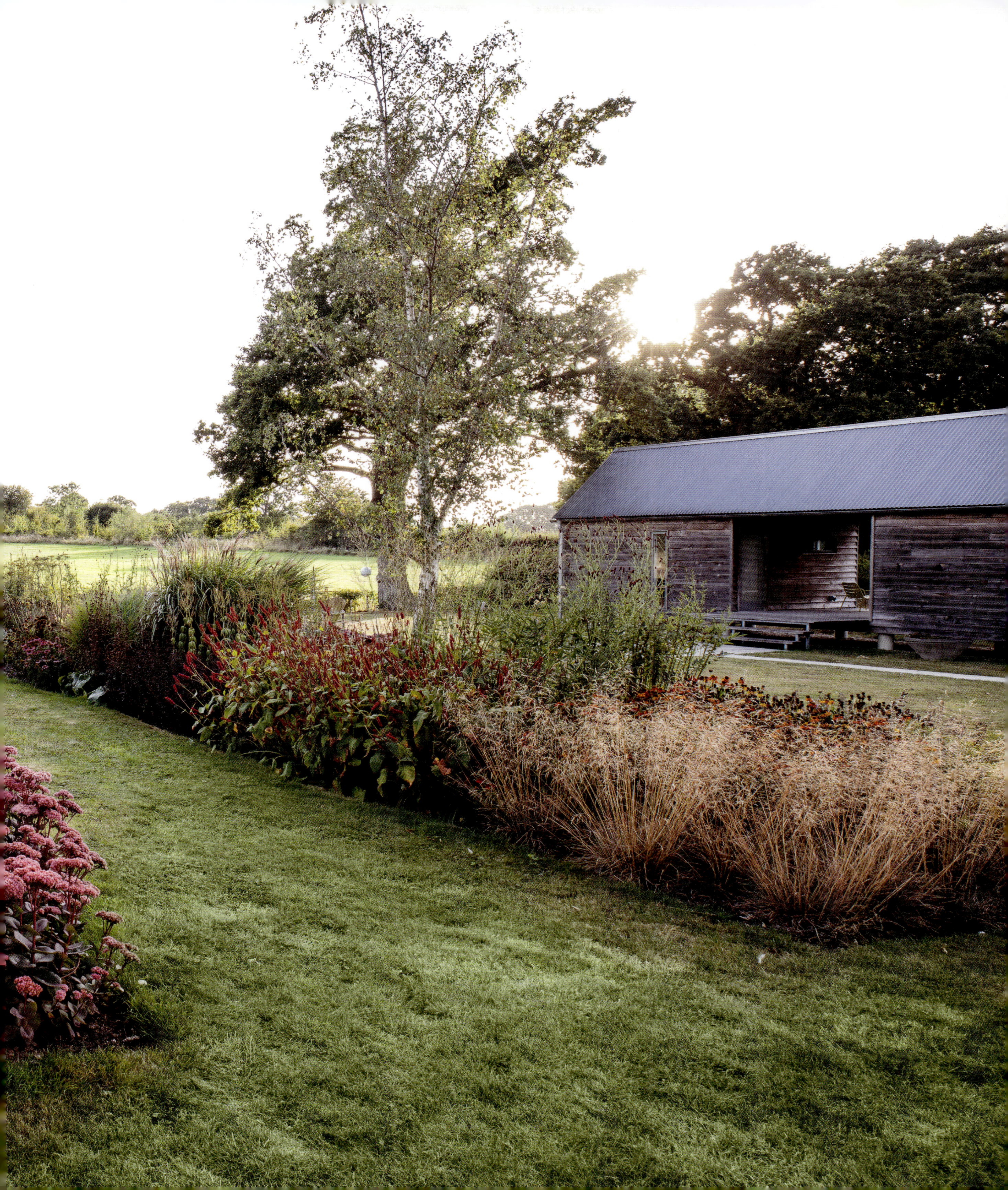

LEFT Fine art photographer Emma Burrill initially fell for the old buildings on this former horse farm in East Sussex, but the land ignited her gardening passion as she altered the seven acres of scruffy pasture into a biodiverse prairie-style haven. A circular mowed path in an old paddock resembles the properties' past while adding a modern element.

RIGHT A dog trot in Burrill's art studio overlooks a wildflower meadow. "To have it half-planned and half-wild links the gardens to the fields and woods beyond, creating connected wildlife corridors," she says.

PAGES 142-143 Ornamental grasses, including Warrior, Karl Foerster, and Goldtau varieties, create softness in beds mixed with pink autumn stonecrop and other sedum. "I'm a tidy person by nature, but I try not to take that into the garden," says Burrill. "I let things be; that's better for wildlife."

144   ENCHANTING GARDENS

RIGHT Purple coneflower is a favorite pollinator, and it punches up the lavender and lilac hues throughout the garden.

COUNTRY ESCAPES 145

Glin Glory

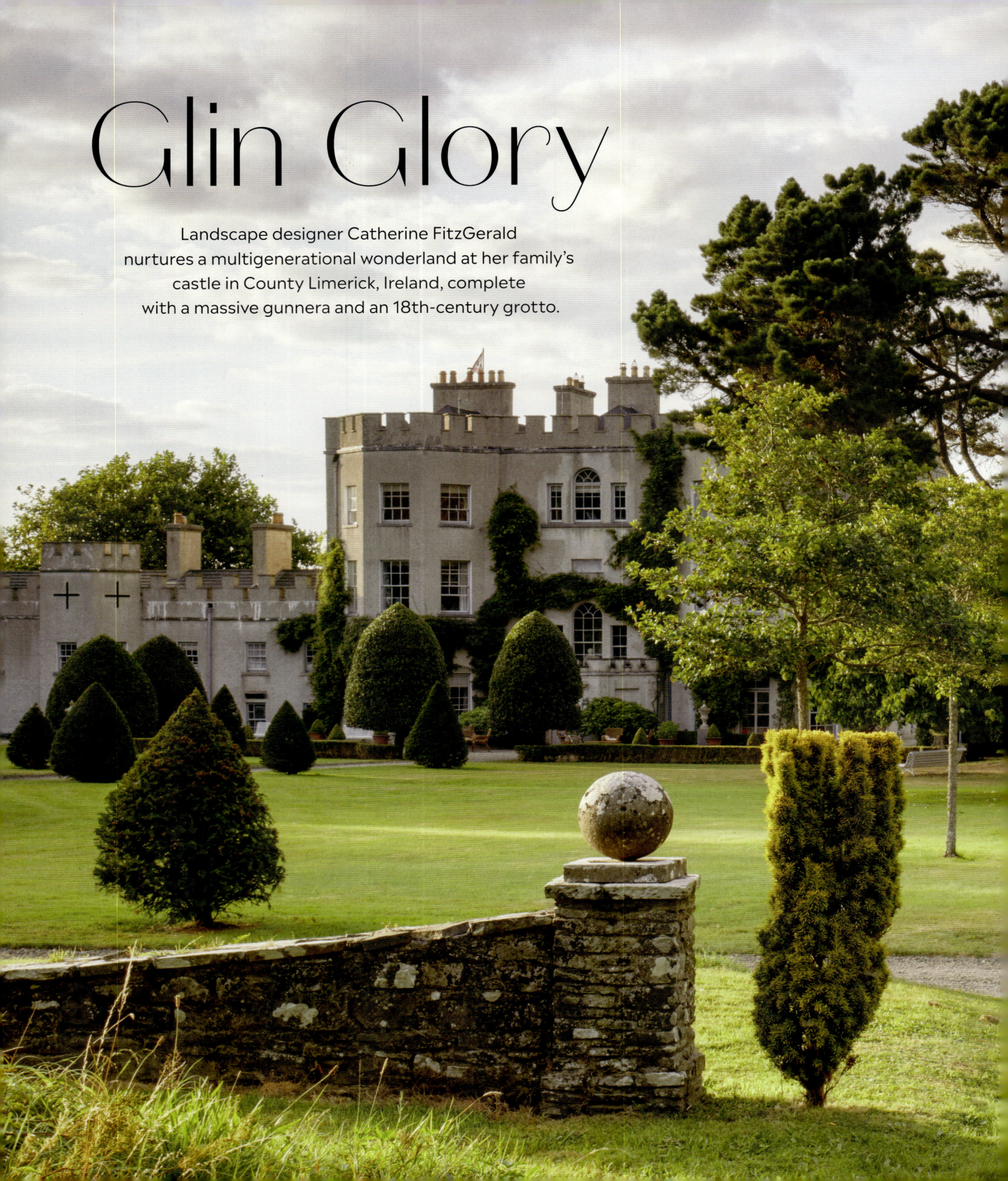

Landscape designer Catherine FitzGerald nurtures a multigenerational wonderland at her family's castle in County Limerick, Ireland, complete with a massive gunnera and an 18th-century grotto.

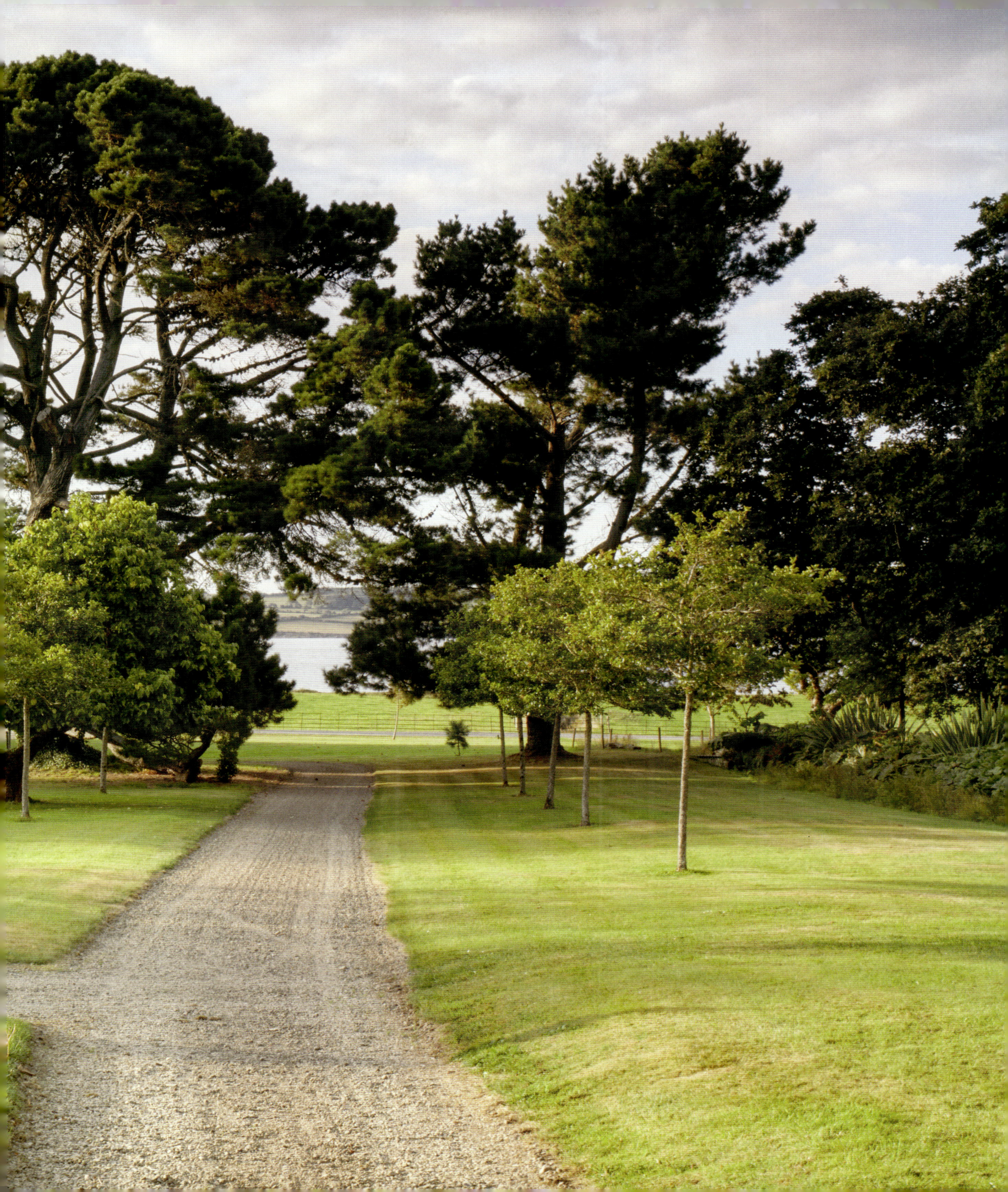

148 ENCHANTING GARDENS

PAGES 146-147 Catherine FitzGerald grew up roaming the circa 1870 Glin Castle, which her parents ran as boutique hotel. Gnarled and twisted sessile oaks are descendants of the Killarney forest that once extended down to the River Shannon estuary. FitzGerald's landscape design career got its start here, and today she tweaks her childhood stomping grounds.

LEFT Tightly clipped bay, boxwood, and yew stand sentry on the path nearest the castle, the castellations of which owe more to the Gothic fantasies of the 24th knight rather than any defensive need. The gardens are open to the public, and the castle often hosts events.

ABOVE A Persian ironwood, planted by FitzGerald's mother in the 1930s, forms the central axis of the garden. It's one of the first things to come into leaf and among the earliest to color in fall. "It gets a pink tint by the end of August, and that is how I know it is the end of summer," FitzGerald says.

COUNTRY ESCAPES 149

150   ENCHANTING GARDENS

LEFT The walled garden is where FitzGerald expresses creativity, embellishing a formal layout designed by her mother in the 1970s with long double borders on either side of the path by the south-facing stone wall. Irish yews maintain order among more boisterous herbaceous plants in a joyous jig of color and form, while the towering stems of tender Tower of Jewels thrust toward the heavens.

RIGHT A stone outbuilding is camouflaged by climbing Pink Perpetua roses. Numerous other perennials and annuals thrive in this mild but damp microclimate, thanks to the warm Gulf Stream air.

PAGES 154-155 "It is all about Glin's unique atmosphere; it has such a powerful spirit," says FitzGerald. In addition to the bountiful perennial and cut flower gardens, there's a large, productive walled kitchen garden, which visitors are welcome to harvest from. "The garden is for mooching in and enjoying," says FitzGerald.

ENCHANTING GARDENS

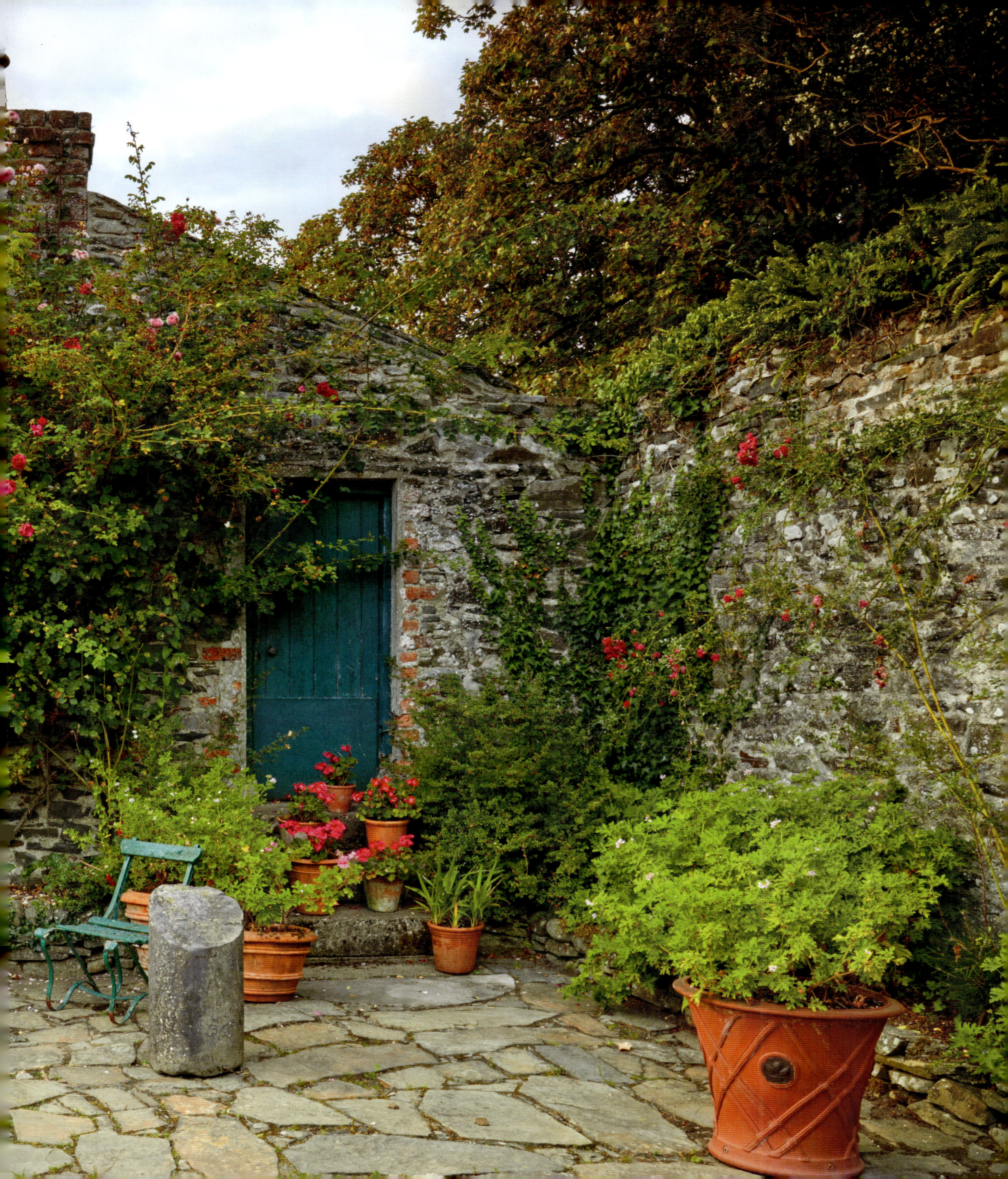

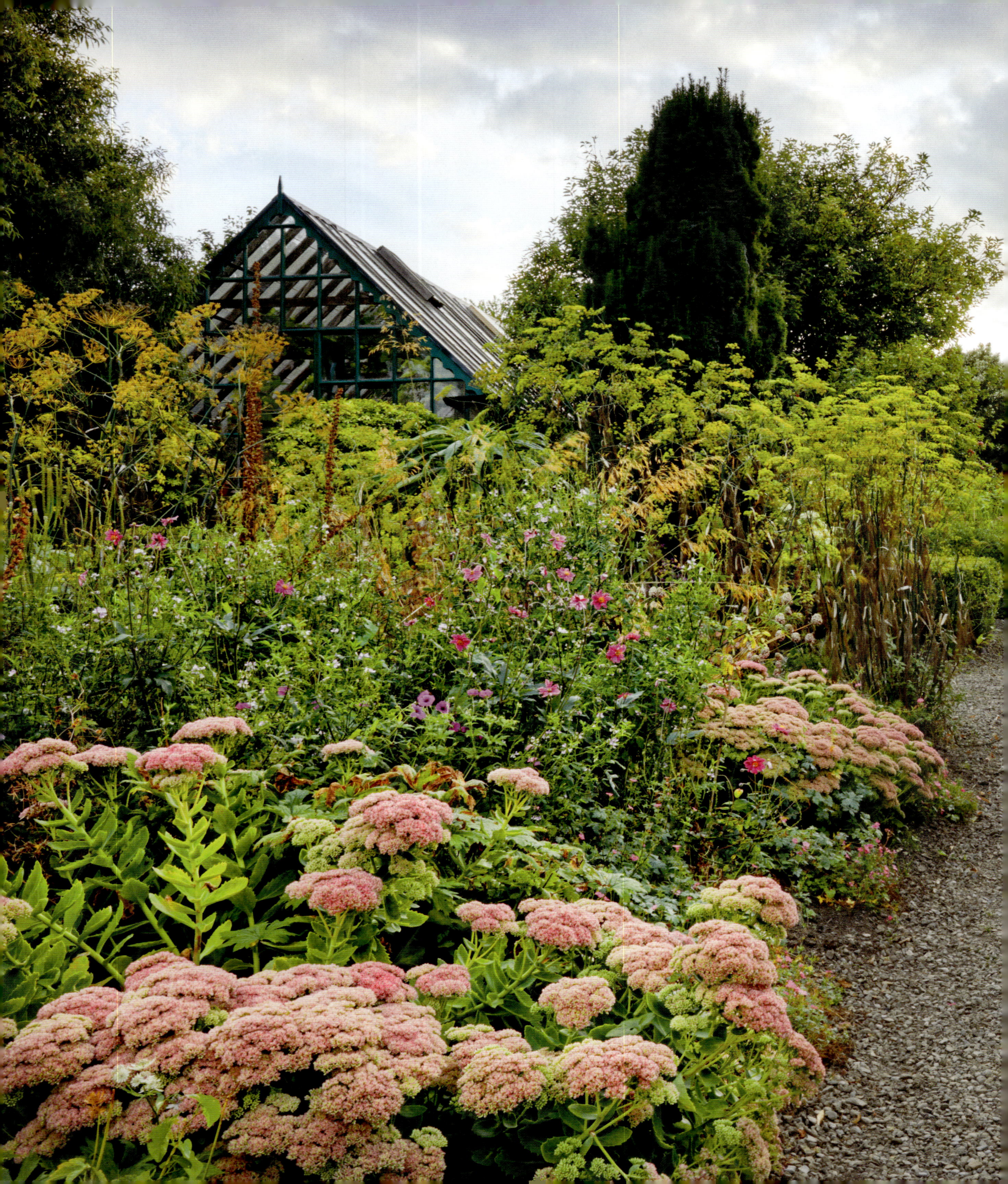

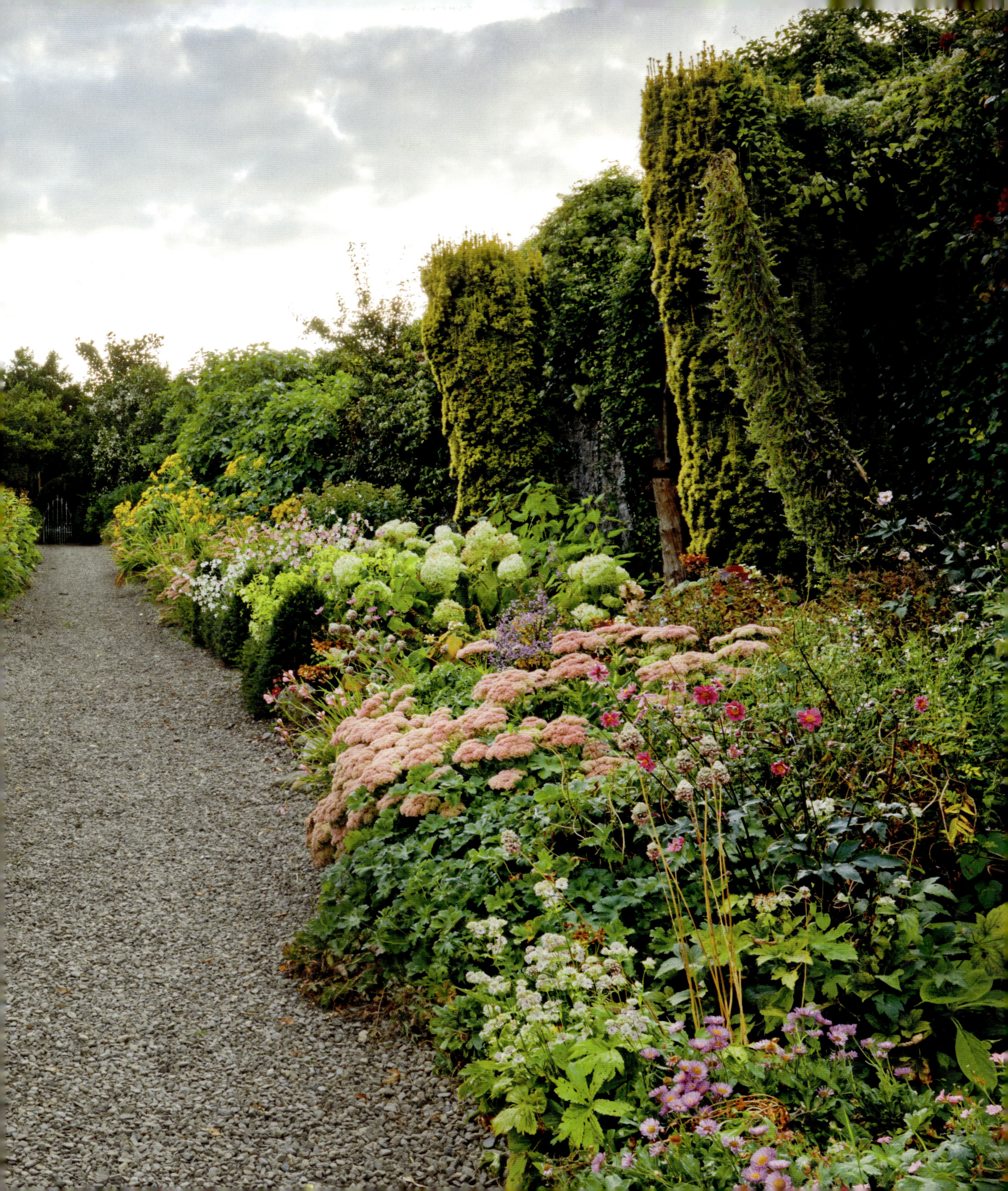

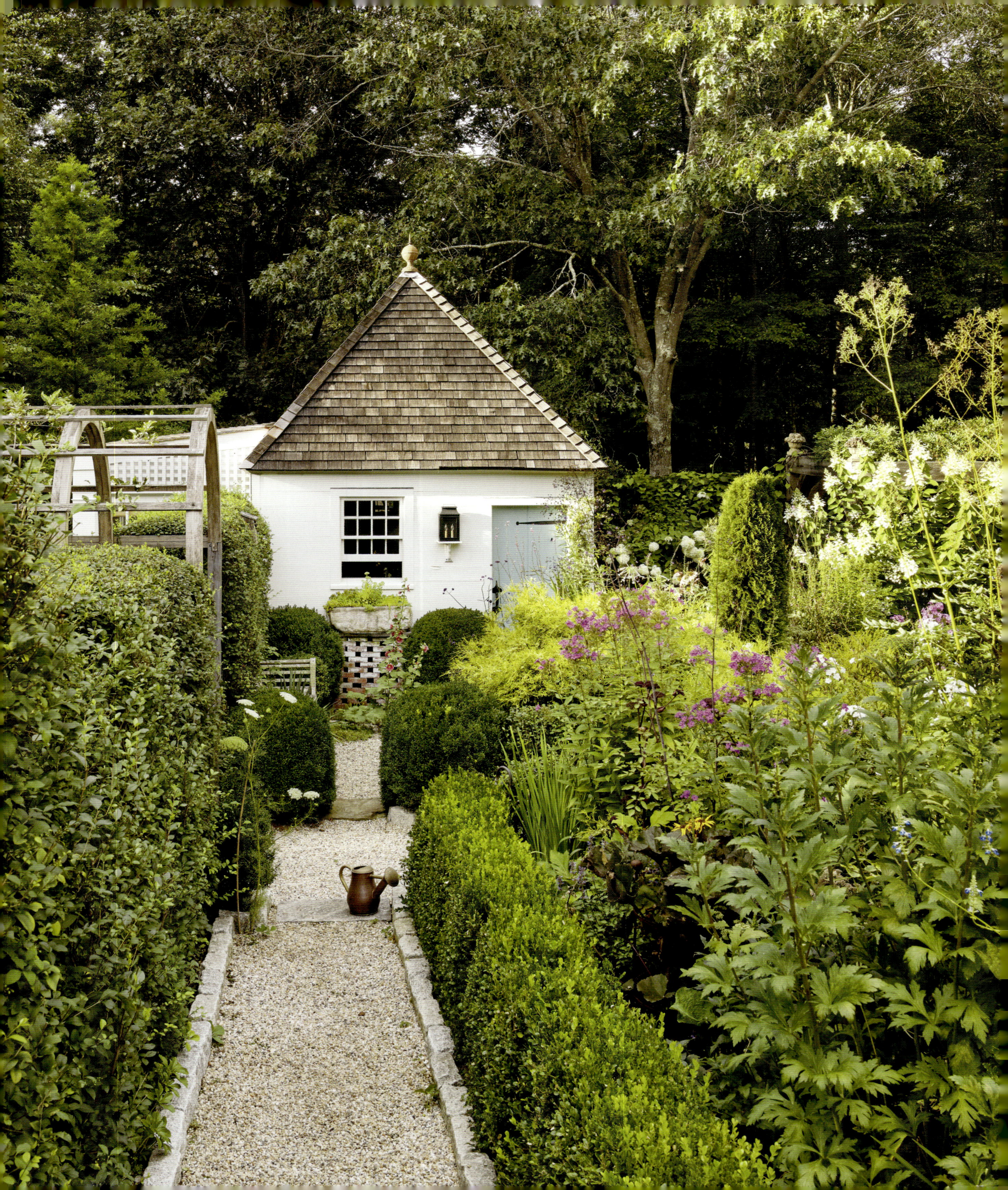

Connecticut Carte Blanche

A move to New England spurs creative new growth, and multiple garden nooks, for two hands-on gardeners.

LEFT After moving to Southeastern Connecticut from Atlanta, Bill Reynolds and Robb Nestor began daydreaming about what their 11-acre property might become. "We imagined a fountain in a flattened-out area and sketched a little garden house in the corner, and things slowly evolved," says Reynolds. The steep-pitched cedar-shake roof of the garden shed designed by Reynolds is a nod to Southern vernacular outbuildings.

RIGHT A playful parterre introduces fun clipped-hedge shapes within a pebbled circle. Reynolds and Nestor do all the garden design, planting, and maintenance themselves. "Long days spent weeding and pruning are the best days," Nestor says.

COUNTRY ESCAPES 157

LEFT "We loved that the property was so pure, just an old farmhouse and a field," Nestor says. They also adored that it was a tabula rasa, with no preexisting garden. Keeping the front natural and simple, they added heirloom apple and pear trees to what had been a small orchard. The back is a warren of delight.

RIGHT "You'd never know this is back here. It unfolds in a series of surprises as you walk from room to room," Reynolds says. Japanese pachysandra, giant butterbur, and English boxwoods form an evergreen passage from the pool garden to a potting shed and greenhouse.

RIGHT "Given the simplicity of the house, we didn't want the gardens to be too rigid and formal," he adds, noting that structural hedges are mixed with casual plantings. The Vita Sackville-West–inspired perennial garden blooms with a carnival of alliums, phlox, and Aruncus.

ENCHANTING GARDENS

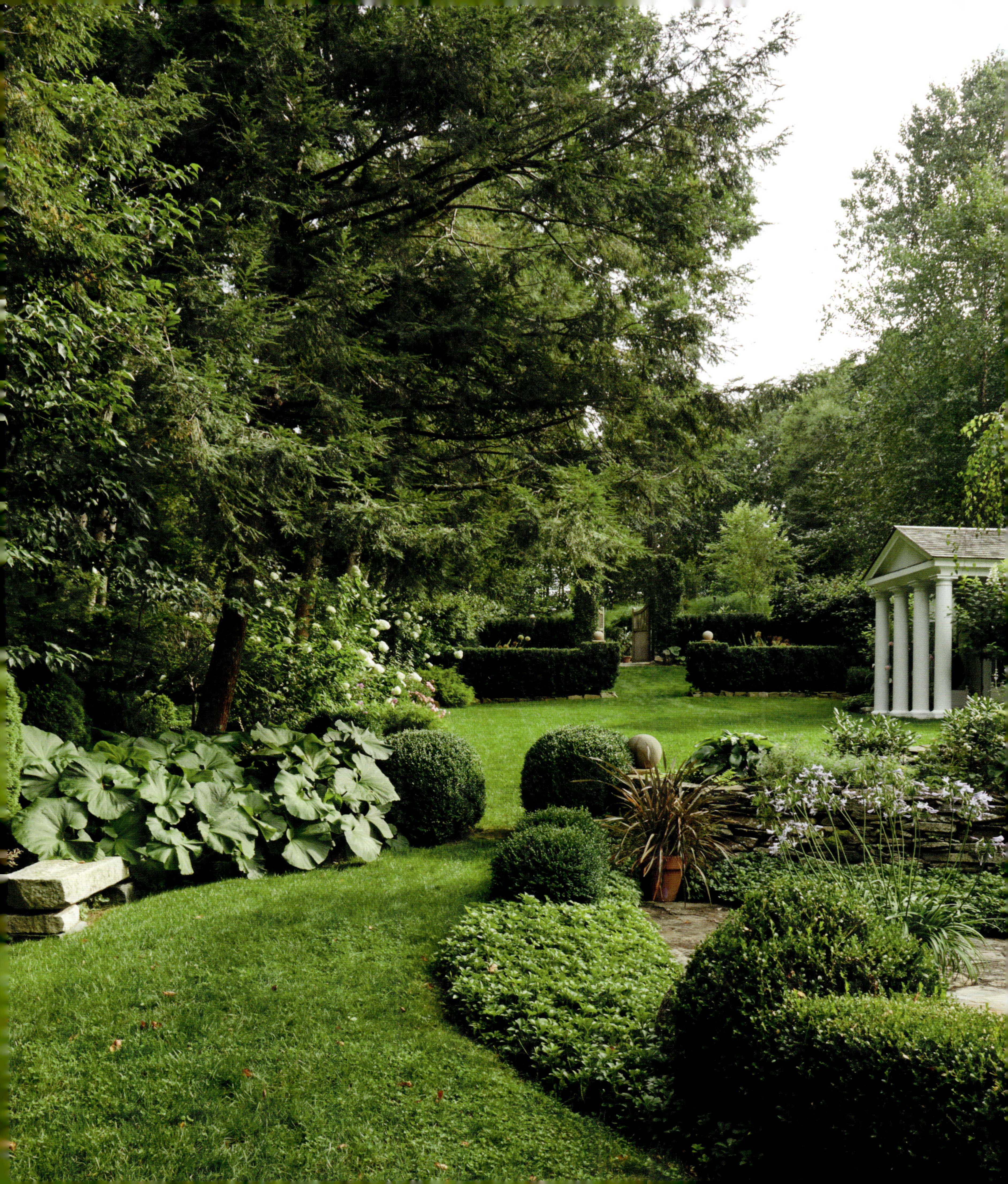

LEFT In the potager, cabbage—along with herbs, lettuces, and leeks—bursts forth from elegant, geometric boxwood hedges. Willow wattle fencing and Belgian blocks form linear borders.

RIGHT Stone from an on-site quarry comprises stacked-stone walls and the small pool area in the shaded side yard, which is punctuated by potted agapanthus and boxwoods. "Much of the garden is on an axis with eye-catchers to draw you to the next room," Reynolds says. "We like things a little offset."

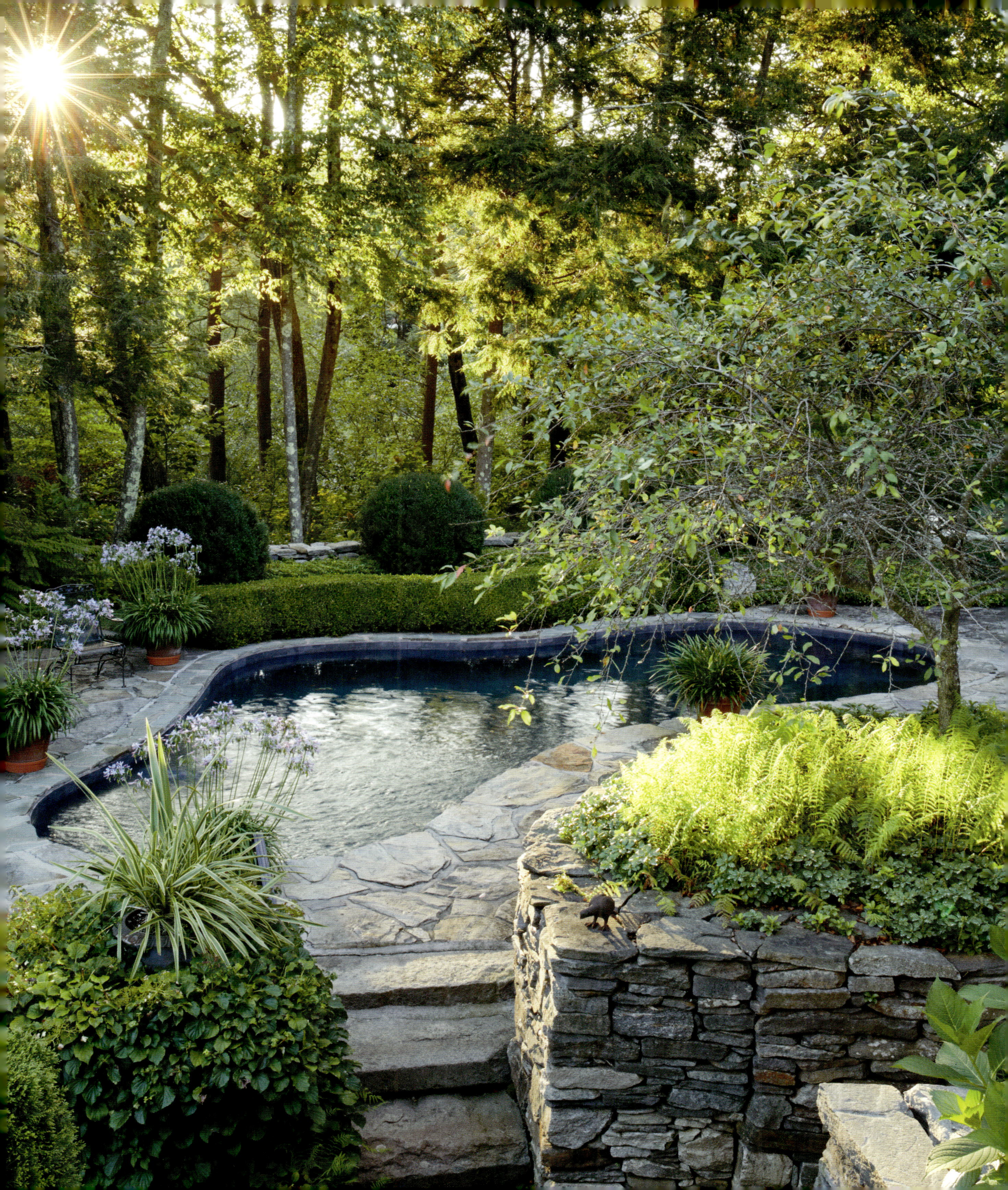

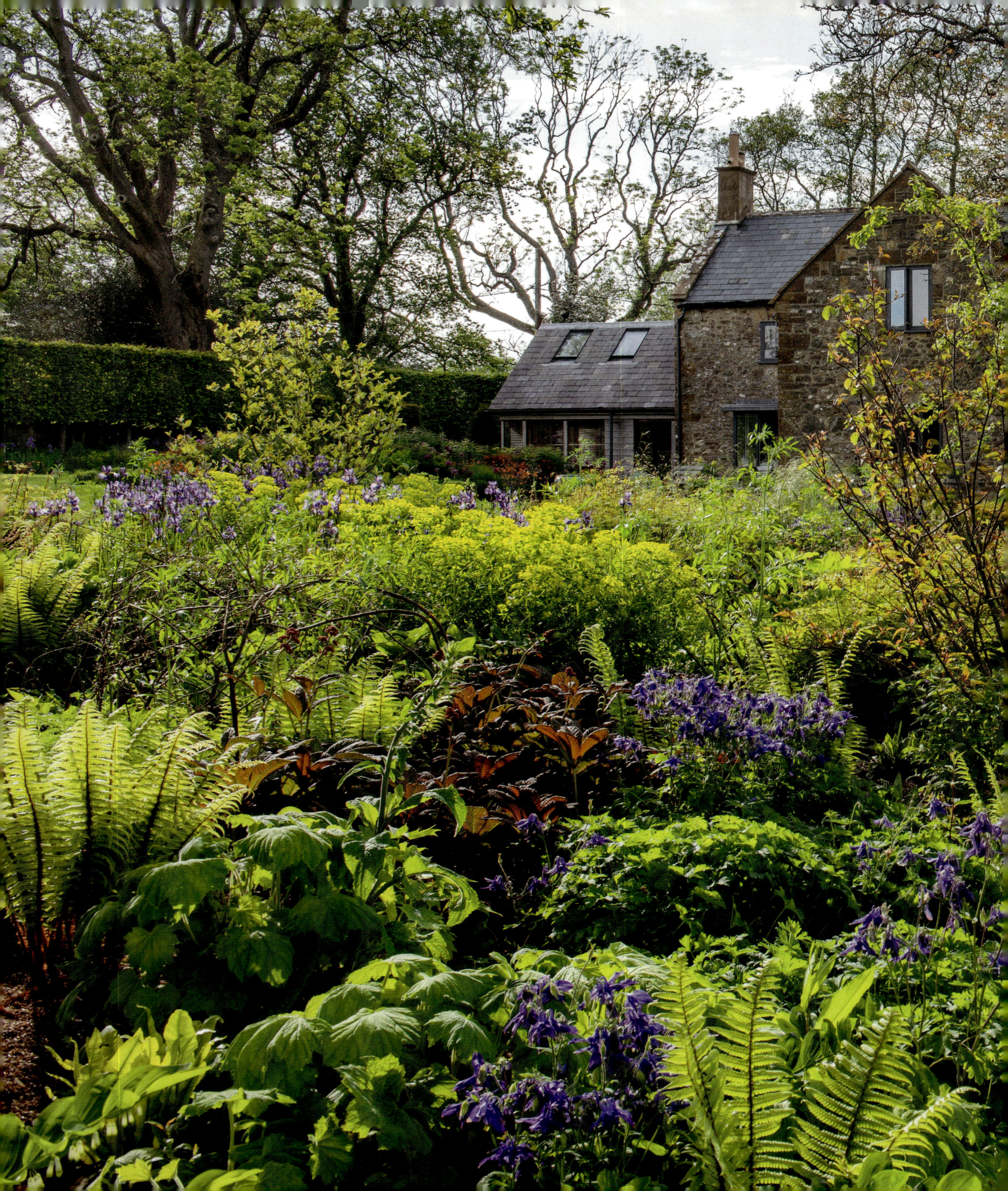

The Long View

In the Dorset countryside, landscape designers Hugo Bugg and Charlotte Harris bring back the ha-ha, opening up vistas and planting for longevity.

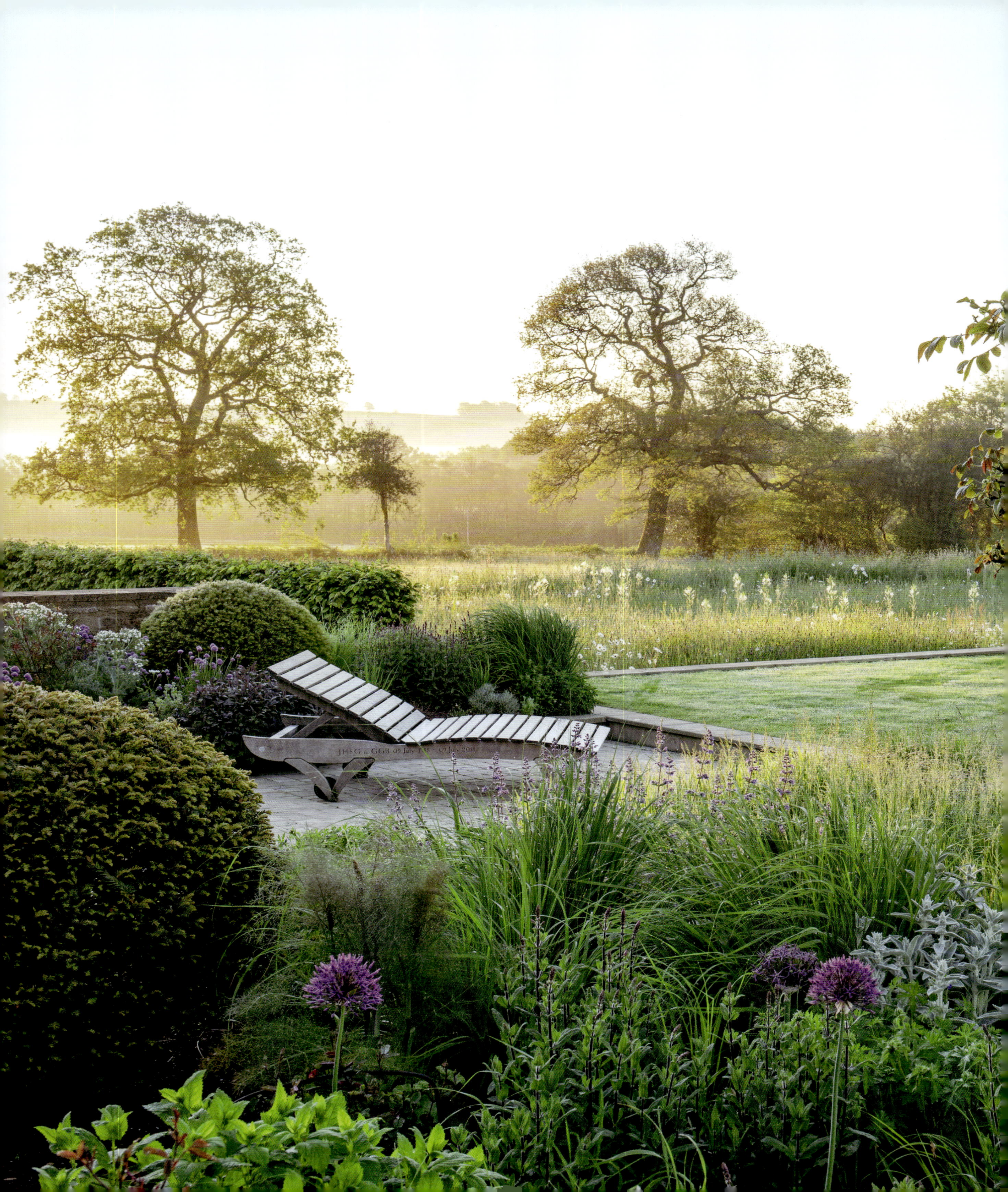

PAGES 162-163 In this officially recognized United Kingdom "Area of Natural Beauty," London-based landscape architects Hugo Bugg and Charlotte Harris redesigned this farmhouse garden "to open it up and invite people into the garden," says Harris. A mixed bed of Siberian iris, columbine, Solomon's seal, and Wallich's wood fern hugs a dining terrace, connecting the outdoor space to the residence.

LEFT In the distance, a ha-ha—a sunken fence common in 18th-century French landscapes—camouflages a tennis court, while yew domes, ornamental onion, Korean feather reed grass, and herbs huddle around a terrace overlooking meadows of white-flowered quamash.

ABOVE "This garden is not a fixed space; it breathes and changes," says Harris. Obelisk plinths of yew are a repeated motif, signaling a transition to the orchards of young apple, walnut, hazel, and other fruit trees.

COUNTRY ESCAPES

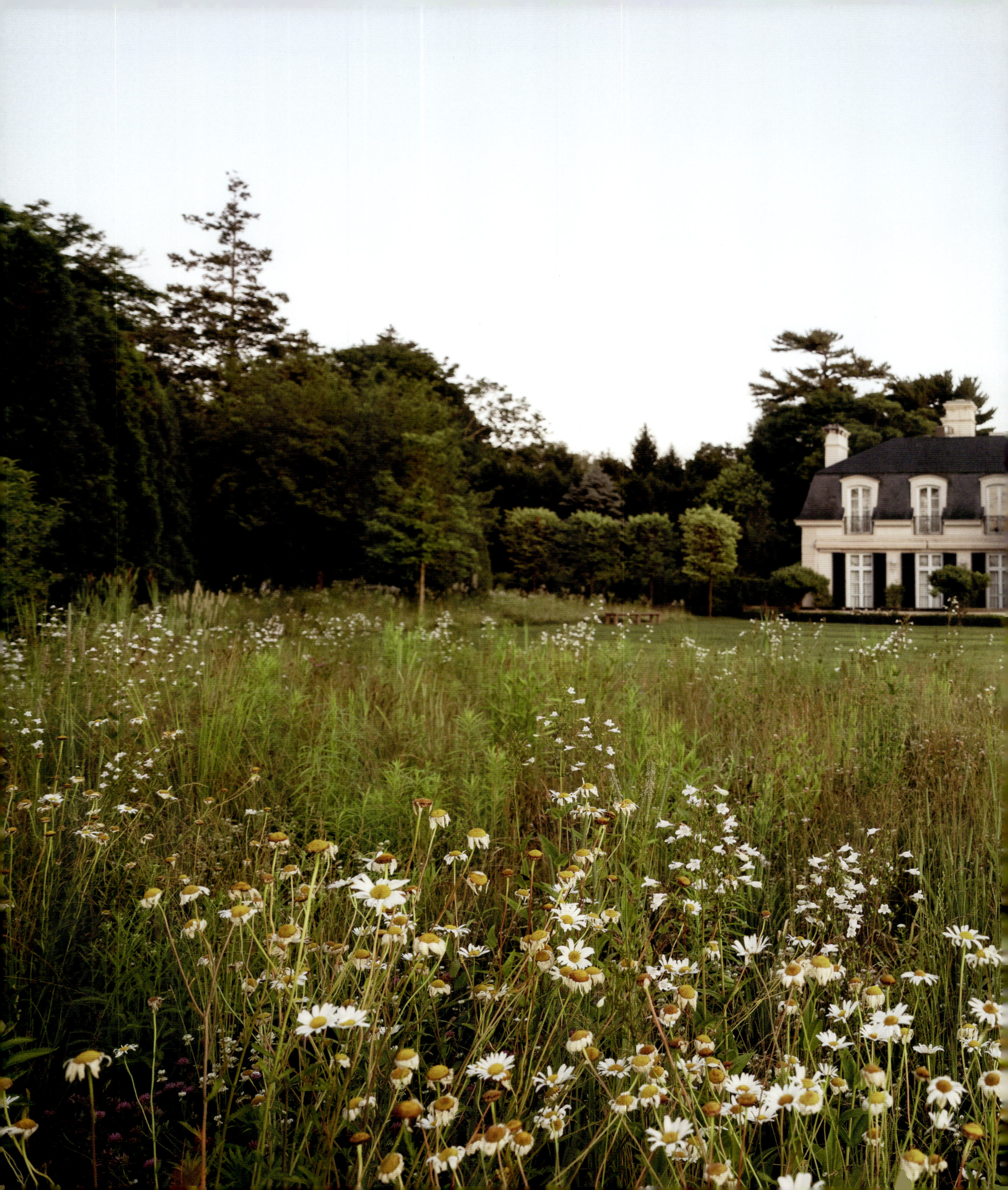

Unrepentant Romantic

In a return to the classics, landscape architect Kathryn Herman trades "static" lawns for meandering meadows, plus terraces and towering *tuteurs*.

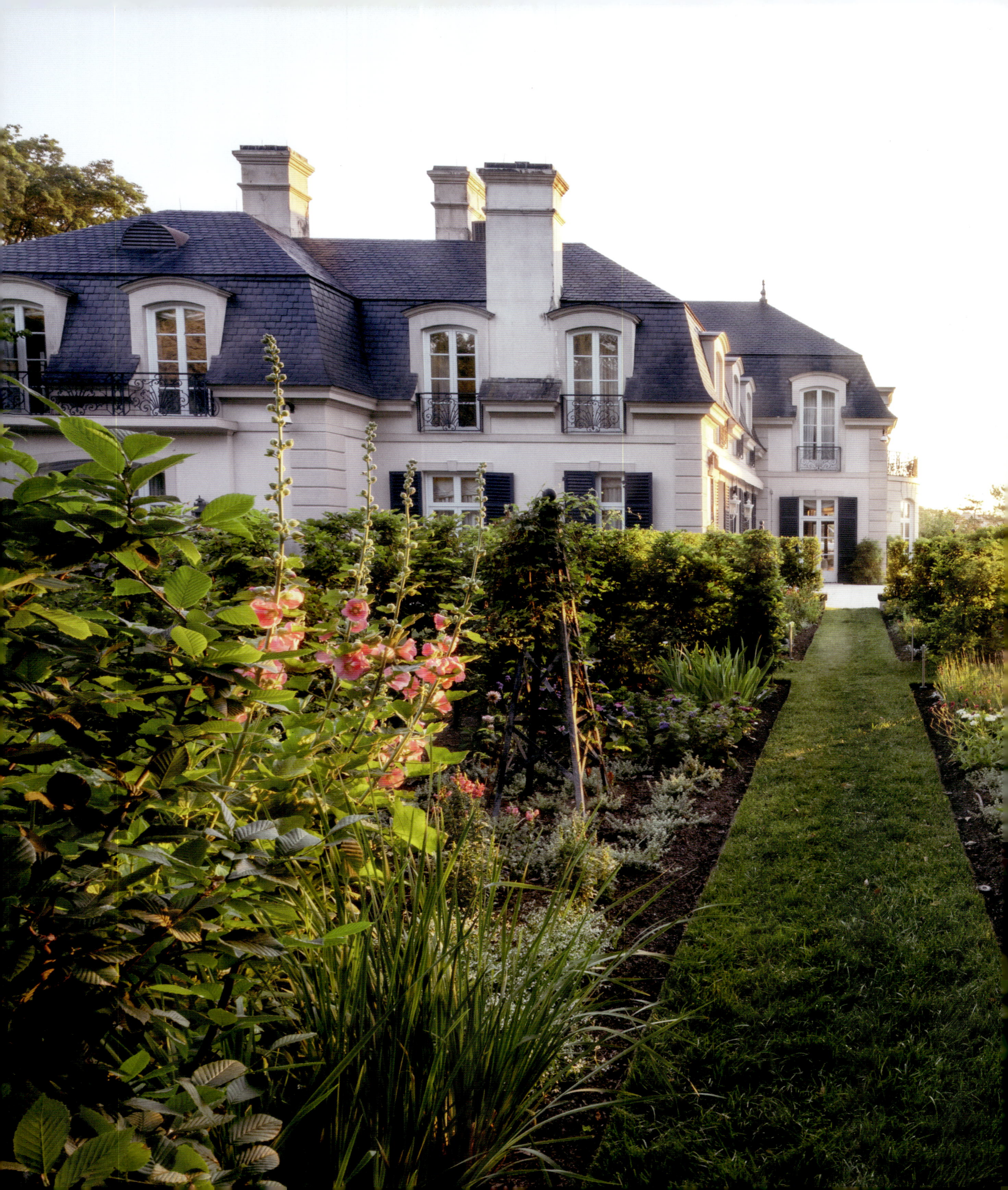

LEFT In response to the grandness of a harborside, French-style manse, "we created a garden that was both French and American," says landscape designer Kathryn Herman. She balanced more formal spaces, like this series of outdoor rooms full of Franco elements (*tuteurs*, hornbeam hedges, and rows of linden trees) along the rear and sides of the house, with spirited expanses of lawn and meadow sloping toward the sea.

PAGES 166-167 Herman invoked a loose, dynamic meadow that opens behind the house tapping into the pastoral Connecticut setting. "There's a wildness to it that's unexpected and terribly romantic," she says. "Lawns are static, but the meadow is ever changing."

COUNTRY ESCAPES 169

LEFT Terraced limestone steps cut through the sloping meadow to a dining area where pollarded London plane trees sprout from a gravel patio and offer shade, "like you see at the Jardin des Tuileries," says Herman.

RIGHT The original 1960s-era pool rests beside Greenwich Harbor, surrounded by an elegant *Ilex crenata* Green Lustre hedge and border of White Carpet roses. A screen of water-tolerant pitch pines give privacy. "You really have the best of both worlds here, formal and informal," Herman says.

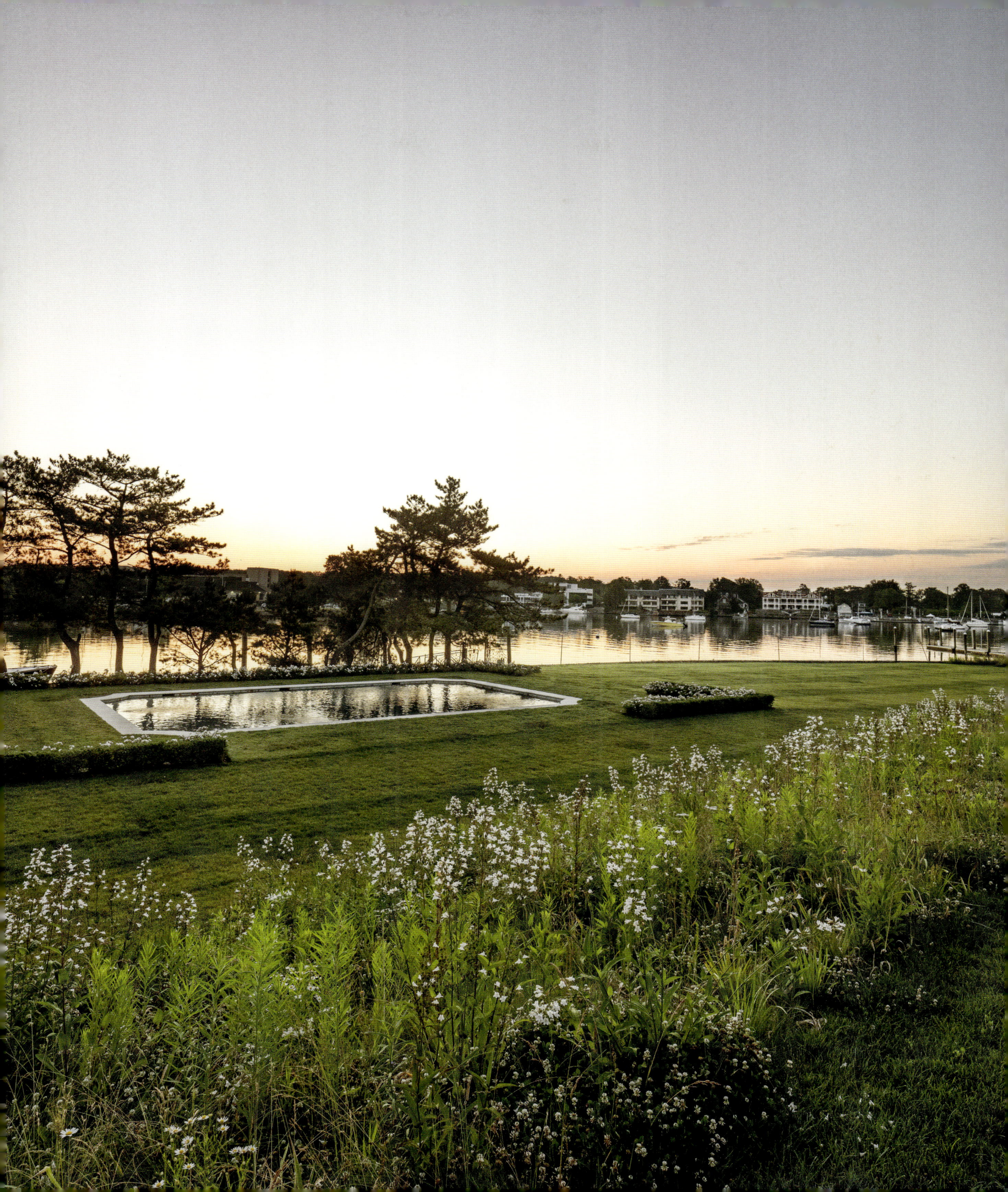

CHAPTER 4

WATERSIDE IDYLLS

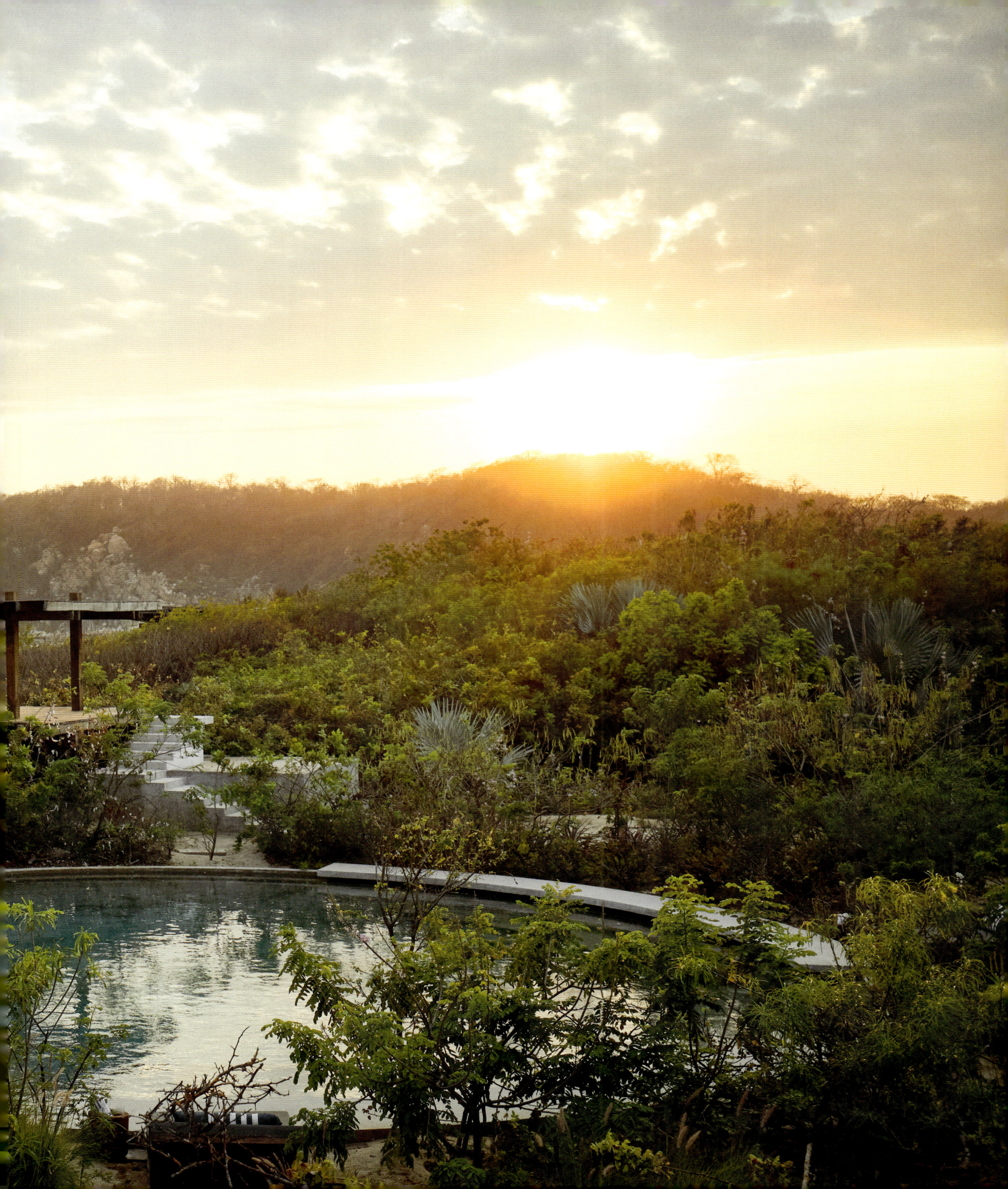

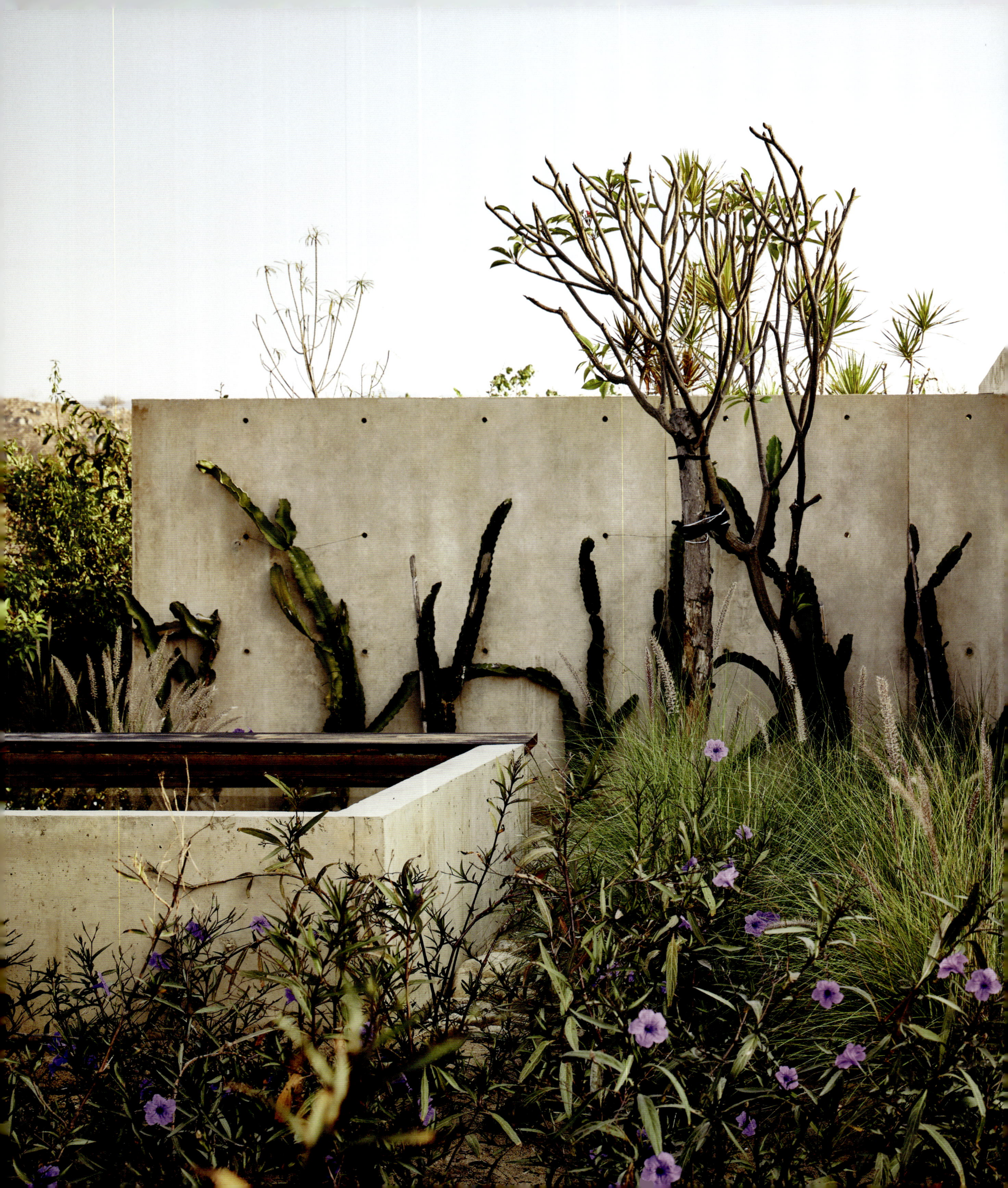

WATERSIDE IDYLLS

LEFT In Oaxaca's Puerto Escondido, a mirador (from *mirar*, to gaze) surrounded by Mexican petunias brings reflective calm to this plaza where cacti grow, looking almost like deep green graffiti against a garden wall.

PAGES 172-173 Landscape architects Maria Kalach and Gabriela Salazar create a "sense of harmony" between the mountains, sea, garden, and architecture (which was designed by Maria's father, Alberto Kalach). The pool, sited in the center of the landscape, references Italian villa design. By stepping the home back from the shore, there's room for a garden in between, making "your view more expansive," says Kalach.

SWIMMING POOLS, OCEANS, RIVERS, HARBORS, PONDS—water is not just essential to keep gardens growing, but often it's the most central design element in one. "Water is its mater and matrix, mother and medium," writes Hungarian biochemist and Nobel Prize winner Albert Szent-Györgyi. "Life is water dancing to the tune of solids." When it comes to waterside gardens, perhaps it's more like plants dancing to the tune of trickles, splashes, and waves.

Humans, by our own aqueous makeup, are waterlogged creatures, clocking in at upwards of 60 percent H-two-O. We are seduced and soothed by water, cleansed and quenched by it, and thus inviting water elements or views, water sounds and experiences into the garden, as those here prove, is one of the surest tricks in the successful gardening handbook. In hot, humid Houston, architect Bill Curtis makes a circular pool an anchoring centerpiece. On the Pacific shore of Mexico, landscape designers Maria Kalach and Gabriela Salazar embrace the arid alchemy of a coastal property, introducing mirror pools to cool and calm the senses. In Montecito, California, landscape architect Steve Gierke compliments contemporary architecture with a sculpted landscape and arbor that frames the Pacific Ocean, treating that ever-shifting vista as the work of art it is.

Water holds the fluidity of time, the ebbs and flows of past and future, the sea's eternal rhythms and the river's shifting currents. It shapes our landscape and geography, and perhaps even, stretching back to the womb, our personhood too. Whether or not that holds water is up to you to decide, but according to the designers within this chapter, the power of water to transform a garden is incontrovertible. Come take a dip, and see if you agree.

Embracing the Wild Coast

Mountains tumble down to the sea in Oaxaca, where landscape designers
Maria Kalach and Gabriela Salazar ground a pavilion-style villa in coastal harmony.

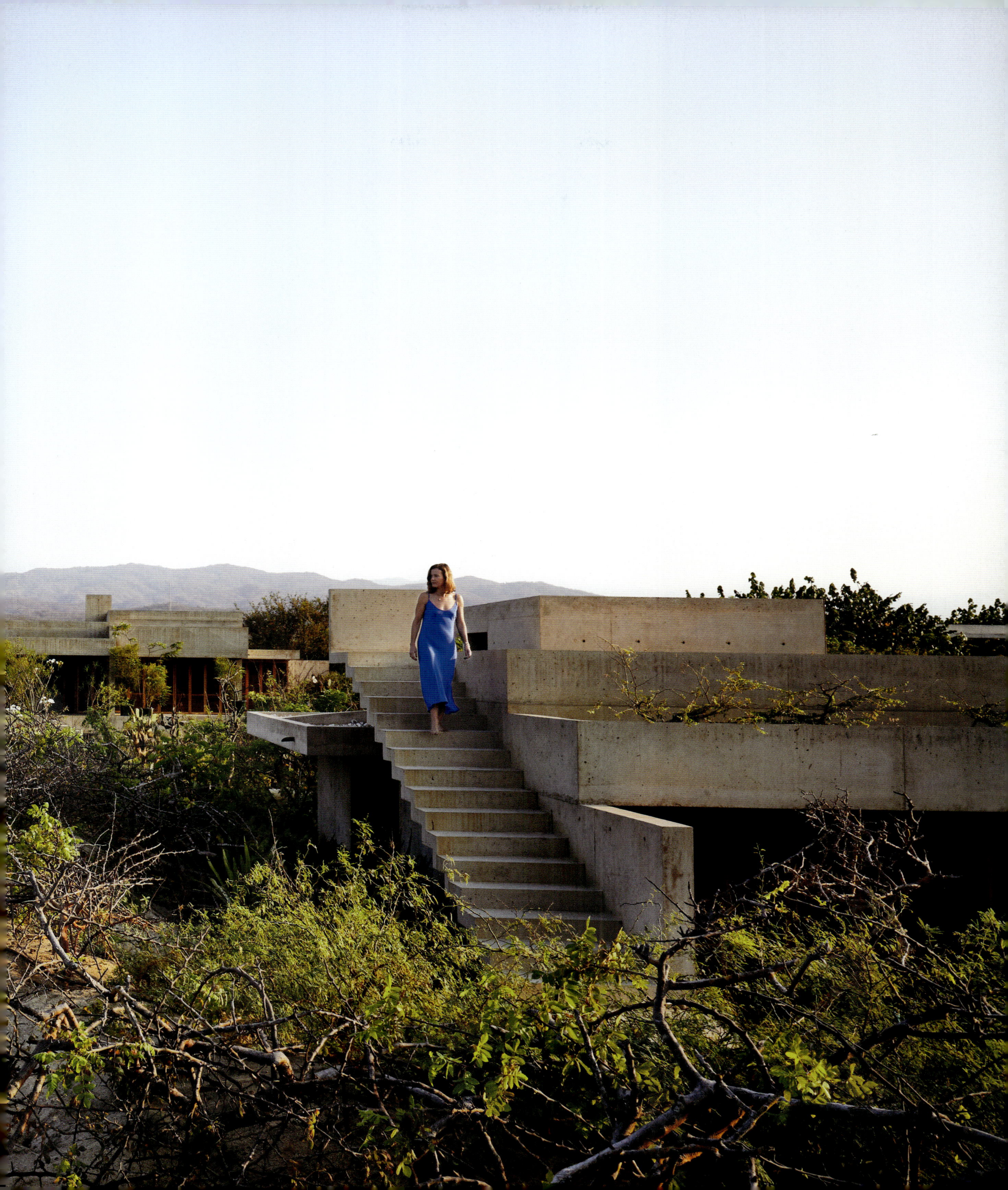

PAGES 176-177 For father/daughter duo Alberto Kalach and Maria Kalach, architect and landscape architect, respectively, equanimity between house and garden is the prime objective. From the vantage of the casitas' sculptural stairs, "you have a complete sense of place," says homeowner Pablo Velasco Sodi.

ABOVE The open-air *palapa*—a pavilion of concrete, pine, and thatched palm fronds—is furnished with stone and rugged wood tables and sofas made by Pablo Velasco Sodi, the homeowner. The arid conditions can be challenging for plants, but not for alfresco living. "You are not a spectator here, you are contributing to the experience," adds Sodi.

LEFT Salazar encouraged an intimate connection with the landscape, planting ornamental grasses and new cacti to give more sculptural definition to pathways. "I envisioned a garden that could be walked in with boundaries and textures you could engage with," she says.

BELOW "The plants protect each other from harsh winds, high salinity, and intense sun and heat, so the only way for them to grow is to grow together," explains Kalach. Late afternoon sun casts geometric shadows thanks to the angles and curves of the 18th-century table and chairs.

WATERSIDE IDYLLS 179

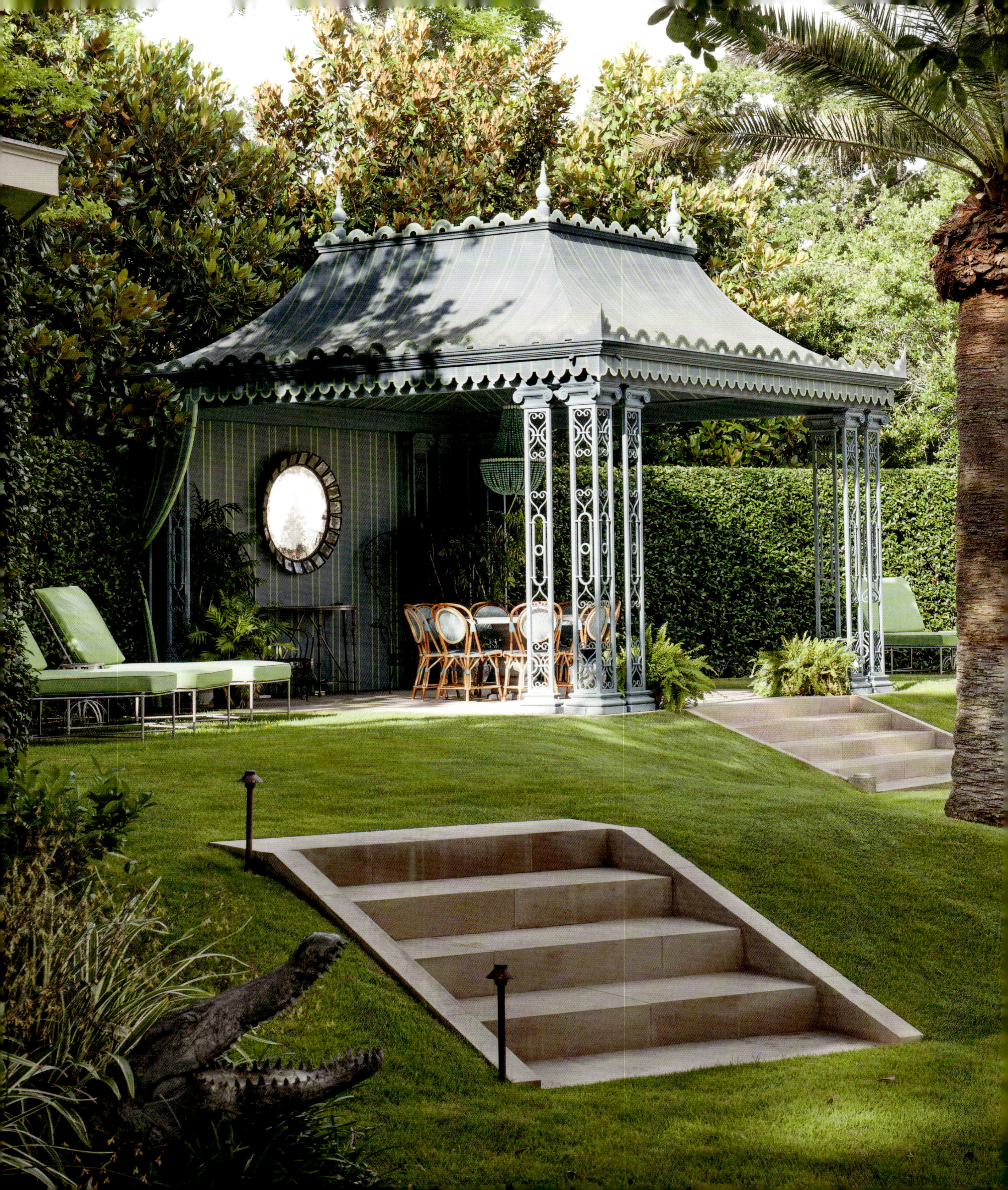

French Folly

Taking cues from Versailles, and executed in true Texas fashion, architect Bill Curtis centers a grand circus-ring pond around a Parisian-inspired folly.

LEFT Architect Bill Curtis of Houston-based Curtis & Wyndam Architects designed this precision-cut pergola as a focal point for this pool garden. The flair is decidedly French, reminiscent of tented guard shacks at Versailles. It also harkens back to local Texas craftsmanship traditions popular in the 1930s and '40s.

RIGHT Ornate detailing in copper and steel is as functional as it is fancy. The steel is cast in sand, which results in a form that's textural and imperfect. The "tented" details, by contrast, are intentionally smooth, including the subtly sloped roof of precision-cut cooper. All these materials will hold up in the harsh climate.

WATERSIDE IDYLLS

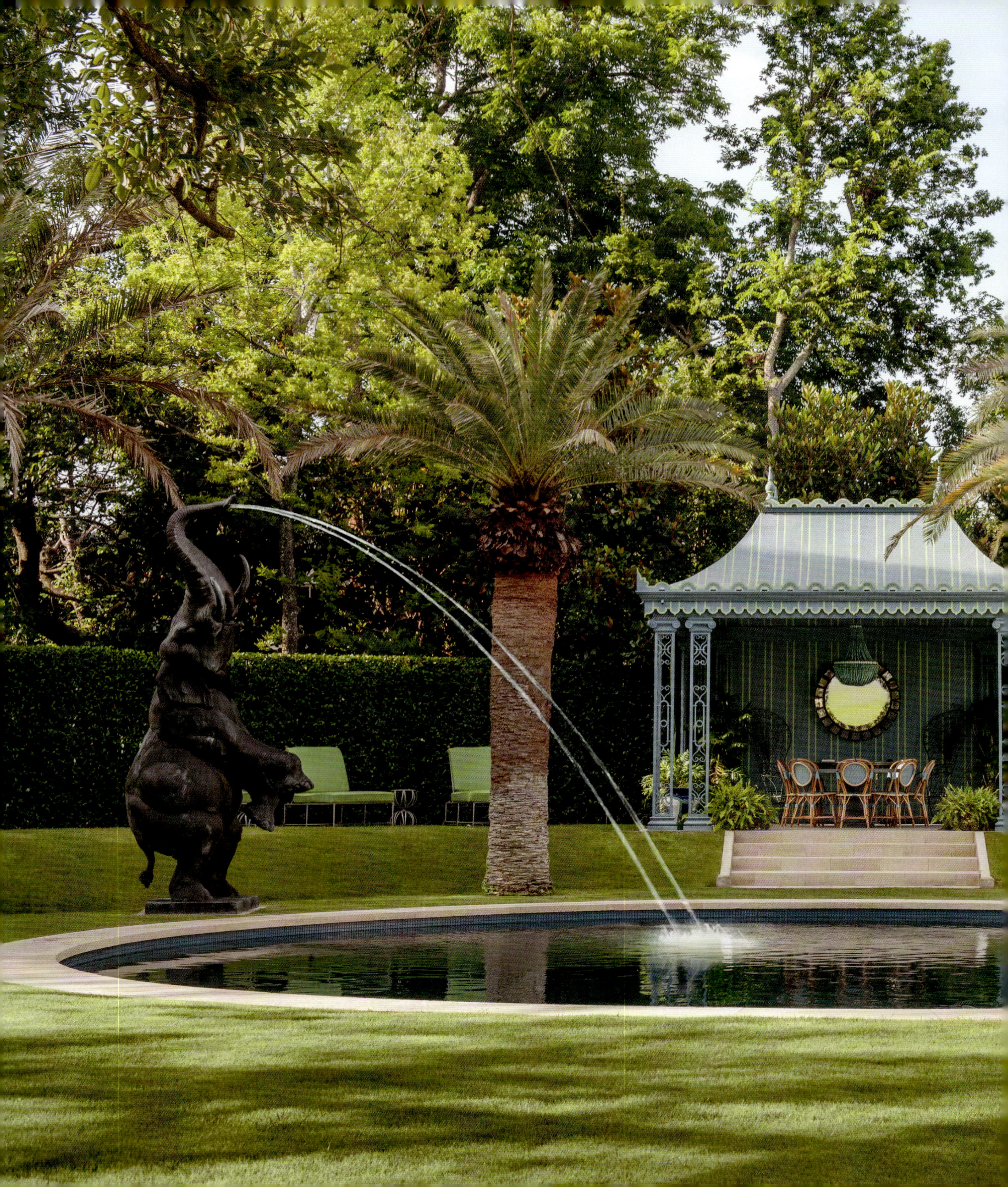

LEFT Another Paris landmark, the Rodin Museum, inspired the pool. A bronze elephant fountain by Dan Ostermiller adds a circus-like playfulness. The graceful arc of Canary Island date palms lends an air of tropical exoticism framed against curved star jasmine ivy-clad walls.

WATERSIDE IDYLLS

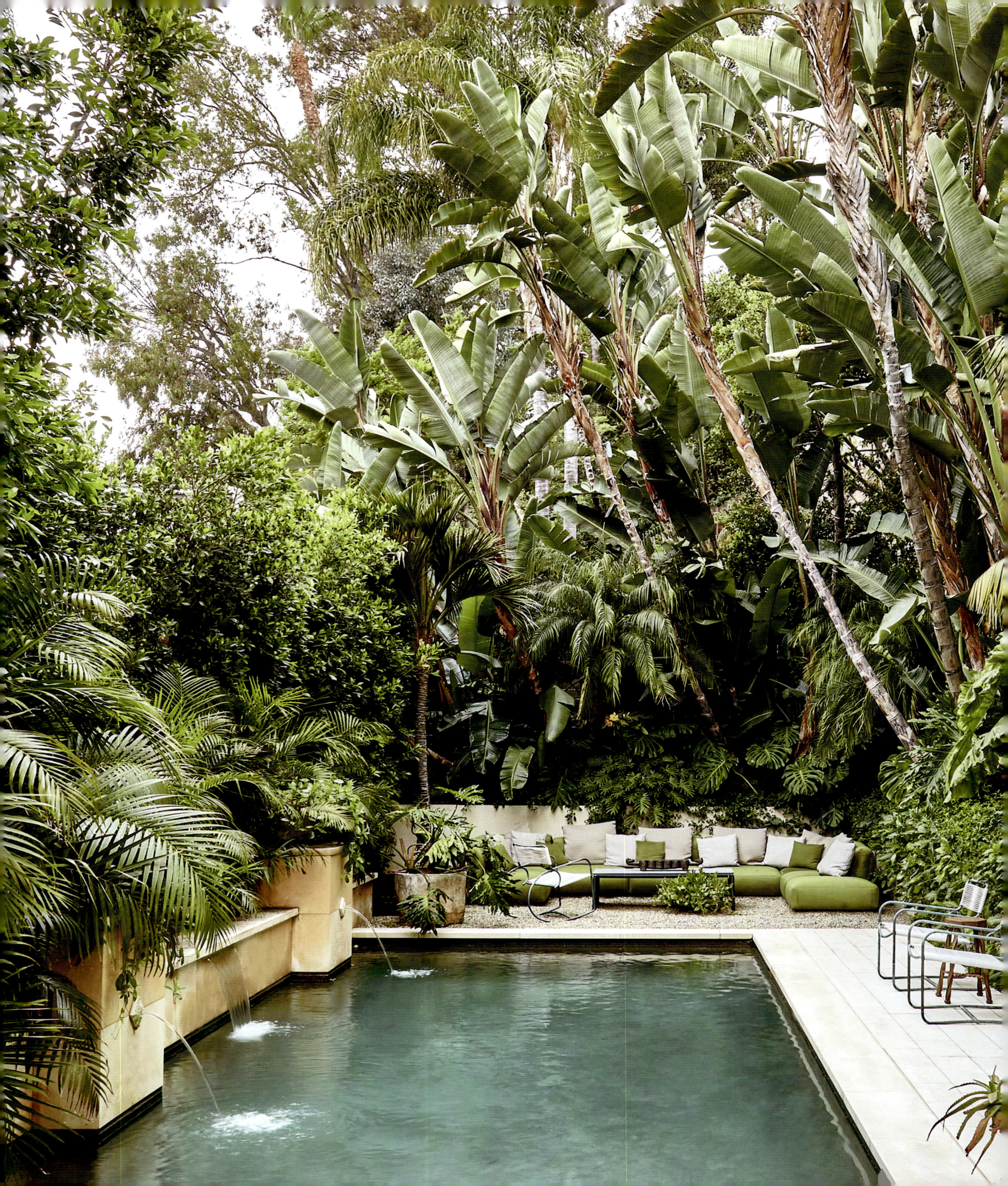

Tropical Whimsy

Fanciful objets d'art and lush tropical plantings elevate a sunken California garden to a playground of discovery.

LEFT For this wild wonderland carved into a Los Feliz, California, hillside, landscape designers Stephen Block and Kimberlee Keswick of Inner Gardens enlarged the pool area and enveloped it with lanky Kentia palms and bold, leafy evansii, creating an unexpected, exotic fantasyland. "It's really a sunken garden, with trees rising like art," says Keswick.

RIGHT The homeowner, an art collector, welcomed a garden infusion of rare outdoor furnishings, art, and vintage pieces, like this Italian lion's head fountain, circa 1820, and a French limestone trough, surrounded by climbing fig.

WATERSIDE IDYLLS 185

RIGHT "These clients have a great sense of humor," says Block, who knew adding a giant Belgian toadstool would be a "home run." "Sometimes a concept begins with plants, but here the objects really informed the design," he adds.

ABOVE Happy yellow angel's-trumpet and glossy leopard plant hug the 1940s-era stairs that inspired other faux-bois elements in the garden. Elsewhere wisteria and stephanotis invite fragrance, while wild orchids and staghorn ferns nestle in trees.

ABOVE A firepit nook canopied by 15-foot-tall Australian tree ferns is one of several intimate pausing places scattered throughout the garden. The two amoeba-like Willy Guhl chairs were a starting place for Block, "an invitation to sit and hang out," he says. "The rest of the garden evolved from there."

WATERSIDE IDYLLS 187

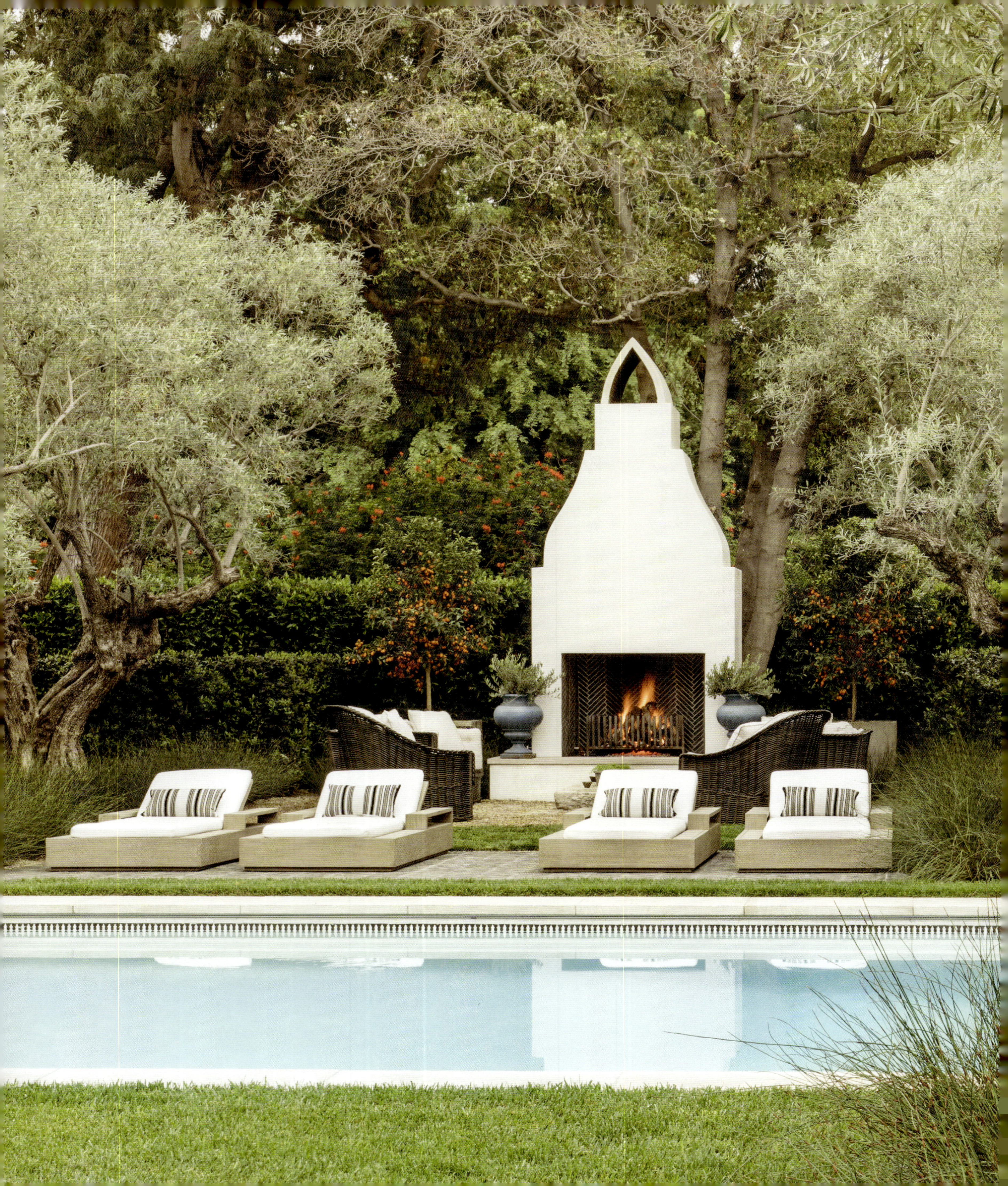

Inside Out

Landscape designer Scott Shrader blurs the lines between interior and exterior with masterful hedges and a poolside courtyard at this Moroccan-inspired oasis.

LEFT For a Spanish-meets-Moroccan-style home in West Hollywood, California, landscape designer Scott Shrader makes a Moorish fireside seating area a centerpiece by the pool, where mature kumquats and old-growth olive trees add character. "It's my job to get people out into the garden and keep them there," he says.

RIGHT To fully immerse people in the garden requires that they "slow down," says Shrader, who designed the entry to do just that. After entering a walled garden, visitors then promenade through an allée of olive trees and limestone columns salvaged from a Frederick Law Olmsted–designed estate. Stephanotis vines and potted gardenias make the space fragrant.

WATERSIDE IDYLLS

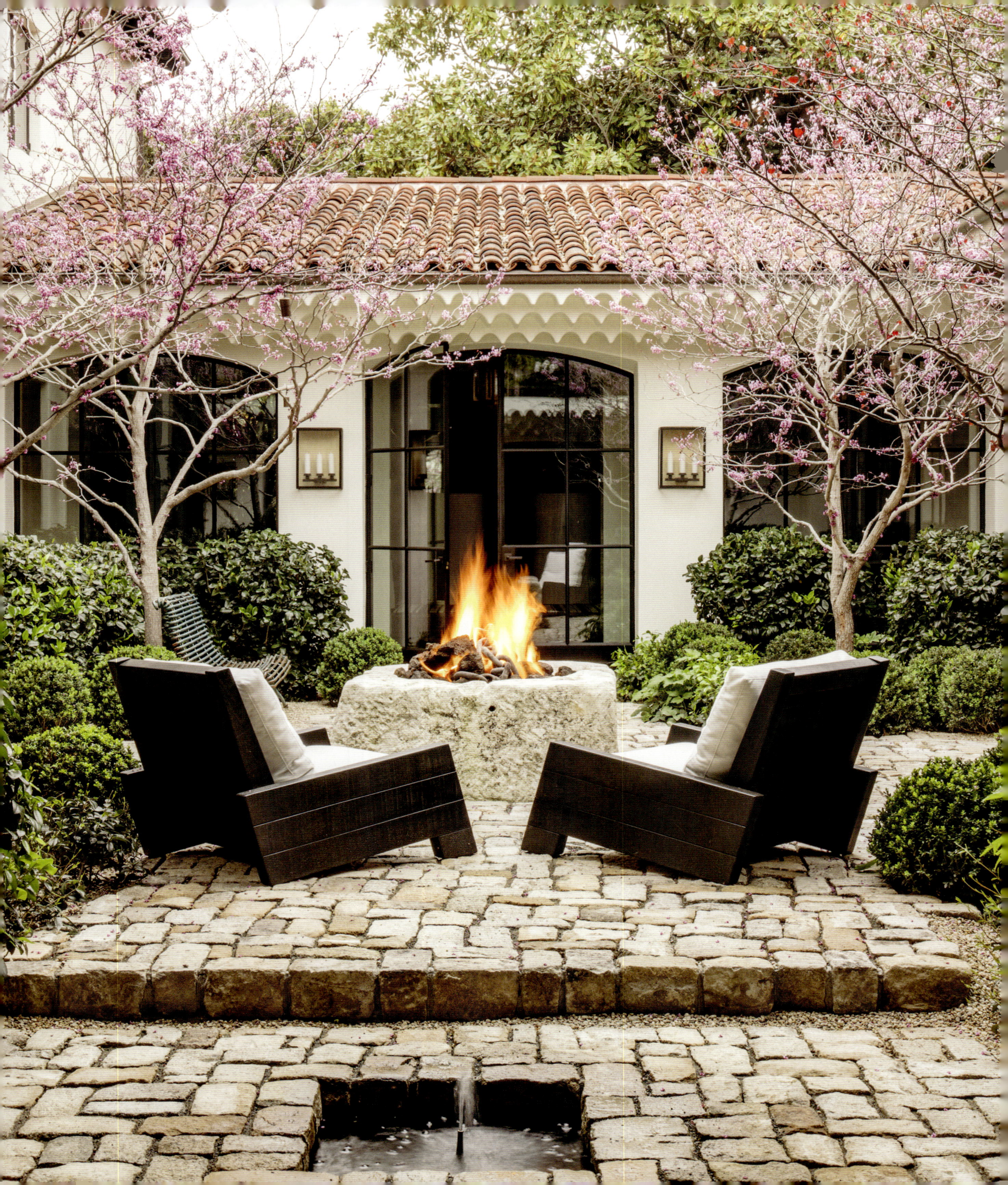

LEFT In the inner courtyard, Forest Pansy trees show off their early spring pink blossoms, flanking a 13th-century well reclaimed as a firepit. Numerous gathering and entertaining spots center the garden. "I am always looking for a new arrangement to engage people and give them something to do, even if it's simply spending time together," Shrader says.

ABOVE Nearly every room in the home extends into the garden. The family room opens to an outdoor dining room and bar area featuring a 25-foot steel trellis of bamboo fencing with inset overhead lighting. Espaliered Mission fig trees offer shade.

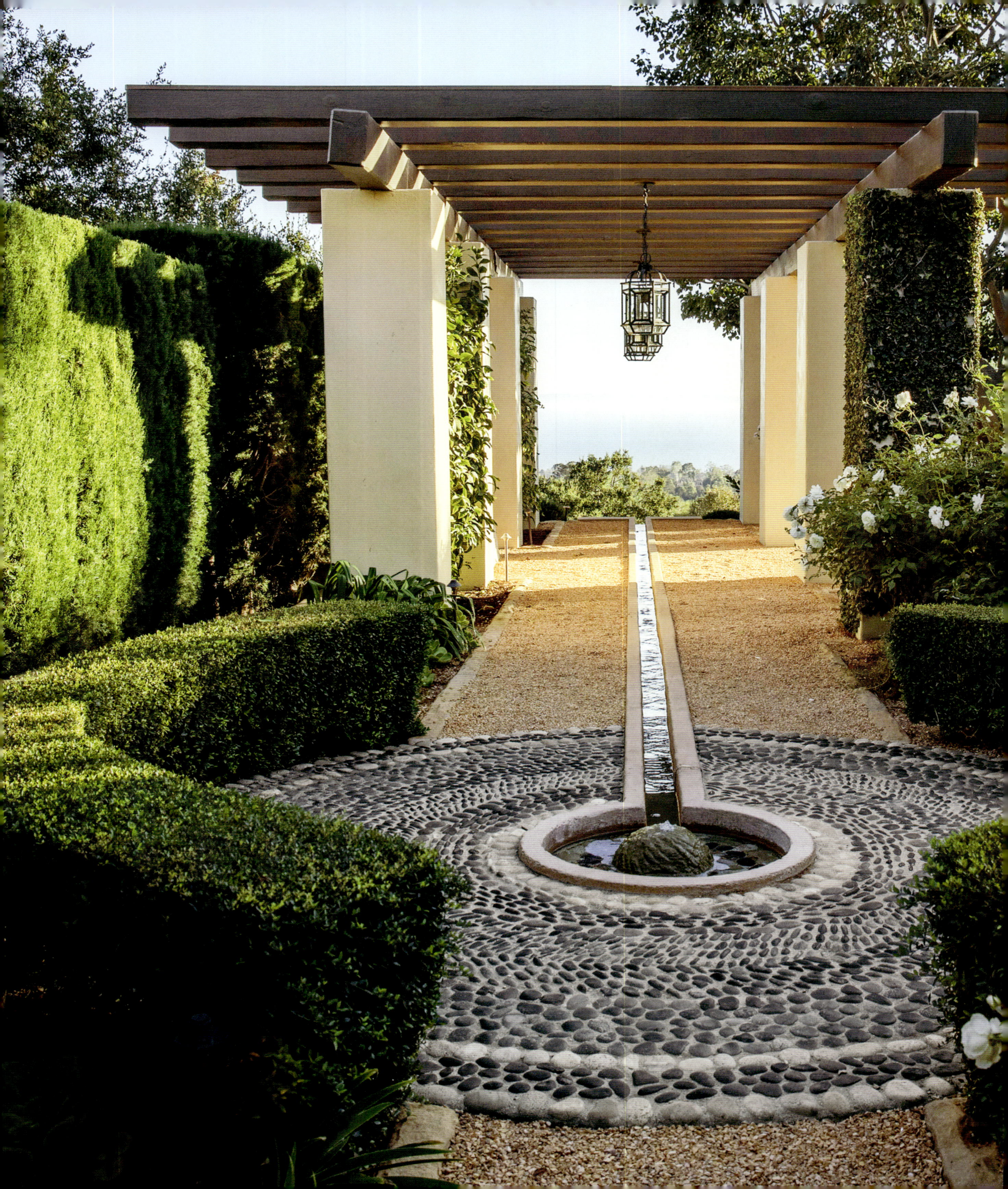

Montecito Magic

In this contemporary garden on the California coast, Steve Gierke blends elegant order and wild seaside beauty with an innovative mix of materials.

LEFT In this three-acre garden overlooking the Pacific, landscape designer Steve Gierke played up the property's duality—it abuts the wooded Santa Ynez mountains yet has "these wide-open views of the ocean and Montecito," he says. A cedar pergola frames that view, edging the bluff alongside a round pebble mosaic bordered by Iceberg roses, clipped boxwood, and cypress.

WATERSIDE IDYLLS 193

ABOVE Zinc planters filled with drought-resistant plants like echeverias, sedums, aeoniums, and Blue Glow agave punctuate a corner, adding contemporary flair. "The property had great bones, but much of the original design hinged on plants that wanted more water and had failed, so we needed a more realistic plan," says Gierke. The resulting garden, with its array of succulents and native plants, is both region-appropriate and fitting for the mod planters.

BELOW Boxwood globes and articulated olive trees are like minimalist pop art in the gravel courtyard (formerly paved) leading to the entry. The garden redesign incorporated cooling, pervious surfaces wherever possible and prioritized shade, tucking a dining area beneath California live oaks and pepper and coral trees.

ABOVE Vibrant color, thanks to violet Santa Barbara sage and citrus trees bearing bright yellow lemons, jazz up the terraced lawn where the owners' children and dogs can run and play. Gierke refers to this property as "king of the mountain," he says. "In the wilder landscape, you can really become immersed in the natural beauty of Southern California."

CHAPTER 5

WALLED SANCTUARIES

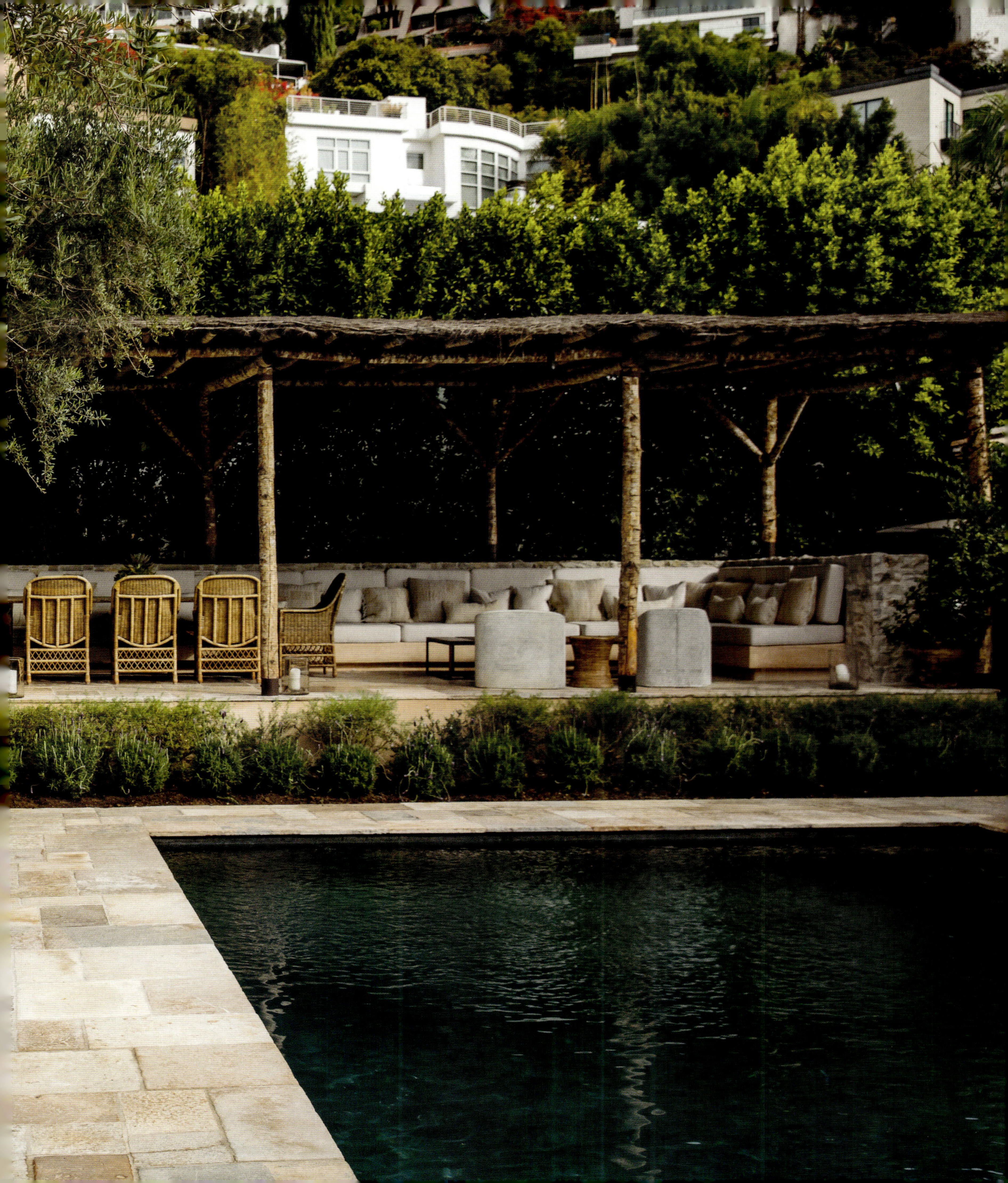

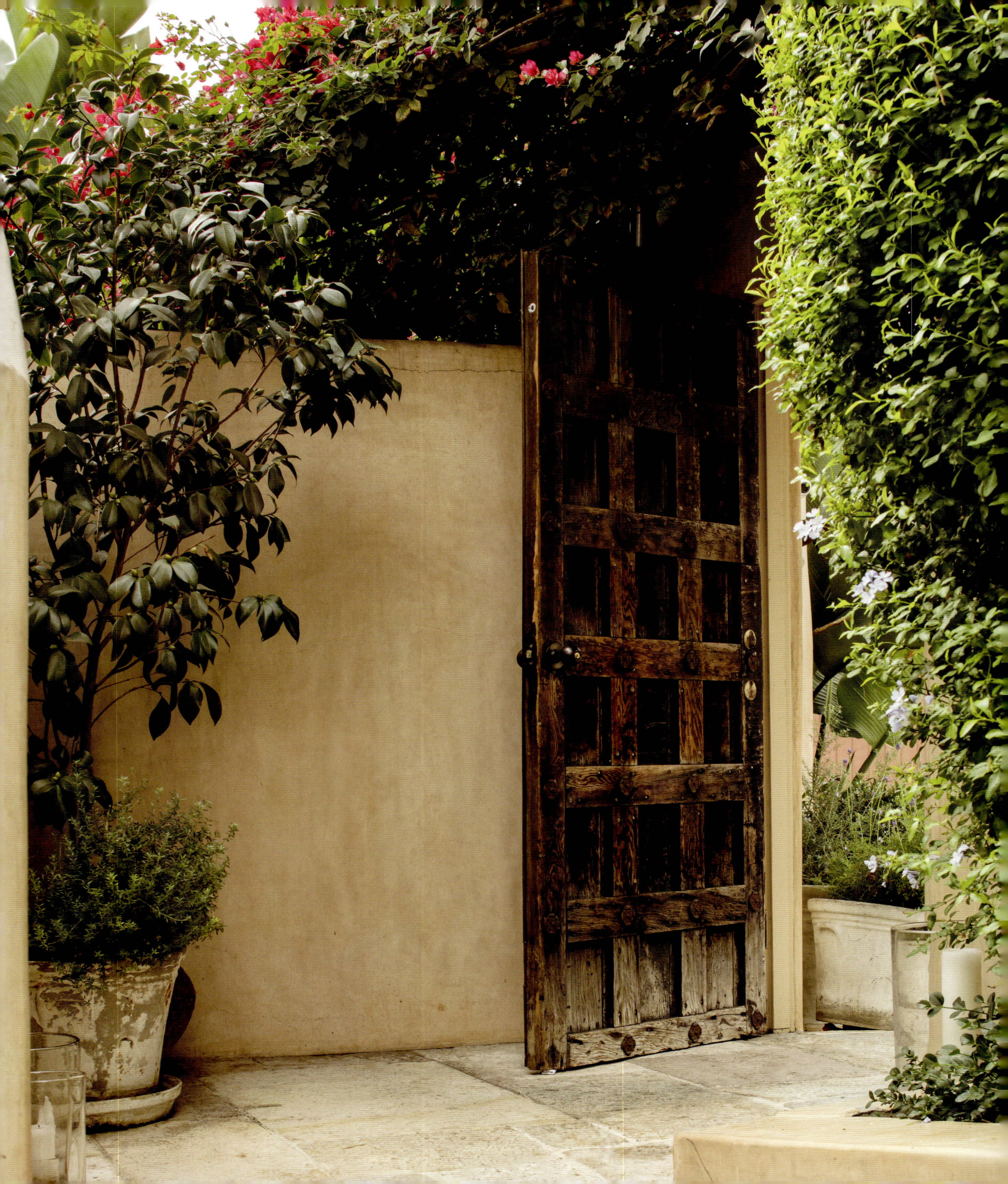

WALLED SANCTUARIES

gO AHEAD, HOIST YOURSELF UP; shimmy up to the wall's edge and peek over. It's okay—we all want to do it. Who's not intrigued by the mystery of what might be on the other side of, say, an aged brick garden wall? Or maybe a moss-covered stone wall, or a crumbling plaster one?

Michelle Nussbaumer sure was. Climbing up an old limestone wall to look beyond it was how the Dallas-based interior designer and home goods purveyor first discovered, then restored and reimagined, the fabulous ruins of an old hacienda on the outskirts of San Miguel de Allende, Mexico. There, she revived the garden walls and built new ones to make a series of inviting garden rooms. If fences make good neighbors, then walls, as Nussbaumer understands, make good gardens.

"Before I built a wall I'd ask to know/ What I was walling in or walling out," wrote Robert Frost in his poem, "Mending Wall." It's a valid question, philosophically and practically. Walls can keep out deer and other garden pests. They can be like arms that hug you, giving the garden space a sense of definition, protection, and intimacy. In the Charleston, South Carolina, garden of preservationist Ben Lenhardt, two of his three garden "walls" are borrowed walls—that is, they belong to the abutting neighbors' homes and property. He loves a small garden— "it's like a magnifying glass," he says. In the bustle of Los Angeles, Anna Hoffman uses stucco walls, plus ancient olives and old-world limestone, to whisk us away to southern Italy. And in Bridgehampton, New York, garden designer Charlie Marder asks privet and hornbeam hedges to do enclosure duty, creating a cozy envelopment around a pool-centric outdoor living and entertaining space.

Walls help modulate a garden's scale; they provide boundary and definition. Like a wrapped gift, walled garden sanctuaries hold enticing secrets of enclosure. Shall we venture in?

LEFT Mature bougainvillea and airy plumbago grace an antique garden gate door. Inside the stuccoed walls, a Tuscan-inspired garden overlooks Hollywood's iconic Chateau Marmont.

PAGES 196-197 An alderwood pergola gives shade, privacy, and hints of Tuscan flair to this poolside enclave that feels worlds away from its busy Los Angeles locale. Old gnarled olive trees and French limestone pavers add to the Italian flavor.

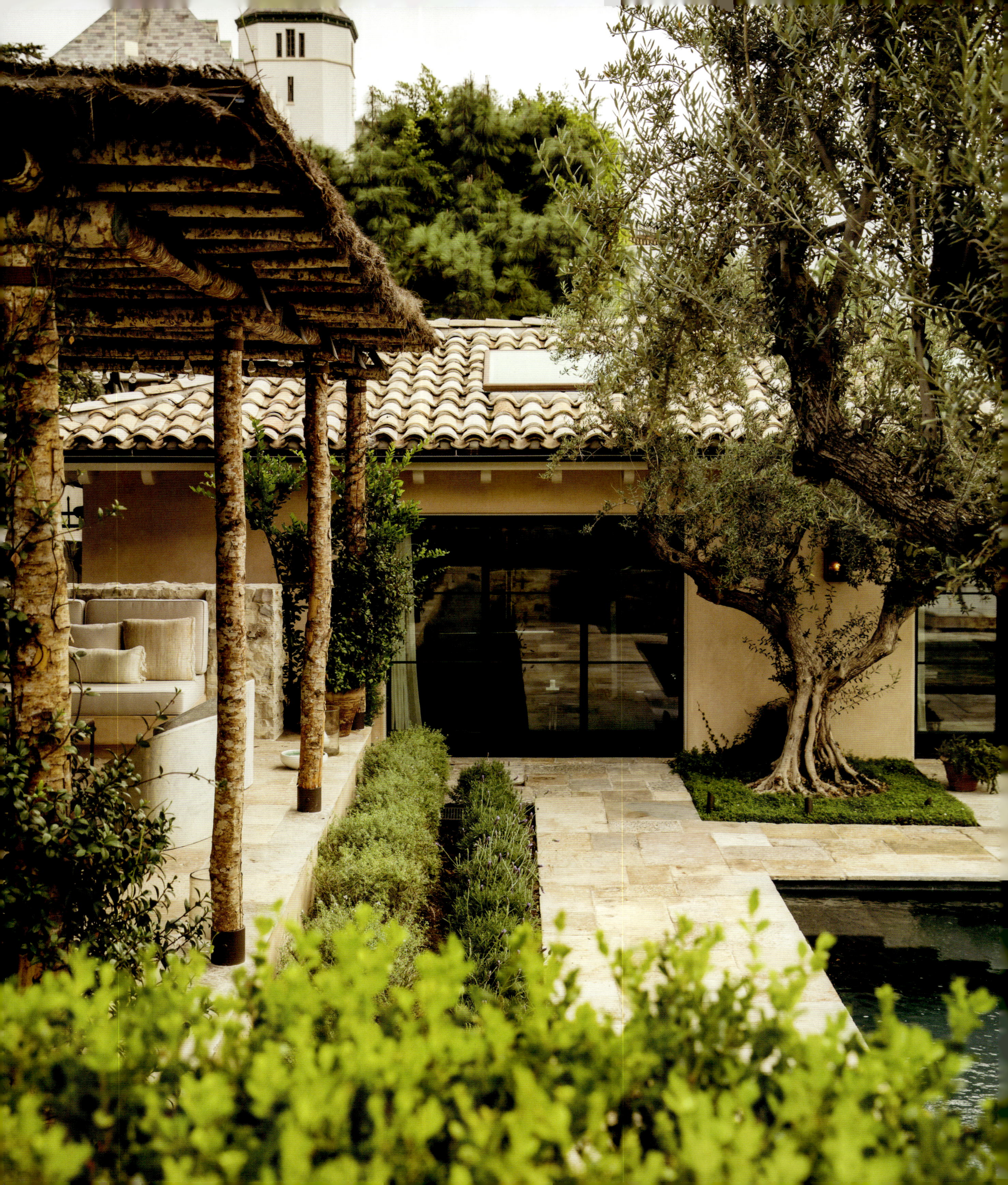

Tuscan Hideaway

In the heart of West Hollywood, city bustle vanishes into an Italian-infused landscape, thanks to Anna Hoffman's stone-and-stucco wizardry.

LEFT In designing a new pool and pool house for an L.A. family who desired a Tuscan-inspired sunken garden, landscape designer Anna Hoffman chose reclaimed French limestone for the hardscaping, and for the pergola, alderwood in lieu of Californian redwood, because it's similar to the poplar popular in Tuscany. It's "a way to make it feel like the Italian countryside," she says.

RIGHT A stucco fountain along the garden walls feels old world and introduces ambient water song that masks whatever street noise isn't muffled by the property's surrounding 20-foot-tall ficus trees. Terra-cotta pots and an old farm table add to the Mediterranean ambiance.

PAGES 202-203 Five century-old olive trees craned in from northern California ground the garden and pool area with a sense of history, while relaxed boxwood hedges delineate borders. While the predominately green palette creates cohesion and serenity, dabs of blue and pink from plumbago and bougainvillea add variation closer to the house.

WALLED SANCTUARIES

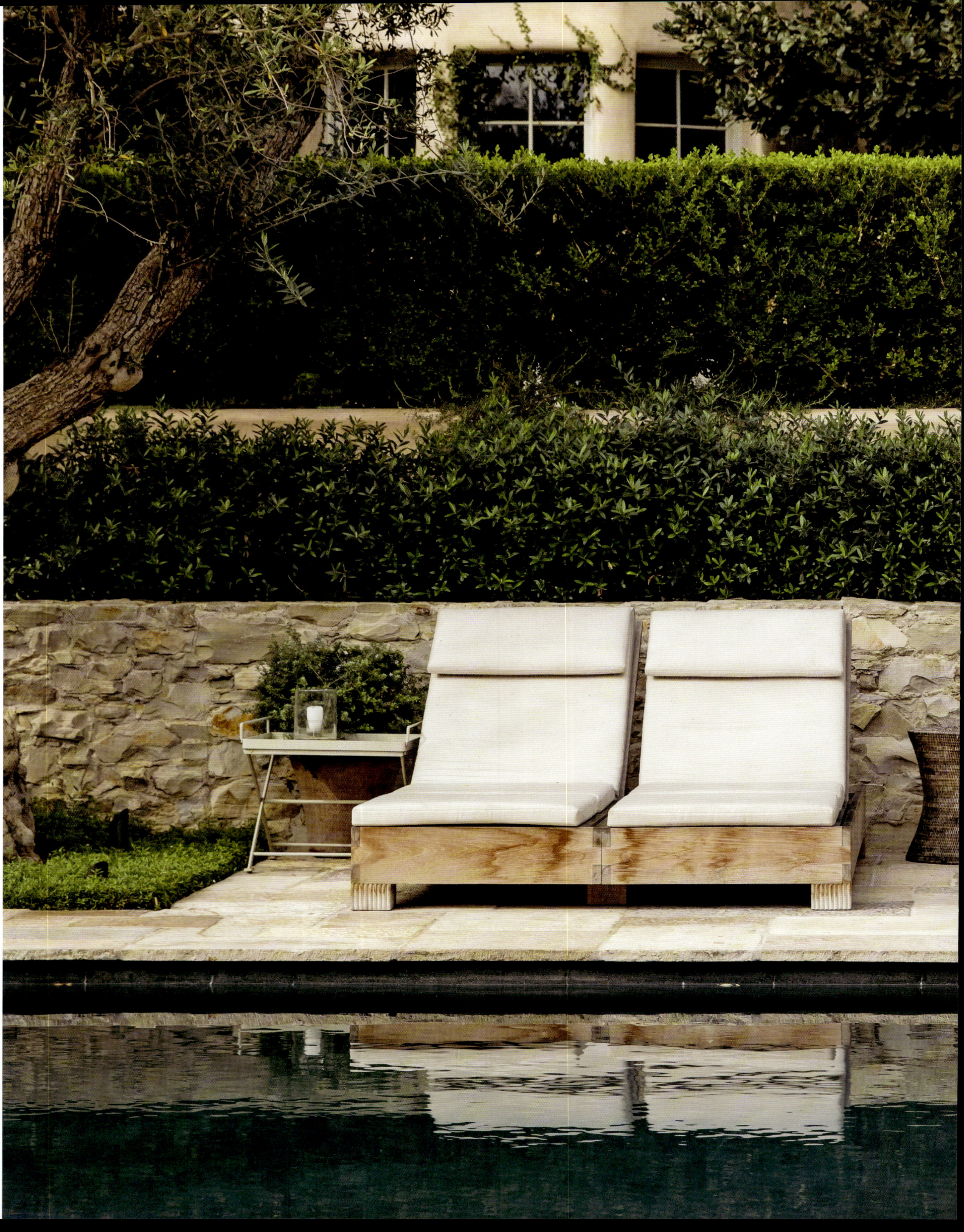

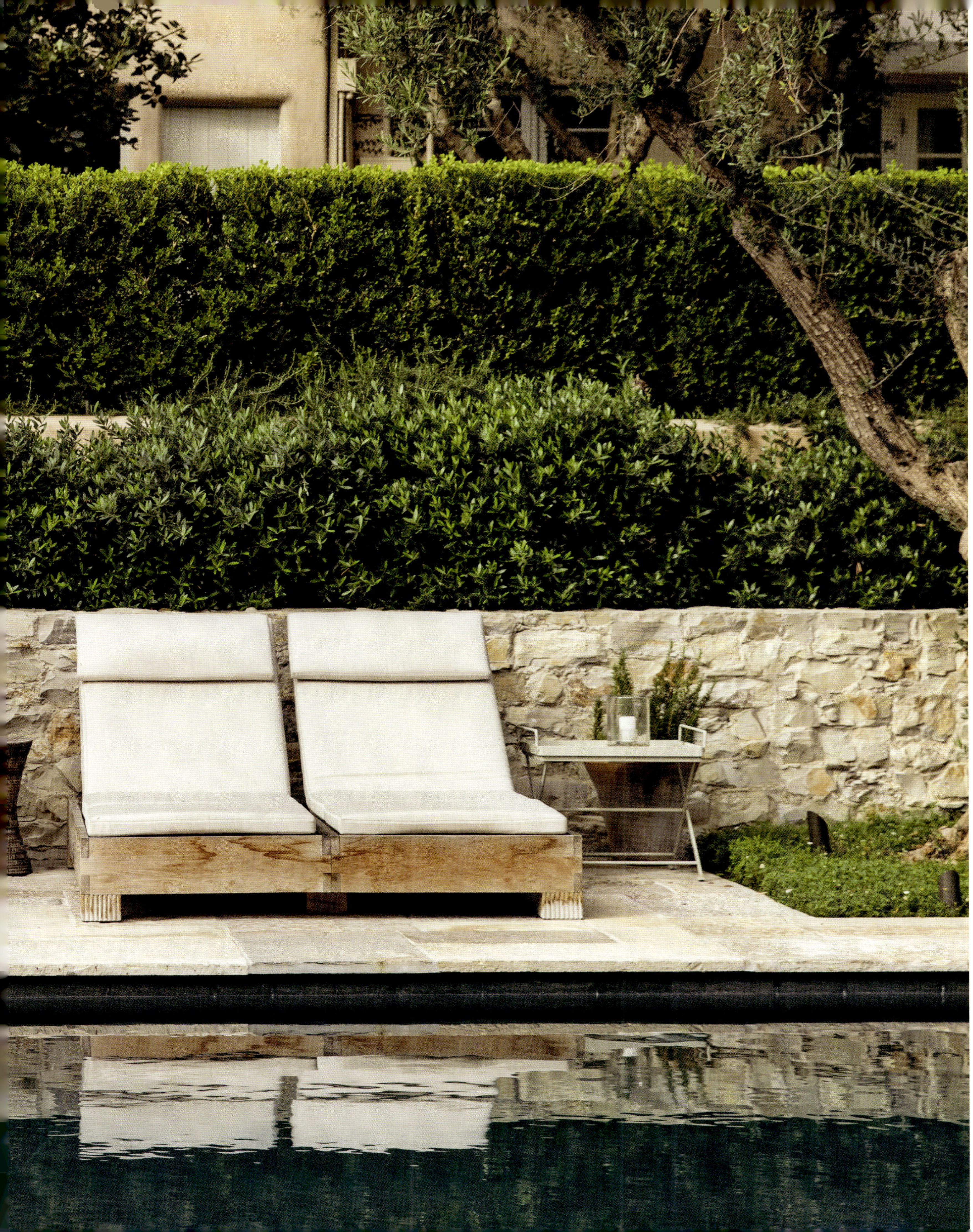

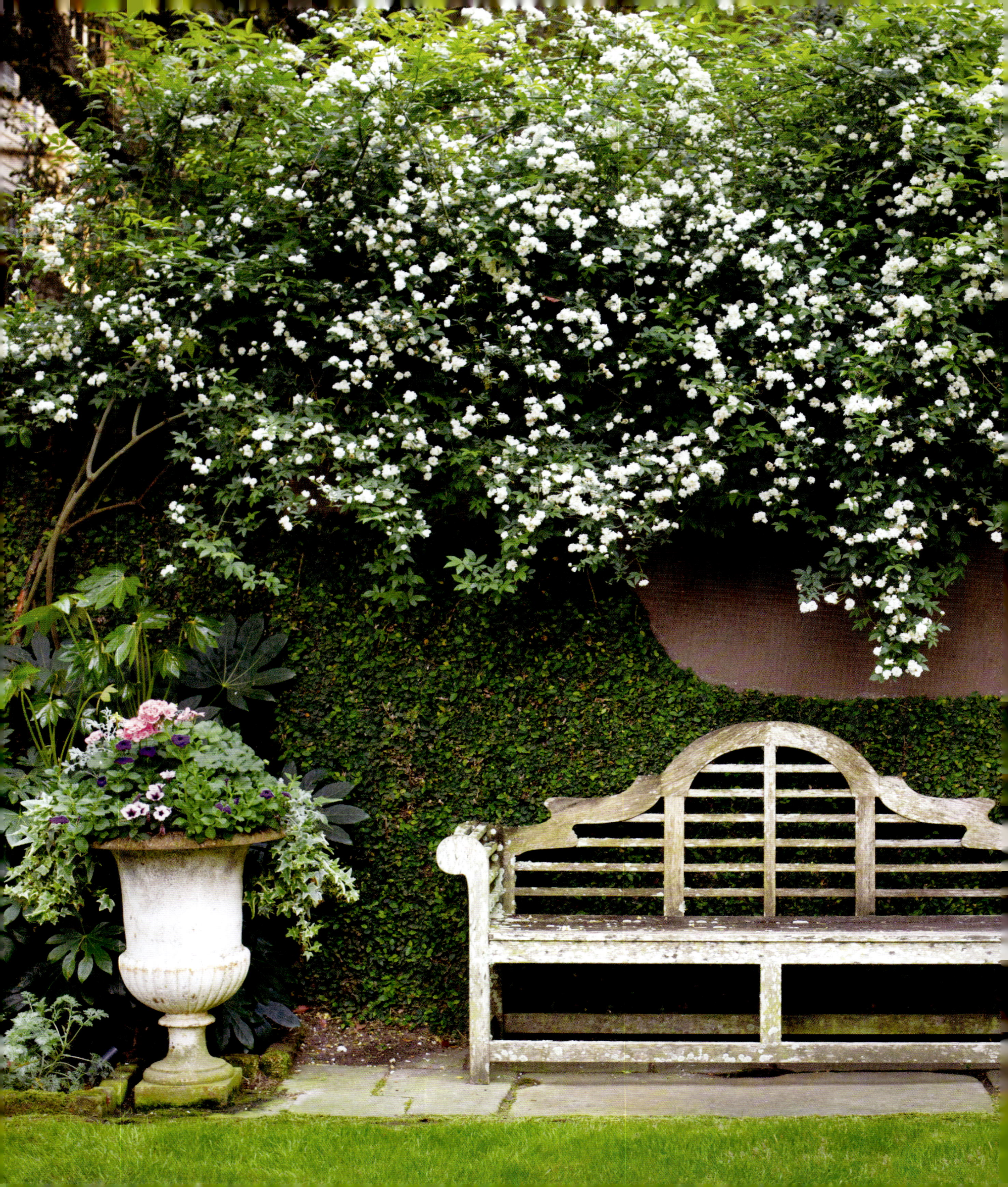

Parterre Perfection

In Charleston, South Carolina, a preservationist revives formal hedging and a restrained palette to conjure 18th-century splendor.

LEFT The formal Charleston garden restored by preservationist Ben Lenhardt surrounds his 1743 home with refined precision. Along a back wall covered in creeping fig, white Lady Banks roses tumble over a garden bench. Dual urns hold pink geraniums, a "usual suspect" in a Southern garden, says Lenhardt.

RIGHT A smaller parterre front garden features a double border of white gardenias framing the perfectly clipped geometry of Kingsville littleleaf boxwood. An old pruned Ligustrum stands guard in the back.

WALLED SANCTUARIES

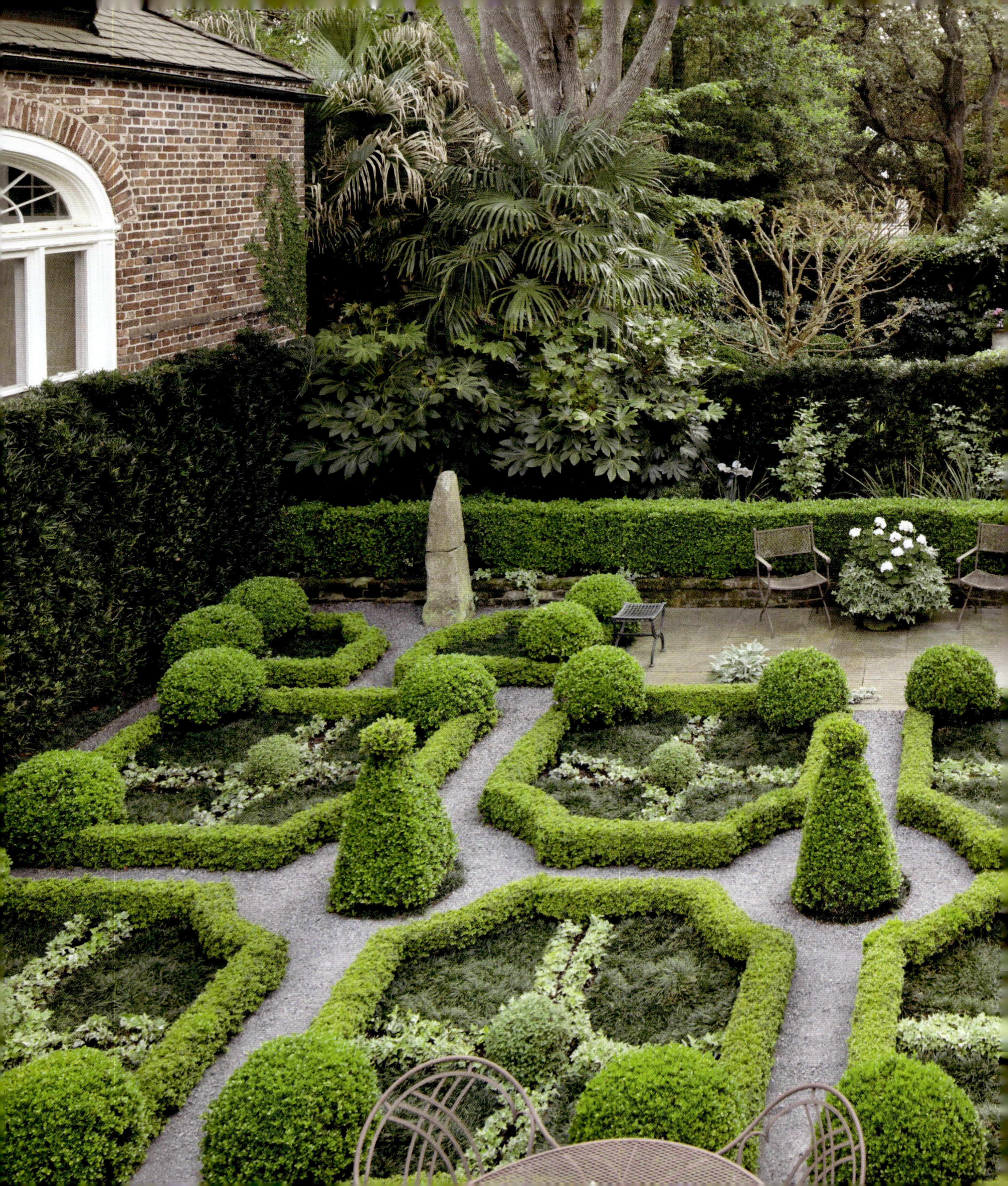

LEFT "Parterre gardens are meant to be enjoyed from above, designed so the lady of the house could gaze from a piazza," explains Lenhardt, who designed this intimate space from scratch, with Kingsville boxwood borders, corner globes of Japanese boxwood, and Asiatic jasmine knots tucked inside. Attention to detail is paramount: "A small garden is like a magnifying glass," Lenhardt says. "You can see every error."

WALLED SANCTUARIES

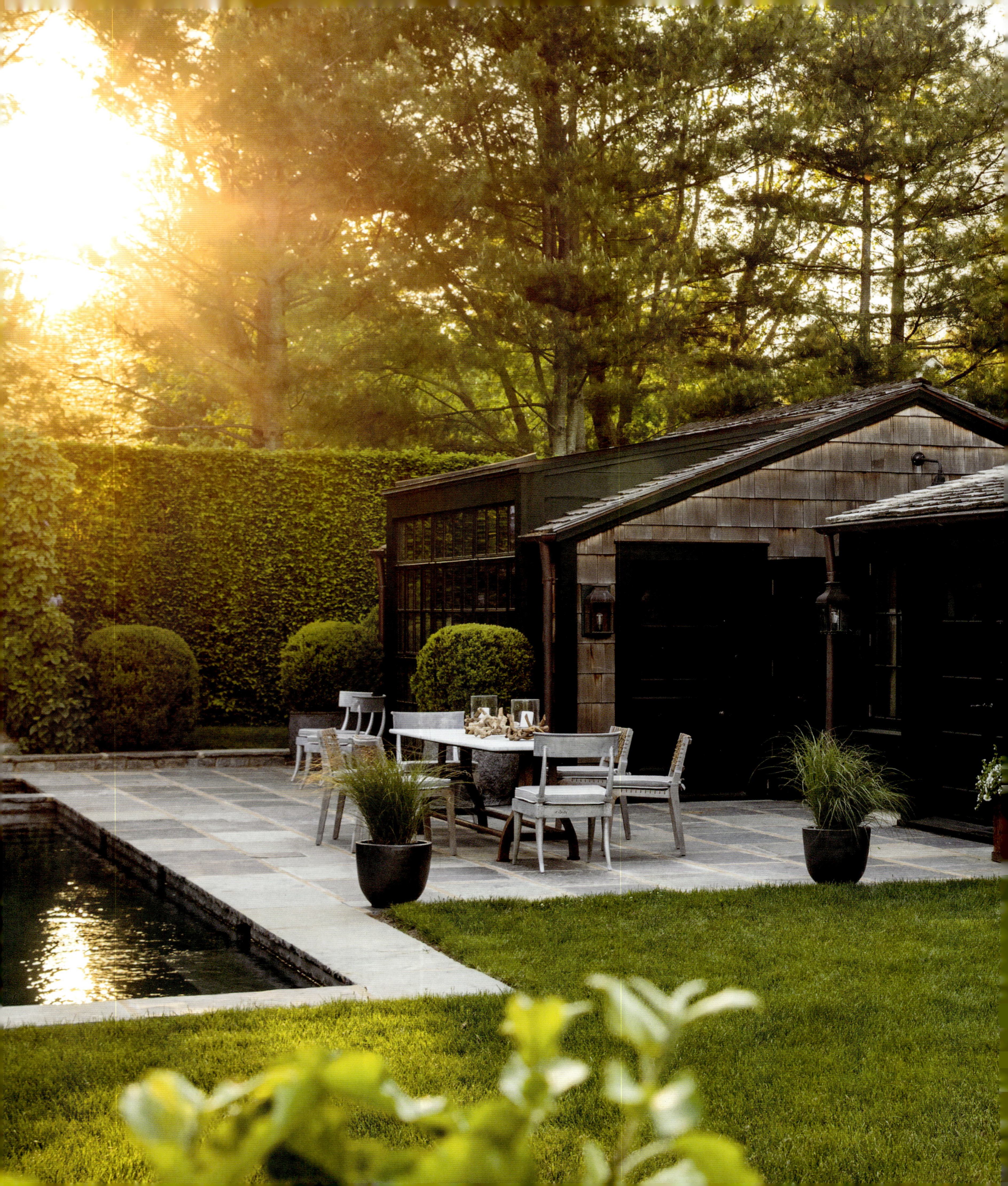

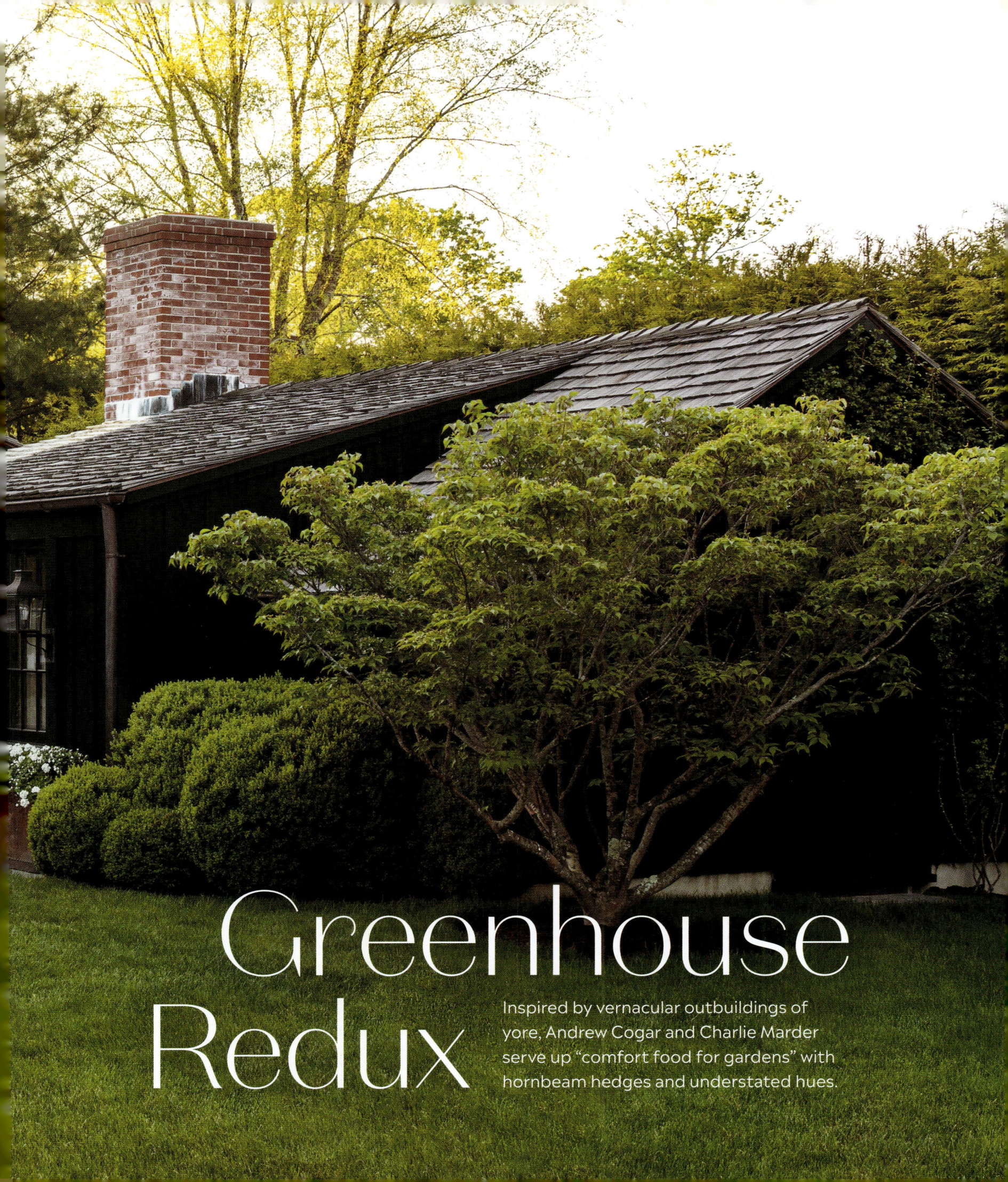

Greenhouse Redux

Inspired by vernacular outbuildings of yore, Andrew Cogar and Charlie Marder serve up "comfort food for gardens" with hornbeam hedges and understated hues.

ABOVE Architect Andrew B. Cogar and garden designer Charlie Marder teamed up to tease out a fictional backstory for this poolside compound for an 1840s Bridgehampton, New York, home, imagining it as a farm shed-turned-garage-turned-greenhouse. The Kota stone terrace is surrounded by a lawn of fescue and bluegrass. "It's unexpected, and that's precisely what makes it feel just right," says Cogar.

PAGES 208-209. A saucer magnolia oversees a bank of boxwood, adding contrasting textures and softening the tall hornbeam hedges that enclose this poolhouse courtyard.

LEFT Steel and glass casement windows give a greenhouse aura while offering ample views of the pool and garden. "The view to the pool is so clear that it's like watching a movie," Cogar says. Hornbeam hedges and glossy boxwood soften the sturdy steel.

BELOW Dark green paint on board-and-batten walls and fencing allows the building to recess into privet hedges, so the poolside dining terrace can stand out. "It's a restrained palette designed to blend in," says Cogar. "It's understated, which is what makes the area so welcoming."

WALLED SANCTUARIES 211

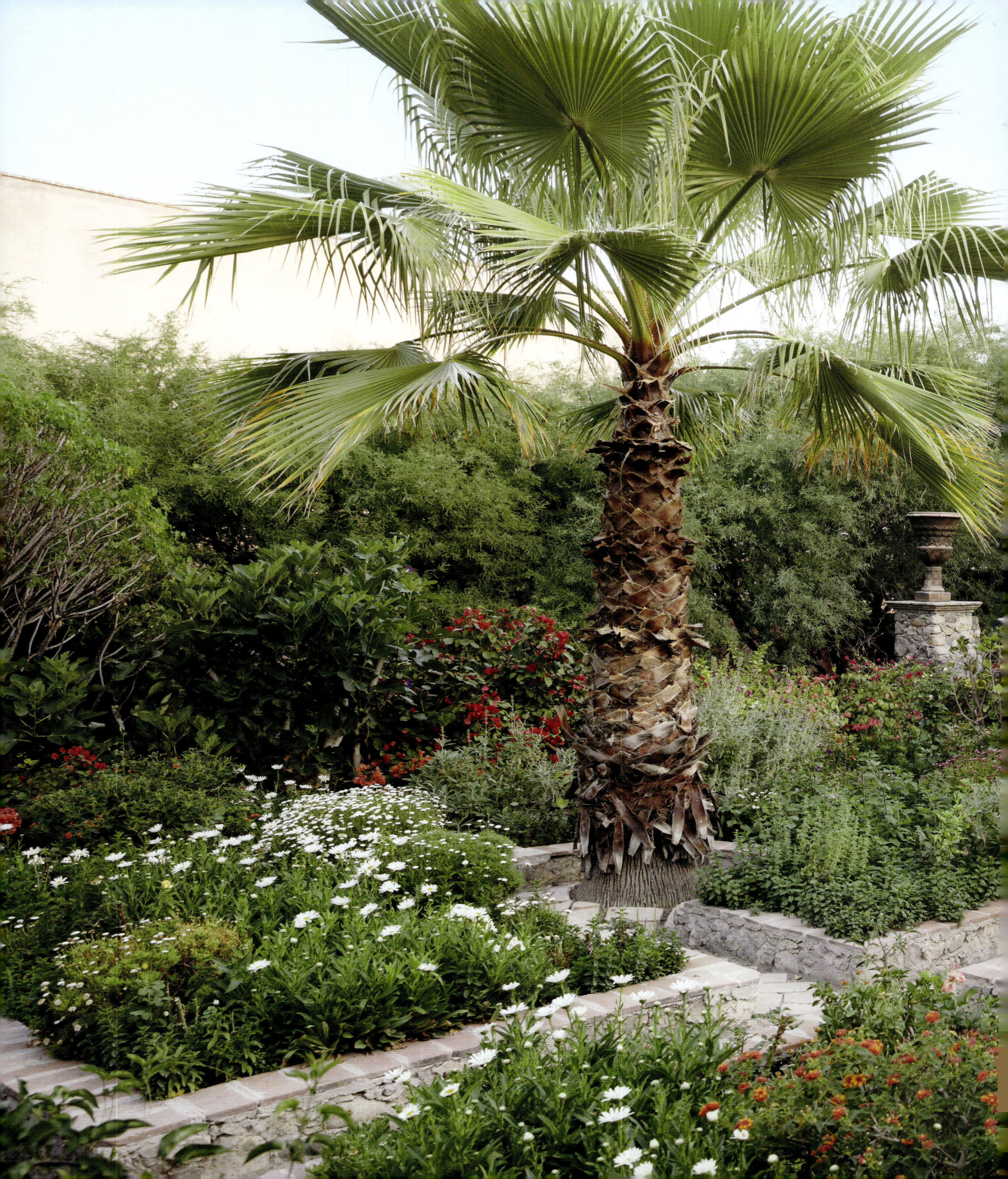

Hacienda Haven

Michelle Nussbaumer's San Miguel de Allende wonderland of roving donkeys, roses, and old stone walls is a masterpiece of symbiosis.

PAGES 212-213 A dilapidated uninhabited hacienda from the 1600s and 1700s ready for its revival appealed to interior designer and gardener Nussbaumer. Inside the walls, she created a series of garden rooms, including this vegetable and cutting garden, where a fan palm stretches out over raised beds overflowing with herbs, marguerite daisies, and roses.

ABOVE Nussbaumer set about creating 20-foot stone walls to delineate courtyards and brace meandering pathways leading to terraces and intimate enclaves, plus a pen for rescue donkeys Apache (pictured here) and Mirabel. Local artisans did all the masonry and stonework.

RIGHT A cocktail perch anchored by a vintage Moroccan table looks out onto Nussbaumer's gray garden, designed for succulents and desert-tolerant plants. Another garden features the seven varieties of nopal (prickly pear cactus) native to San Miguel, as well as endangered golden barrel cactus, some 200 years old, transplanted from elsewhere on the property.

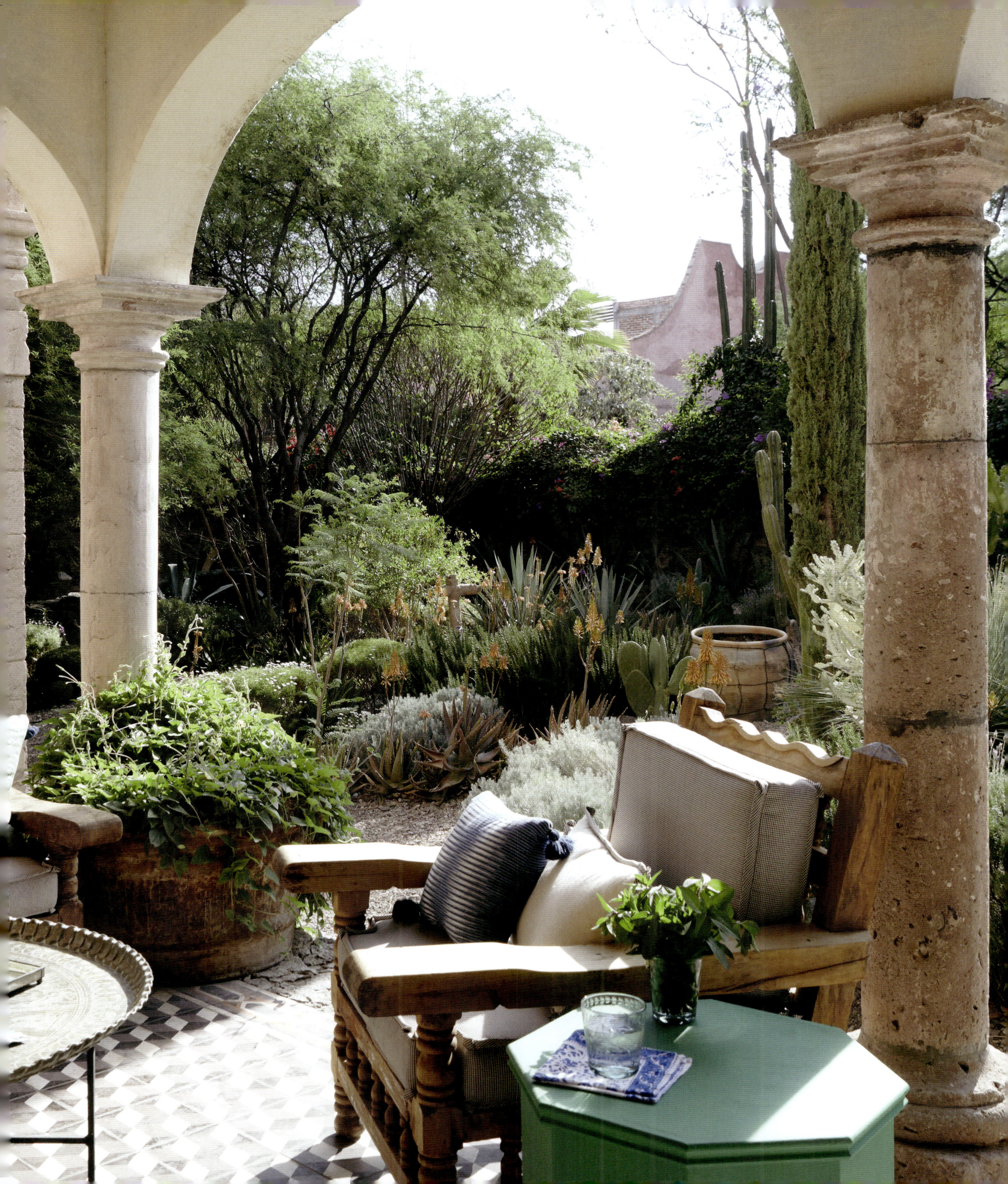

LEFT A magnificent chicken coop inspired by Dunmore Park's Pineapple folly in Scotland was handcrafted by artisans carving cement on site. "It's like a giant piece of pottery," Nussbaumer says. "These maestros are skilled in centuries-old techniques. Their immense capabilities really let my imagination run wild."

RIGHT Stone, wood, and architectural elements were scavenged from the site and from nearby troves and repurposed throughout the gardens in unexpected ways. Here, 18th-century mesquite beams prop up a terrace in the lower pavilion, a later addition built for Nussbaumer's daughter's wedding.

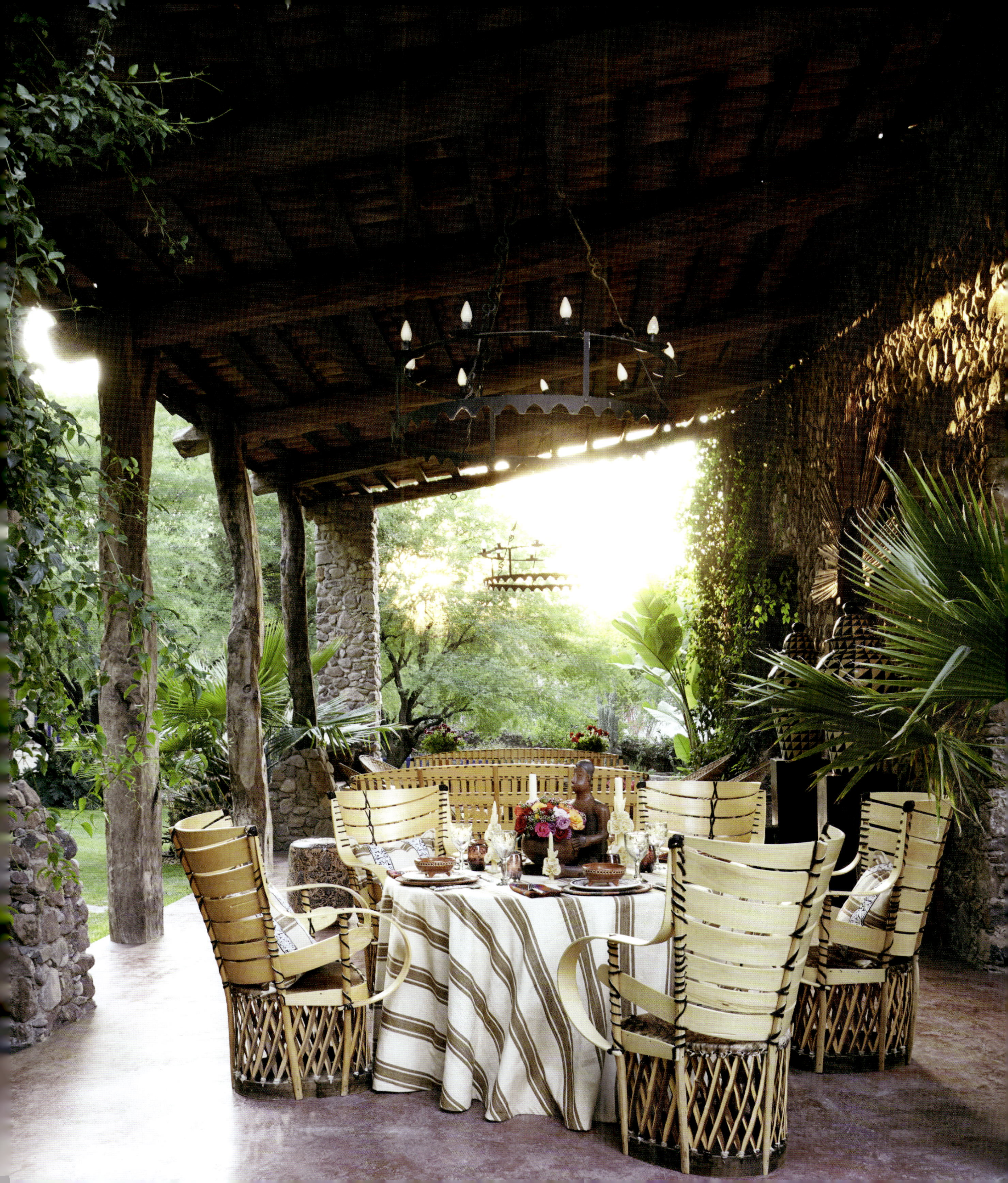

ABOVE A terrace nestled by philodendron features classic arches and ancient tile prevalent in the Yucatán. With a breezeway open to two courtyards, "it's such a lovely cool place on a hot afternoon," says Nussbaumer.

RIGHT Peppertrees and Mudejar arches frame a terrace lounge, where 18th-century colonial Mexican seating centers around a cantera stone mantel that Nussbaumer designed. "What I love about this garden," she says, "is how it came about in a haphazard, symbiotic way, which I think is the way most Mexican gardens are created."

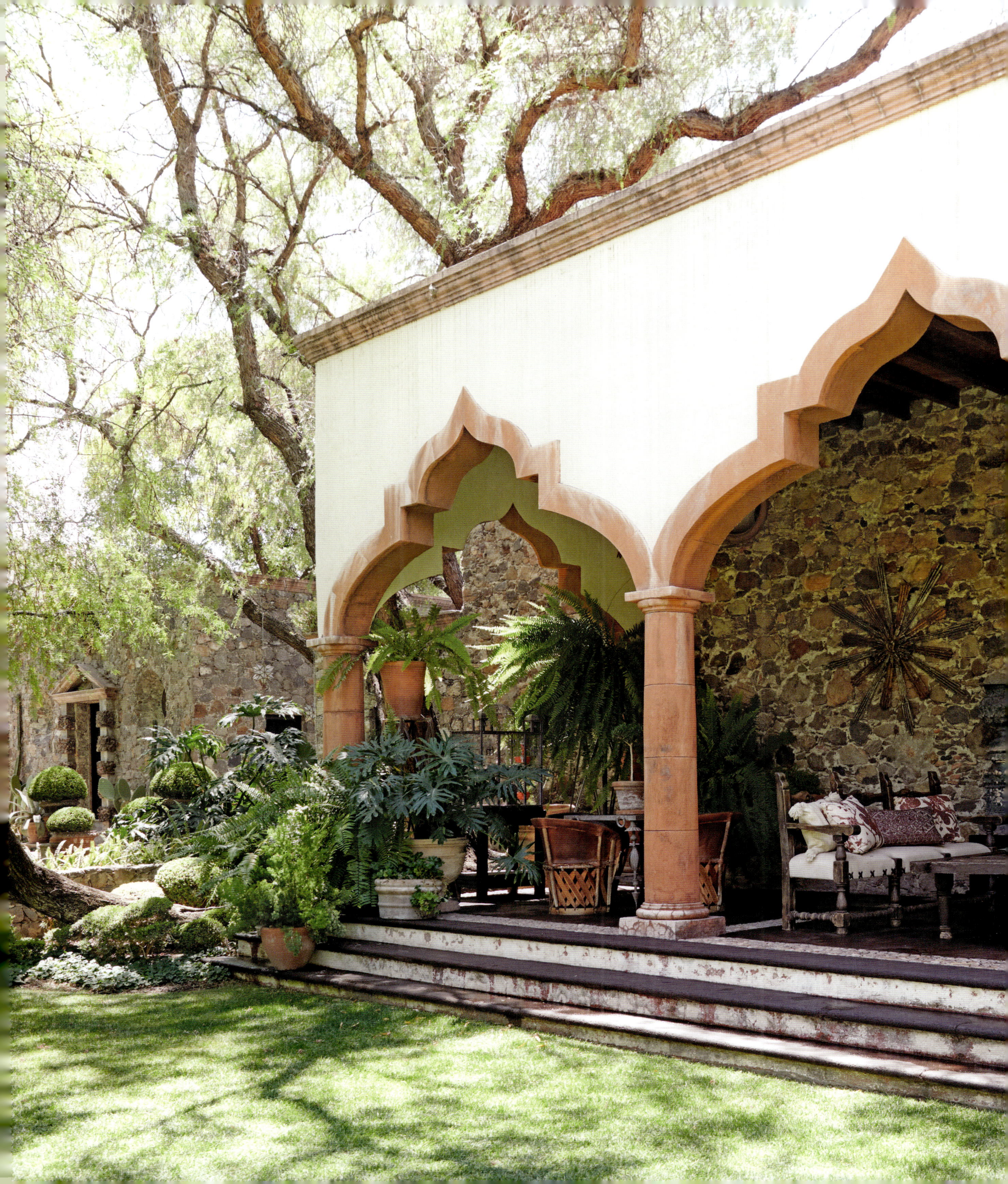

INDEX

RIGHT AND PAGE 1 White Annabelle hydrangeas and Rozanne geraniums pool around a secluded fountain in a terrace garden designed by landscape architect Dan Gordon and project manager Patrick Taylor. For more, turn to page 44.

NOTE: Page references of photos indicate locations of captions.

A

alliums, 22, 25, 47, 103, 158
American sensibilities in British landmark, 21–25
angel's-trumpet, 186
apple trees, 37, 42, 59, 131, 134, 136, 158, 165
arboreta, 25, 40, 42
arborvitae, 115
ash trees, 40, 42

B

Bath, England, Claverton Manor, 21–25
benches, 121, 205
Block, Stephen, 185, 186
bluestone walks, 47, 78
bougainvillea, 28, 199, 201
boxwoods, 16, 28, 39, 40, 47, 52, 62, 103, 125, 149, 158, 160, 193, 194, 201, 205, 207, 210, 211
brick walkways, 40, 74, 116
brick walls, 37, 50, 52
Briger, Cris, 13, 39, 40, 42
Bugg, Hugo, 131, 163, 165
bulbs, 22, 115
Burrill, Emma, 131, 142, 144

C

California
   Carpinteria Valley farm transformation, 92–99
   Los Feliz hillside fantasyland, 185–187
   Montecito embrace of nature, 107–111
   Montecito magic, 193–195
   Northern California delights, 89–91
   Pasadena rose-infused revival, 26–33
   West Hollywood Moroccan-inspired oasis, 189–191
   West Hollywood Tuscan hideaway, 199, 201–203
Canada (Montreal), rural renaissance, 133–141
Cannell, Andy, 22, 24
catmint, 47, 86
chairs and benches, 42, 65, 121, 179, 186, 205
cobblestone path, 121
Codd, Joe, 57
Cogar, Andrew, 209, 210, 211
coneflowers, 84, 145
Connecticut
   English-Italian influence, 121–127
   Falls River sanctuary, 113–119
   Greenwich farmhouse, 83–87
   meandering meadows, 167–171
   Southeastern hands-on spread, 157–161
Conners, Angela, 25
cosmos, 131, 136
cottage romance
   about: overview of, 71
   California farm transformation, 92–99
   California (Montecito) embrace of nature, 107–111
   California (Northern) delights, 89–91
   Connecticut Falls River sanctuary, 113–119
   Connecticut farmhouse beauty, 83–87
   Connecticut garden with English-Italian influence, 121–127
   East Hampton Grey Gardens, 71, 72–81
   English perennial parade, 100–105
cottonwood trees, 40
country escapes
   about: overview of, 131
   Canada, Montreal rural renaissance, 133–141
   Connecticut, hands-on spread, 157–161
   Connecticut, meandering meadows, 167–171
   England, Dorset countryside, 163–165
   England, East Sussex horse farm transformation, 142–145
   Ireland, County Limerick castle, 146–155
Curtis, Bill, 175, 181

D

daffodils, 22
dahlias, 71, 85, 131, 136

Dall'Armi, Danielle, 92, 94, 96, 99
Demesne, Ballyfin, country house, 54–59
Dobyns, Winnifred Starr, 28, 30
Dorset countryside, England, 163–165
Doyle, James, 85, 86, 87
dwarf lemon trees, 91

E

East Hampton Grey Gardens, 71, 72–81
England. *See* United Kingdom
English garden in East Hampton, 71, 72–81

F

fence, sunken, 165
firepits, 186, 191
FitzGerald, Catherine, 146, 149, 151, 152
Forest Pansy trees, 191
fountains, 16, 28, 30, 47, 57, 74, 183, 185, 201
France
    Le Jonchet (de Givenchy estate), 61–67
    Parisian-inspired folly in Texas, 181–183
Frost, Robert, 199
fruit trees, 37, 65, 158, 165, 195
    See also apple trees

G

gardening, meditative act of, 13
garden library, 125
garden/potting sheds, 116, 157, 158
Gierke, Steve, 175, 193, 194, 195
Givenchy, Hubert, Zoë, and Olivier de, Le Jonchet estate of, 61–67
Gordon Castle, 34–37
Gordon, Dan, 45, 47
Gordon Lennox, Angus and Zara, 34, 37
Grace, Margie, 107, 110
grasses, 19, 23, 25, 37, 144, 179
greenhouse, redux, 209–211
Grey Gardens, 71, 72–81
Groft, Eric, 25

H

Hahn, Bill, 92, 94
Harris, Charlotte, 131, 163, 165
Herman, Kathryn, 131, 167, 169, 170
Hill, Anna Gilman, 74
historic revivals
    about: overview of, 13
    California, Pasadena rose-infused revival, 26–33
    England, Bath's Claverton Manor, 21–25
    French estate (de Givenchy), 61–67
    Irish country house, 54–59
    Massachusetts landscape, 45–47
    Mexican hacienda, 39–43
    Scottish garden at Gordon Castle, 34–37
    Spanish estate, 15–19
    Virginia estate (Mellon), 48–53
Hoffman, Anna, 199, 201
hornbeam hedges, 84, 103, 169, 210, 211
Humminghill Farm, 133–141
hydrangeas, 47, 59, 78, 91, 103

I

Ireland
    Ballyfin Demesne's country house, 54–59
    County Limerick Glin Castle glory, 146–155
irises, 19, 87, 110, 165
ironwood (Persian), 149
Italian cypress trees, 16, 19
ivy, 16, 71, 110, 183

J

Japanese anemone, 84
juniper trees, 39

K

Kalach, Maria, 175, 176, 179
Keswick, Kimberlee, 185
Korean lilac trees, 116
Krehbiel, Fred, 57
Kucera, Joseph, 28

L

Ladham House, 100–105
Lamprecht, Barbara, 30
Lange, Liz, 71, 72, 74, 76, 78
lavender, 37, 40
Le Jonchet (de Givenchy estate), 61–67
Lenhardt, Ben, 199, 205, 207
leopard plant, 186
lilacs and lilac trees, 116, 125
linden trees, 16, 78, 84, 169
London plane trees, 47, 170

M

magnolia trees, 52, 105
maple trees, 42, 87, 134
Marder, Charlie, 201, 209, 210
Massachusetts landscape, 45–47
Maynard, Arne, 37
maze, grass, 37
Mellon, Paul and Rachel "Bunny" estate, 48–53
Mexico
    Oaxaca pavilion-style villa, 176–179
    San Miguel de Allende haciendas, 39–43, 199, 213–219
Montecito magic, 193–195
Montreal rural renaissance, 133–141
Moroccan-inspired oasis, in West Hollywood, 189–191

N

Nestor, Rob, 131, 157, 158
Nevins, Deborah, 71, 72, 74, 78
New York
    Bridgehampton greenhouse redux, 209–211
    East Hampton Grey Gardens, 71, 72–81
Nussbaumer, Michelle, 199, 213, 214, 216, 218

O

O'Connell, John, 57
Oehme, van Sweden, 22
olive trees, 13, 28, 189, 194, 199, 201
Ostermiller, Dan, 183
Ouellette, Richard, 131, 133, 136, 139, 140

P

Parisian-inspired folly, in Texas, 181–183
paths and walkways
    bluestone, 47, 78
    brick, 40, 74, 116
    cobblestone, 121
    meandering, 25
    mowed, 144, 150
    old stone, 86
    pebble/gravel, 13, 37
    plants giving sculptural definition to, 179
    shady, 42
pavilion, Mexican coastal landscape with, 178
pear trees, 65, 158
Peed, Charles, 39, 42
pepper trees, 93, 218
perennial gardens, 23, 28, 71, 74, 100–105, 152, 158
pergolas, 74, 76, 103, 181, 199, 201
phlox, 59, 158
pine trees (water-tolerant), 170
pools, 16, 91, 160, 170, 175, 183, 185, 189, 199, 201, 210, 211

R

raised beds, 89, 91, 214
Reynolds, Bill, 157, 158, 160
Reynolds, Jim, 57
roses
    butterscotch, 98
    climbing, 13, 99, 110, 152
    Danielle Dall'Armi and, 92, 94, 96, 99
    Eden, 13
    fragrant arrangement of, 96
    Great Rosarians of the World award, 99
    Iceberg, 193
    Lady Banks, 13, 205
    Madame Alfred Carrière, 13
    Memorial Day hybrid tea, 99
    perennial parade with, 105
    Pink Perpetua, 152

(roses, continued)
    Princess Alexandra of Kent, 96
    revival of rose-infused garden, 26–33
    Rose Story Farm, 92–99
    Secret hybrid tea, 96
    voluptuous wildly fragrant, 94, 96
    White Carpet border, 170

S

Salazar, Gabriela, 175, 176, 179
salvia, 19, 25, 47
Sampedro, Álvero, 13, 15, 16, 19
Scarlet bee balm flowers, 84
Scottish garden at Gordon Castle, 34–37
sculptures, 25, 103, 125
South Carolina, Charleston parterre perfection, 205–207
Spain, estate revival, 15–19
Stick, Charles, 50
stone walls, 47, 59, 86, 126, 160, 214

T

Texas, Parisian-inspired folly, 181–183
Thompson, Jo, 100, 103, 105

Timbrell, Erica, 71, 89, 91
topiaries, 52, 103, 113, 115, 121
Trapp, Michael, 121, 122, 126
trees
    apple, 37, 42, 59, 131, 134, 136, 158, 165
    ash, 40, 42
    cottonwood, 40
    dwarf lemon, 91
    ferns amid, 186
    Forest Pansy, 191
    fruit, 37, 65, 158, 165, 195 (See also apple)
    ironwood (Persian), 149
    Italian cypress, 16, 19
    juniper, 39
    Korean lilac, 116
    linden, 16, 78, 84, 169
    London plane, 47, 170
    magnolia, 52, 105
    maple, 42, 87, 134
    old/mature, 16, 28, 78, 84, 105, 131, 134, 136, 201
    olive, 13, 28, 189, 194, 199, 201
    pear, 65, 158
    pepper, 93, 218
    pines (water-tolerant), 170
    topiaries and, 52, 103, 115, 121
tulips, 37, 59

U

United Kingdom
    Bath, Claverton Manor, 21–25
    Dorset countryside, 163–165
    East Sussex horse farm transformation, 142–145
    Scottish garden at Gordon Castle, 34–37
    Southeast, Ladham House perennial parade, 100–105

V

Vandal, Maxime, 131, 133, 136, 139, 140
Verey, Rosemary, 116
Virginia, Mellon estate, 48–53

W

walled sanctuaries
    about: overview of, 199
    California, West Hollywood Tuscan hideaway, 199, 201–203
    Mexico, San Miguel de Allende hacienda haven, 199, 213–219
    New York, Bridgehampton greenhouse redux, 209–211
    South Carolina, Charleston parterre perfection, 199, 205–207
walls
    brick, 37, 50, 52
    ivy on, 65, 71, 183
    stone, 13, 47, 59, 86, 126, 160, 214
    sunken fence and, 165
water features. See also pools
    fountains, 16, 28, 30, 47, 57, 74, 183, 185, 201
    ponds, 37, 87, 110, 131
waterside idylls
    about: qualities, power of water and, 175
    California, Los Feliz hillside fantasyland, 185–187
    California, Montecito magic, 193–195
    California, Moroccan-inspired oasis, 189–191
    Mexico, Oaxaca villa, 176–179
    Texas, Parisian-inspired folly, 181–183
Williams, Bunny, 71, 113, 115, 116
Willinger, James, 84
Wilson, Bridget, 50, 52
wisteria, 16, 126, 186

Y

Yariv, Gabriela, 13, 26, 28, 30
yews, 103, 115, 149, 151, 165

RIGHT AND PAGES 2-3 Liz Lange and landscape architect Deborah Nevins placed an ornate bench, offering a place for a quiet reprieve, in the new Indian-inspired garden at Grey Gardens. For more, turn to page 72.

PHOTOGRAPHY CREDITS

Annie Schlechter cover, 6, 112–119, 120–127, 156–161
Chris Rucinski 1, 46, 47, 220
Pascal Chevallier 2–3, 9, 68–81, 222
Manolo Langis 5, 196–203
Claire Takacs 10–19, 142–145
Courtesy of Peter Hall Photography/American Museum 20–25
Jennifer Cheung 26–33
Ed Bollom 34–37
Charles Peed 38–43
Neil Landino 44–45, 166–171
Noe Dewitt 48–53
Naoise Culhane 54–55
James Fennell 56–57
Dylan Thomas 60–67
Allegra Anderson 82–87
John Sutton 88–91
Victoria Pearson 92–99, back cover
Rachel Warne 100–105
Holly Lepere 106–111
André Rider 128–141
Britt Willoughby Dyer 146–155
Marianne Majerus 162–165
Brie Williams 172–179
Paul Hester 180–183
Michael Clifford 184–187
Lisa Romerein 188–191
Scott Shigley 192–195
Gross & Daley 204–207
Eric Piasecki 208–211
Max Kim-Bee 212–219
Noel Hunt 223
Becky Luigart-Stayner 223

Stephanie Hunt

is a Charleston, South Carolina-based freelance writer who covers design, lifestyle, and travel for *VERANDA* and other titles. Stephanie also writes environmental stories, personality profiles, and reported features for several publications, including *Charleston Magazine*, where she is editor at large. She's a graduate of Duke University and Vanderbilt Divinity School, and when not chasing stories, she dabbles in her garden and spends time reading, bicycling, and getting fashion tips from her three grown daughters. Stephanie is also the author of *VERANDA At Home in the South* and *VERANDA Simply Chic*.

Steele Thomas Marcoux

is the editor of *VERANDA* and a veteran of the design publishing industry, having served in senior editorial roles at *Country Living*, *Coastal Living*, and *Southern Living*. She is a member of the board of directors of the Alabama School of Fine Arts in Birmingham, where she lives with her husband, two sons, and two dogs.

VERANDA

EDITOR-IN-CHIEF Steele Thomas Marcoux
CREATIVE DIRECTOR Victor Maze
EXECUTIVE EDITOR Ellen McGauley
MANAGING EDITOR Amy Lowe Mitchell
VISUAL DIRECTOR Kate Phillips
VISUAL EDITOR Ian Palmer

HEARST HOME
VICE PRESIDENT, PUBLISHER Jacqueline Deval
DEPUTY DIRECTOR Nicole Fisher
DEPUTY MANAGING EDITOR Maria Ramroop
SENIOR PHOTO EDITOR Cinzia Reale-Castello

AUTHOR Stephanie Hunt
PROJECT EDITOR Leah Tracosas Jenness
ART DIRECTOR Erynn Hassinger
DIGITAL IMAGE SPECIALIST Ruth Vazquez
COPY EDITOR Vanessa Weiman

PUBLISHED BY HEARST
PRESIDENT & CHIEF EXECUTIVE OFFICER Steven R. Swartz
CHAIRMAN William R. Hearst III
EXECUTIVE VICE CHAIRMAN Frank A. Bennack, Jr.

HEARST MAGAZINE MEDIA INC
PRESIDENT Debi Chirichella
GENERAL MANAGER, HEARST FASHION & LUXURY GROUP Alicianne Rand
GLOBAL CHIEF REVENUE OFFICER Lisa Ryan Howard
EDITORIAL DIRECTOR Lucy Kaylin
CHIEF FINANCIAL & STRATEGY OFFICER; TREASURER Regina Buckley
CONSUMER GROWTH OFFICER Lindsey Horrigan
CHIEF PRODUCT & TECHNOLOGY OFFICER Daniel Bernard
PRESIDENT, HEARST MAGAZINES INTERNATIONAL Jonathan Wright
SECRETARY Catherine A. Bostron

PUBLISHING CONSULTANT Mark F. Miller

HEARST HOME

Copyright © 2025 Veranda Publications, Inc.

All rights reserved. The written instructions in this volume are intended for the personal use of the reader and may be reproduced for that purpose only. Any other use, especially commercial use, is forbidden under law without the written permission of the copyright holder.

Library of Congress Cataloging-in-Publication Data available on request

10 9 8 7 6 5 4 3 2 1

Published by Hearst Home, an imprint of Hearst Books/Hearst Communications, Inc.
300 W 57th Street New York, NY 10019

Veranda and the Veranda logo are registered trademarks of Veranda Publications, Inc. Hearst Home, the Hearst Home logo, and Hearst Books are registered trademarks of Hearst Communications, Inc.

For information about custom editions, special sales, premium and corporate purchases: hearst.com/magazines/hearst-books

Printed in China
ISBN 978-1-958395-57-8

Discover Elegance on Every Page

◆ ◆ ◆

Available wherever books are sold.

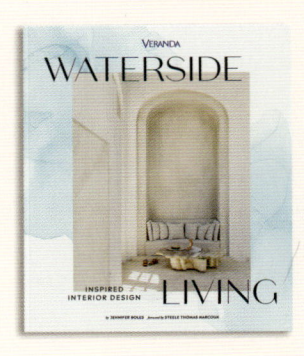

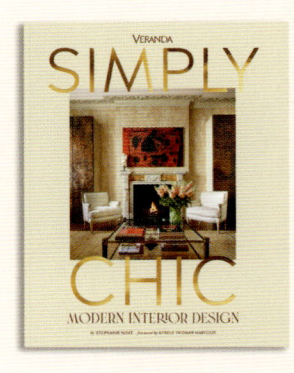

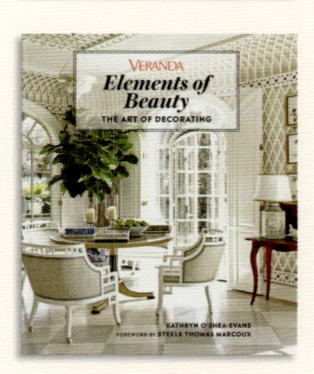

- VERANDA **DESIGNER SECRETS**: Expert Lessons from Top Decorators' Own Homes
- VERANDA **WATERSIDE LIVING**: Inspired Interior Design
- VERANDA **SIMPLY CHIC**: Modern Interior Design
- VERANDA **At Home in the South**: Interior Design Reimagined
- VERANDA **Elements of Beauty**: The Art of Decorating